THE COMPLETE GUIDE TO RUM

THE COMPLETE GUIDE TO RUM

An Authoritative Guide to Rums of the World

Edward Hamilton

TRIUMPH
BOOKS
CHICAGO

© 1997 Edward Hamilton and Triumph Books.

All rights reserved. No part of this publication may be reproduced, stored in a retrieval system, or transmitted, in any form by any means, electronic, mechanical, photocopying or otherwise, without the prior written permission of the publisher, Triumph Books, 644 South Clark Street, Chicago, Illinois 60605.

Cover design by Salvatore Concialdi.
Cover photographs by John Thoeming.
Book design by Sue Knopf.
Illustrations on pp. 2, 28, and 272 by Bruce Smith.
Illustration on p. xiii by Nancy Cook.

This book is available in quantity at special discounts for your group or organization. For further information, contact:
> Triumph Books
> 644 South Clark Street
> Chicago, Illinois 60605
> (312) 939-3330 FAX (312) 663-3557

ISBN 1-57243-205-5

Printed in the United States of America.

*In memory of
Fritz Seyfarth
and Andre DePaz*

Contents

Preface ix
Acknowledgments xi
Introduction xiii

Origins of Rum 2

Rums of the World
    U.S. Virgin Islands 31
    British Virgin Islands 39
    St. Martin/St. Maarten 49
    St. Bart's 61
    St. Kitts 63
    Antigua 65
    Guadeloupe 76
    Marie Galante 100
    Dominica 111
    Martinique 118
    St. Lucia 165
    St. Vincent and the Grenadines 171
    Carriacou 175
    Grenada 179
    Barbados 198
    Trinidad and Tobago 216
    Puerto Rico 228

Dominican Republic 241

Jamaica............................ 248

Haiti 255

United States 259

Cuba 264

Australia........................... 265

England and Scotland 267

Venezuela.......................... 269

Guyana 269

Surinam 270

Africa 270

Guatemala 271

The Pacific 271

Rum Lore............................ 272

Rum Line 295

Recipes 300

Glossary............................ 321

Index 328

Preface

Before you ask, which is my favorite rum, let me ask you, which is your favorite island?

Sure, the French islands of Martinique and Guadeloupe are unquestionably beautiful with their rain forests and intimate beaches while Puerto Rico has a flavor of its own. But anyone who visits Trinidad and Tobago agrees that the exotic blend of cultures make them irresistible too. Everyone is inspired by the Pitons in St. Lucia and the rugged landscapes of Dominica and Hispaniola. For some, Jamaica is the paradise they dream of all year round. In fact, no matter where you travel, you will be rewarded.

Just as it is hard to say which is your favorite island, it is hard for me to say which is my favorite rum. The more than two hundred different rums cataloged in this book vary from raw alcohol right out of the still to matured rums aged for a decade or more in oak barrels. Certainly there are differences that make classification easier, but don't discount any rum until you have tried it! Some rums lend themselves to the colorful, tropical drinks served in the most chic watering holes, others should be enjoyed straight and mixed only with the company of good friends.

In order to decide which is the best rum, you must go to the distilleries and try them. Most have a tasting center where they will proudly let you sample their products. Some of the best rums are available only at the distilleries of their birth. In

PREFACE

order to make this seemingly difficult task manageable, I have included directions and tour information for many of the distilleries. I can't think of a more rewarding way to spend a day than visiting the distilleries and getting to know the spirits they produce.

During the research for this book, I encountered many surprises. Luckily, most were pleasant. Sure, there is some rum that I prefer not to drink. But you will find, just as I did, that there are many excellent rums in the islands that aren't available anywhere else. With the market for rum growing, there are now new rums being distilled and blended all over the world.

It is not my hope that you will drink more than you should—only that you will be a better informed consumer of the fine sugar cane spirits we call rum.

Cheers. To your health!

Acknowledgments

The Complete Guide to Rum was written in appreciation of those who have dedicated their lives to planting and nurturing the cane—turning the fruits of their labor into the finest spirits in the world. Without them, none of this would exist.

I am indebted to the many people who took the time to help me understand what they do and why, to those who offered technical assistance, and to the people who saw the value in permitting me to include the labels of their rums. I also want to acknowledge the people who helped me translate pages of French history and distillery information and those who read the countless drafts and offered their criticisms.

I must also thank Mitch Rogatz, Siobhan Drummond, and Laura Moeller of Triumph Books for executing an almost impossible task.

Many people encouraged me from the start, but I am most grateful to you—the person taking the time to read this book. I hope that it will give you a better understanding and appreciation of the fine cane spirits we enjoy.

Introduction

This book was conceived at a full moon party on the small island of Culebra in the spring of '93. I had nearly completed preparing the sloop *Tafia* for sailing south and was hoping to discover a few of the secrets of the islands that have drawn people from the corners of the world for the last five hundred years. A few days later, without a schedule other than that dictated by hurricane season, I weighed anchor and set sail.

Like most of those before me, I was looking for adventure. But more importantly, I was in search of treasures left unnoticed by the hordes of others before me. What better place to begin than at the birthplaces of the rum we drink?

I approached the distilleries like any other interested tourist and was quickly surprised how much the distillers I met wanted me to understand everything about the rum they made. No one was at a loss to tell me why he or she made the best rum in the world. From the beginning, I was encouraged and soon came to know some of the magic of the islands.

As part of the research for this book, I bought at least one bottle of rum from each of the distilleries and consumed it with friends along the way. Some of the distilleries gave me bottles of rum, others offered to help pay some of the expense of publishing this book. Of course, I accepted the rum; my hosts would have been insulted if I refused. But in order to remain objective, none of

INTRODUCTION

the money to publish this book came from anyone connected with the manufacturing or marketing of this celebrated spirit.

This story is told as I remember it being told to me. Undoubtedly, I have made errors in reporting the facts and, more than once, the story told to me was just not true. I tried not to be insulted when I knew the facts to be different than what I was being told and I have attempted to give you what I believe to be the most correct account. It would serve no purpose to tell you that this or that person tried to mislead me in my research. When you detect inconsistencies in a few details of this story, accept that making rum is an art interspersed with more than a little magic. Surely you wouldn't expect a magician to tell you all of his secrets without a twinkle in his eye. If you knew all the secrets, it wouldn't be magic, would it?

To minimize the distortion of the facts (while sampling exotic liquors in the tropics), I visited most of the distilleries twice and several more than three times. I also interviewed local customs officials and surveyed numerous records of imports and exports. As you read this book, I hope you appreciate the simple fact that this is supposed to be entertaining—for both of us. When it no longer continues to be so, I have failed. For that, and only that, I apologize from the bottom of my empty glass.

I have not attempted to judge each rum by its rich, fruity, nutty, passionate nose or its full-bodied, warm, dry, sweet taste. I have tried to tell you everything you need to know to begin to understand what makes the spirits different. By understanding what goes into these spirits, you will be better able to appreciate them. But there is no substitute for going

INTRODUCTION

to the distilleries and trying the products after seeing for yourself how they are made.

I have seen the taste of my favorite rum described by an expert journalist as "leather." Although we did agree that this was an exceptional rum, I would hardly describe it as leather. (Nor would I want to drink something that tasted like leather.) I hope you will taste each rum for yourself and not rely on me or anyone else.

The Caribbean basin produces the majority of the world's rum but this versatile spirit is also produced in many other countries around the world. It would be nearly impossible to visit every distillery in the world but I have tried to include information on as many distilleries and their products as possible. In a project of this dimension, there will surely be oversights and omissions; I have tried to give you the best information available at the time of publication. I hope any such shortcomings will not reflect on the distillers or on the spirits they produce.

Finally, I have included one of my more memorable nights of research. As I watched the first drops of alcohol drip from a humble island still, my mentors shared their years of experience on turning the sweet juice of the sugar cane stalk into rum. Hours later, when the last drops of that potent liquor had been collected, it was obvious that I had only begun to appreciate the magic that has been performed in the Caribbean for nearly five centuries.

Today, apart from the opportunity to taste the differences in the various products, each distillery offers the traveler something unique. I hope that you will visit the birthplaces of rum and meet the people who so proudly make their spirits. The experience will surely enhance your appreciation of this celebrated drink.

INTRODUCTION

Many recognized health experts around the world acknowledge that an ounce of alcohol per day is actually beneficial for a long and healthy life. During the research for this book, I drank too much rum by any measure. And at least one relationship suffered as a result. Just as many drugs, including alcohol, can be beneficial in small quantities, almost anything is bad for our health and well-being when consumed in excess.

Few things are more rewarding in life than a good rum punch while watching a magnificent sunset from the cockpit of a yacht at anchor, but too much of anything tends to diminish our appreciation of the passions that drive our lives.

Coral Bay
March 20, 1997

Origins of Rum

Columbus claimed most of the Caribbean Islands for the king and queen of Spain. But the Spanish never took one ship of gold from these islands. The explorers did, however, bring with them a simple plant—sugar cane. Ironically, the sugar and rum produced in these islands became more valuable than the gold the conquistadors had originally sought. Even today there are treasures to be discovered by the modern traveler.

The birthplaces of the rum made during the last three centuries are places not to be missed on your next Caribbean expedition. Each of the Caribbean distilleries offers a unique view of the history of these enchanting islands. You can see an ox-drawn cart being weighed before it is emptied of its cargo in Marie Galante, a two hundred-year-old water wheel slowly crushing the day's harvest of cane in Grenada, or polished copper columns producing the most popular rhum in Guadeloupe.

Believed to have originated in Papua New Guinea, sugar cane was brought from China to the Indian subcontinent about two thousand years ago. Over the next thousand years, this hearty plant was dispersed across Northern Africa by traders to the Canary Islands. In the early sixteenth century, Spanish and Portuguese explorers brought sugar cane to Brazil. Since that time, sugar cane has been grown on nearly every island in the Caribbean.

In the 1600s, the European demand for sugar as a sweetener and preservative prompted Caribbean planters to experiment with the sweet grass as a source of much needed trade. The warm climate

ORIGINS OF RUM

was ideal for the hearty grass and soon every island, no matter how small, was growing cane.

To process the sugar cane into a marketable commodity, the stalk was crushed and the sweet juice was cooked with a little lime to help precipitate the impurities. Once cooked the thick, dark brown liquid was transferred to clay pots where the sugar crystallized and the remaining liquid drained out of a hole in the bottom of the pot. After several weeks, the pots were broken and the dark sugar that remained was shipped to the insatiable European markets.

The thick molasses collected from the bottom of the sugar pots contained sugar that could be fermented. To aid the process of fermentation—converting the sugar into alcohol and carbon dioxide—water and yeast were added and the wash was set aside for a couple of weeks. Once fermentation was complete, the alcohol formed during fermentation was boiled off in a simple pot still which resembled a large tea kettle with a long spout. The alcohol-rich vapor condensed from the still was thought to have great medicinal value and could ward off disease which was the work of the devil, hence the name kill devil.

Because Britain and France forbade the export of alcohol from the colonies in order to protect their domestic alcohol markets, much of the molasses was shipped to North America where it was distilled. By the mid-1700s, there were over forty distilleries in Boston alone. What wasn't consumed in New England was shipped to Africa and traded for slaves to provide the labor to grow more cane in the Caribbean islands.

Even though it was illegal for most of the Caribbean colonies to export crude rum, it was sold at bargain prices to the navies stationed in the *islands to deter the pirates that ravaged the merchant ships. West Indies rum soon gained popularity with the sailors and, in 1687, the Royal Navy officially adopted a pint of rum as the sailor's daily ration. Thus began the long-standing naval tradition linking Caribbean rum and the sea. In spite of the large distilling capability in New England, Caribbean rum was considered superior to the locally distilled product. When George Washington was inaugurated as president, he ordered a barrel of the best Barbados rum for the party.*

Although the commercial production of rum has changed since the seventeenth century, the traditions of rum remain as threads of history woven into the fabric of the Caribbean. The first planters used animals to drive their cane presses. Soon windmills dotted the countryside, from St. Croix to Barbados, taking advantage of the easterly trade winds that blow in this part of the world. By 1690, Barbados alone had 460 windmills.

The remains of the thousands of windmills and sugar factories of the last three centuries can be seen from almost anywhere in the islands. The small boiling houses and pot stills of the past have been replaced by larger sugar factories and distilleries that have become the new treasures of the islands.

Less than half of the over one hundred and fifty rums produced in the Eastern Caribbean today are widely distributed. While you are in the islands, visit the distilleries and see for yourself how the best rums in the world are made. In fact, each of the distilleries offers the traveler something unique, apart from the opportunity to taste the differences in the various products. No matter where you go in the islands you won't be far from a distillery and a chance to gain a greater appreciation of the process and the people that make the celebrated spirit of the Caribbean.

If you've ever dreamed about sailing the Caribbean and tasting the finest spirits the islands have to offer, join the crew of the sloop Tafia *and set sail with* The Complete Guide to Rum.

The Name "Rum"

There is little agreement on the origin of the word *rum*. For thousands of years, the Malays have made a drink called *brum* from the juice of the plant we know as sugar cane. However, the word *rum* is claimed to have been born in Barbados.

The sugar cane sprouts, which proved to be a valuable addition to the crops of Barbados, were brought to the island from the Dutch settlements of Brazil and Guyana. Since the alcohol was being made by South American planters, it is not beyond reason that their name for it also would find its way to the islands.

The Dutch seamen, who brought their large drinking glass, or *rummer*, to Barbados in the seventeenth century may also have had an influence on the name. In 1654, the General Court of Connecticut ordered the confiscation of "whatsoever Barbados liquors, commonly called rum, kill devil and the like" to protect the distilleries in New England. This is the first official recognition of Barbados rum in the new colonies.

In addition to the word *rum*, or *rhum*, there are many other words in the islands for this spirit. *Rumbullion* also is seen in historical accounts in Barbados. *Kill devil* had its origin in beliefs that this strong spirit, stronger than any other in the islands, could cure many of the afflictions that were prevalent in the tropics. Slaves were given kill devil to cure colds, tiredness, sunstroke, or whatever else interfered with work.

In the French islands, *rhum*, *tafia*, *flibuste*, and *guildive* are commonly used to describe the spirit distilled from the fermented juice of the sugar cane stalk. The word *strong* usually implies an overproof rum. Strong is also used in drink recipes for rum of whatever strength you fancy or, perhaps, whatever you have on hand.

Other words for the spirit that come from the local still are simply *local rum*, *forest preserve*, *hogo*, *hammond*, *culture*, and *babash*.

No matter what you call it, there is no dispute that the alcohol distilled from sugar cane is the most versatile spirit of all. The more you know about this diverse liquor, the more you will enjoy it.

Sugar Cane

Sugar cane was grown for the production of sugar, serving as the primary source of this sweet commodity, until 1787 when Franz Karl Archard developed the process to extract sucrose from sugar. Today, a little more than a third of the world's sugar comes from sugar beets. In this century, sugar cane went from being the economic focus of the Caribbean to a crop of far less importance, but certainly not one to be forgotten in the history of the islands.

In a process called photosynthesis, all green plants combine carbon dioxide, absorbed through their leaves, with water to form carbohydrates in the presence of chlorophyll and sunlight. In most plants, the primary sugar, glucose, is converted to sucrose and then stored as starch. Sugar cane and sugar beets are unusual in that they generate large quantities of sucrose and then store it unchanged.

Like the other members of the grass family, sugar cane reproduces by sending off shoots from the roots. Unattended, sugar cane will become a very dense cluster of stalks, impeding new growth and resulting in a less profitable crop. In order to maximize production, farmers generally plow the roots under after the harvest about every five years.

To recultivate the plowed fields, mature cane stalks are cut into short pieces called sets, or plants, and are placed in prepared furrows a few inches under the ground. Each set contains several joints where new shoots will emerge as buds after a couple of weeks. Replanting is usually done at the beginning of the rainy season to insure that the new shoots will not suffer due to a lack of water.

New plants mature in about a year under favorable conditions, but some are harvested in as little as six months depending on the climatic conditions and the demand for cane juice. When harvest time arrives, the stalk is cut close to the ground by hand with a sharp machete or with a cane-cutting machine. The leaves are removed in the field and the stalks are transported to the distillery or sugar mill to be processed.

Throughout the islands, many different species and hybrids of sugar cane are cultivated depending on the expected rainfall, soil, drainage conditions, and the availability of new sprouts. The Department of Agriculture in Barbados maintains the most up-to-date research facility in the Caribbean; providing sprouts and support for many of the cane growers in the islands.

Fermentation

Man has fermented sweet juices for more than six thousand years. Nearly every civilization has made and consumed alcohol in one form or another. The first alcoholic beverage was the result of fresh juice being left unattended; the naturally occurring yeast in the juice fermented, or turned the juice's sugar into alcohol.

Fermentation is the process of yeast, either naturally occurring or introduced from the outside, consuming the sugar in a liquid and producing alcohol and carbon dioxide gas. This transformation of sugar into alcohol and carbon dioxide continues until all the sugar is consumed or the alcohol produced reaches a concentration that actually kills the yeast. To ferment grains or corn to make beer or other distilled spirits, the raw material must be ground and cooked. Enzymes must then be added to convert the starch to a sugar that can be fermented.

During fermentation, heat and carbon dioxide gas are given off. In a small container, this heat is quickly dissipated but, in large vats, this heat can raise the temperature of the fermenting liquid high enough to kill the yeast.

Distillation

Distillation is simply a process of separating and concentrating a certain component of a liquid mixture. Originally used in the preparation of medicines and later to produce perfumes, distillation was used in Europe in the thirteenth century and is believed to have been accomplished in China as long ago as 800 B.C. Until the distillation process was understood, alcohol content was dependent on the ability of the yeast to survive in the increasing alcohol of the fermenting juice.

Condensed vapor, which collects under the lid of a simmering pot of stew, demonstrates the process of distillation. Water vapor is driven from the stew by the heat of the stove. When the lid is removed from the pot, the condensed vapor that has collected on the underside of the lid can be seen as a clear liquid. If this condensed vapor is dripped into a glass and allowed to cool, it looks and tastes like water, with only a slight indication that it was distilled from a flavorful stew.

During distillation, a liquid mixture is heated to the boiling point of the liquid. The vapor is collected and condensed and has a high percentage of the component with the lowest boiling point. The components of the liquid with the higher boiling point are left behind, along with any solids that may have been present.

The condensed vapor, or condensate, under the lid of the pot of stew is mostly water because water has the lowest boiling point. This condensate is clear because it doesn't contain any of the solids in the stew. In another example, salt water is heated to its boiling point and the vapor is condensed to produce drinking water from sea water.

If heat continues to be applied after the component with the lowest boiling point has been evaporated, the temperature will rise and the component with the next highest boiling point will be driven off. When heated in a controlled manner, a liquid mixture can be separated into its components by distillation. Although distillation is not an absolute separation, high component purities are possible. In the case of rum, sugar

Pot Still

The earliest still was simply a pot resembling a tea kettle with a longer spout. The spout was later extended to a tank of cool water to increase the yield. The components of this improved pot still are the kettle, or still pot, where the fermented juice is heated, the condenser that cools the vapor driven from the kettle, and the gooseneck that connects the kettle and the condenser. (Still pot refers to the part of the still that is heated and pot still refers to the entire apparatus.)

When the fermented juice, known as the wine, or wash, is heated in the kettle, alcohol is vaporized in the still pot and then condensed in the condenser. If the still pot is heated too quickly, the fermented juice will boil over and spill out of the condenser like a pot of rice boiling over on the stove. The heat source for this process is typically a wood fire that must be expertly tended. As the alcohol is boiled off from the wash, the volume in the still is reduced. Likewise, the fire must be reduced or the kettle will boil over, reducing the effect of the distillation.

The earliest pot stills could hold only a few gallons. Later, larger ones were built that could hold a few hundred gallons. A still of this type yields only about a gallon of rum for every 15 gallons of fermented wash.

The ethyl alcohol we drink has a boiling point of 78.5°C, slightly lower than the lighter products of fermentation—esters and aldehydes. The first drops of condensation from the still, known as high wines, contain more of these light alcohols, which account for the fruity aroma of the distilled spirit. The fermented wash contains only small quantities of these light compounds, and soon the still begins producing mostly ethyl alcohol, or simply ethanol, the desired product. Once most of the ethanol has been boiled from the wash, flow from the condenser slows down. The condensate contains more of the fusel oils—isobutanol, n-propanol, amyl, and isoamyl alcohols, which are also produced during fermentation.

The last condensate from the still is known as the low wines. High wines and low wines are also known as heads and tails, respectively. The distiller's job is to control the distillation so that the heads and tails are separated from the ethanol. What the distiller wants to collect from the still is between the heads and the tails, and is called seconds.

The simple pot still is capable of producing rum that is about 70% alcohol by volume. By collecting the condensate and then distilling it again, alcohol concentrations of more than 80% by volume are possible. Twice-distilled rum contains more alcohol and less of the other products of fermentation than single-distilled rum. In his *History of the Island of Barbados*, Richard Ligon describes rum being distilled twice in a pot still as part of the rum making process in Barbados in 1651.

Over the next one hundred years, distillation equipment evolved to include retorts and made it possible for the wash to be double distilled in one operation. In this configuration, fermented wine is heated in the cooking kettle. Alcohol-rich vapor from the kettle bubbles through the liquid in the retort. When the liquid in the retort is heated by

ORIGINS OF RUM

the hot vapor from the kettle, the alcohol is vaporized again. The condensate, collected from the condenser, has effectively been double distilled. The addition of another retort further refines the distillation.

The still pot with two retorts is capable of distilling alcohol to about 85% by volume, an increase of about 15% over the simple pot still. By the late eighteenth century, this type of still was in widespread use in the Caribbean. Two wood-fired pot stills with retorts continue to be used along with modern steam-fired versions of this still.

Continuous Distillation Column

The work of filling the kettle and the retorts, boiling the wash, then emptying the kettle and the retorts is called a batch process. Besides the labor and time required, the condensate varies significantly from start to finish. The continuous distillation column was developed in the nineteenth century.

Originally constructed of wood and later of copper, most modern distillation columns are constructed of a combination of stainless steel and copper. The column consists of a number of trays or sections, which form a maze of plates, holes, and mushroom-shaped caps.

In a continuous distillation column, the fermented wash enters the top of the column and is heated directly by the steam as it makes its way down through the maze. As the wash is heated, the alcohol contained in it is vaporized. By the time the wash reaches the bottom of the column, it contains no alcohol and is removed from the column through a float valve. Steam, from an external boiler, enters the bottom of the column. As the steam moves upward, it is saturated with the alcohol vaporized from the wash and is collected from ports near the top of the column.

As in the earlier stills, the alcohol-rich vapor is collected from the top of the still and condensed in a water-cooled heat exchanger. In some configurations, the hot alcohol vapor leaving the still heats the wash before it is introduced to the bottom of the column. Preheating the wash increases the efficiency of the column.

The advantages of the continuous distillation column are greater production capacity and greater consistency of the product stream. If the condensate from the pot still is not the correct alcohol content, it is collected and then used to fill the retorts or added to the next wash to be redistilled. In the continuous distillation column, the effluent is also monitored. If it is not the right alcohol content, it is simply pumped back to the tank that feeds the column and redistilled along with the remainder of the wash. The heads are redistilled as part of the distillation process.

The continuous distillation column is constructed so that it can be taken apart for periodic maintenance and cleaning. During the normal course of distillation, the still is operated for several months with only a good flushing with water.

Coffey Still

Although many single-column continuous stills are in operation, several distilleries employ two-column stills. This generation of distillation equipment was patented by Aeneas Coffey in 1832.

Between the two columns, the effluent vapor is condensed before it is redistilled. By incorporating two columns in series, the wash is double distilled in a continuous process to a higher purity of alcohol than is possible in a single column. In this configuration, the first column is known as the analyzing column and the second as the rectifying column.

After distillation, the condensed rum also contains other products of fermentation. In small quantities, these congeners are generally not harmful and add significantly to the taste and aroma of the raw rum. With further distillation, the alcohol content increases, the congeners are reduced, and the product retains fewer of the characteristics of the fermented wash.

There are many more configurations besides the two-column distillation still. A few distilleries operate four- and five-column stills. (One of the distilleries in this book is considering the installation of a three-column still.) The addition of taps allow other product streams to be recovered from the column and some of the congeners to be separated during distillation.

Continuous distillation columns operate at temperatures of between 80°C, at the top of the column, and 110°C, at the bottom. In a single distillation column, alcohol purities of up to 80% are possible by carefully manipulating the temperature and pressure of the still. In a two-column still, purities can be increased to above 90%. Since water and alcohol are easily mixed and form very stable compounds called azeotropes, purities above 95.5% alcohol by volume are not possible by simple distillation. To attain a higher purity, other substances must be added to the high purity alcohol that attracts the residual water and leaves the alcohol. This process is used primarily for alcohol intended for medical purposes.

The cost of a multicolumn still easily exceeds a few million dollars and is out of the question for small distilleries that do not have the capacity necessary to keep such a large still operating efficiently. The four-column still at Trinidad Distillers Limited in Port of Spain, for example, operates twenty-four hours a day, seven days a week, and is capable of producing over 40,000 liters of alcohol a day.

Classification of Rum

The rums you will encounter are as varied as the islands themselves. There is no uniform measure to compare the spirits made in different nations. It is possible, however, to classify them according to the raw ingredients, the bottled strength, and whether or not they are aged. These classifications can generally be made by reading the label. Other less apparent differences are influenced by the distillation purity and fermentation time. The taste of the spirit also depends on the freshness of the cane, cleanliness of the fermentation, consistency of the distillation process, storage or aging conditions, and any treatment done to the rum prior to bottling.

By understanding the variables, it is possible to

form opinions about the finished product. Bear in mind that some of these opinions will be valid and some will not. During the research stages of this book, I tried not to judge the spirits until I knew as much as possible about them. But even after seeing how they were made, there were more than a few surprises. Much more important than classification is taste. Even with all the sophisticated equipment used to make and monitor these spirits, every distillery makes the final decision on the quality of its product by tasting it. I hope you will too.

Cane Juice/Molasses

The primary factor affecting the taste of the spirits you will encounter is the raw ingredients. Rum is made either from fresh sugar cane juice, cane syrup, or molasses. Cane syrup is cane juice that has been boiled or vacuumed to remove some of the water. Molasses is the black liquid that is left after all the commercially producible sugar has been removed from the juice.

Until this century, nearly all rum was distilled from fermented molasses and other by-products of the sugar-refining process. In the English-speaking islands, most rum is still made from molasses—the exceptions are noted in this book.

In the French islands, rum is spelled "rhum," and is designated as either rhum agricole or rhum industriel. Rhum agricole is distilled from fresh cane juice before it has been processed to remove any of the sugar. Most of the alcohol you will encounter in the French islands will be rhum agricole and will have the word *agricole* on the label. Rhum industriel, on the other hand, is distilled from fermented molasses.

Even though the raw materials used in the production of rhum industriel are similar to the ingredients used in the English-speaking islands for the production of rum, the proportions of molasses, water, and yeast, as well as the distillation equipment, vary considerably. As you might expect, rhum industriel from the French islands and rum made from molasses on the other islands are very distinct products which are consumed differently. In deference to the people who work hard to produce these spirits, I have chosen to refer to the spirits made in the French islands as *rhum*. I hope that this distinction will serve you well when comparing the products of the distilleries.

Heavy/Light

Rum can also be classified as heavy or light, depending on the purity to which it was distilled. As alcohol is concentrated in the distillation process, the concentration of the other products of fermentation is reduced. The taste associated with these congeners is also reduced and results in a lighter rum.

Generally, the product of a pot still or single distillation column is considered a heavy rum. Multiple-column stills are capable of producing both heavy and light rums, depending on where the spirit was taken from the still.

As a general rule, rum that is condensed from the first column is considered a heavy rum. If it comes from one of the later columns, it is considered a light rum. The purest alcohol that can be produced by distillation is 95.5% alcohol by volume and is called a neutral spirit. Even aged, this is not a very good drink. In the distilleries where both light and heavy rums are produced, they are blended to yield a rum that has the desired characteristics.

The classifications heavy and light are also dependent on the fermentation time and are a function of the type of yeast used. A wash that is fermented quickly will yield a rum that is somewhat lighter than a rum distilled from a wash that has fermented for a week or more. In a slow fermentation process, while the yeast is turning the sugar into alcohol, other contaminating bacteria are reproducing that may affect the taste of the final product. Most of this contamination will be removed in the distillation process, but small amounts of other unwanted products may be evident even after distillation.

Some yeast can produce rum with light characteristics even though the fermentation time is relatively long. The trend, in the Eastern Caribbean, is toward yeast that is capable of facilitating complete fermentation within twenty-four hours or less.

To monitor the various products, analysis can be made by gas chromatography. This entails the injection of a liquid into a packed column that enables a technician to heat the sample under very controlled conditions. In this apparatus, the components of the rum can accurately be separated according to volatility. In a modern gas chromatograph, even the type of yeast used in the wash can be distinguished, giving the distillery engineer a fingerprint of the rum.

As you read this book, remember that a longer fermentation time and a lower alcohol purity from the still tends to yield a heavier rum. Reducing the fermentation time and increasing the purity of the product stream will generally produce a lighter rum. Heavy and light are relative terms and not things that can be easily measured. They must be tasted.

Aging

The liquid condensed from a still is always clear, the same as the drops of condensation under the lid of the pot of stew. This high strength alcohol is known as raw, unaged, or current rum. Most distillers dilute this spirit with at least a little water and bottle it as clear, or white rum, although not all white rum is unaged.

When the distilleries began producing more rum than was being consumed, the rum was stored in barrels where the spirit mellowed and improved in taste. As ships carried the raw rum on the long passage to Europe, it improved even more and darkened in color. By 1660, rum was being distilled to be aged. Because it was both difficult and expensive to build a barrel that would hold the volatile liquid for many years without leaking, most aged rum in the eighteenth century was only a few years old at the most.

Today, all the aging takes place in oak barrels from the United States, Canada, or France, where they were used for aging cognac, bourbon, whiskey, scotch, or even wine. Most barrels used for distilled spirits are charred before they are filled the first time. After the barrels are used once for aging other liquors, they are employed in the rum industry as once-used barrels. Before they are refilled with rum, some are charred again while others are scraped to remove the previously charred wood.

The barrels may be as much as fifteen-years-old, and occasionally older, depending on their condition. Nowhere did I find new barrels being used in the Eastern Caribbean. Regulations that require other liquor manufacturers to use barrels only once assure a steady supply of once-used barrels for the rum industry.

The aging process is not fully understood, but many changes take place that give the spirit a darker color and smoother taste. Oak is a hard, but slightly porous, wood that interacts with the rum in a fairly predictable manner. Some of the oils and alcohol in the rum are absorbed by the barrel and are lost to the atmosphere through evaporation. The longer the rum is aged, the greater the losses. These losses are also dependent on the alcohol content of the rum in the barrel. A higher alcohol content will result in greater losses, but requires fewer barrels and less space for storage.

The effects of aging are also dependent on the strength of the alcohol to be aged. If one barrel is filled with rum that is 90% alcohol by volume and another is filled with rum that is only 65% alcohol by volume, the effects of aging will be most discernible in the barrel that started out at the lower strength.

There is much discrepancy among the distillers I have talked to concerning the ideal conditions for aging rum. Some distillers credit higher evaporation rates with improved flavor in a shorter time, others maintain that a lower evaporation rate will yield a smoother alcohol. Again, the best way to determine the effects of aging is to taste the rums yourself.

Blending

Mixing rum from different stills, purities, or aged barrels can produce remarkable results when properly done by a skilled blender. Almost every distillery in the English-speaking islands blends its rums. In the French islands, the practice is far less prevalent. Many of the rums in this book are blends; I have tried to identify them as such.

It is important to note that, in addition to blending, some distilleries add spices or flavorings, which also affect the taste of the bottled product. Only one distillery in this book bottles its spirit directly from the still. At the other distilleries, water is slowly blended with the rum to reduce the alcohol content while preserving the characteristics of the spirit.

Labels

The label, as well as being a testimony to the product by the people who made it, often reveals more than just a name. When you pick up a bottle of rum, read the label. There is a lot of information there for you. Sure, you don't need directions to drink rum, but if you want to be an informed consumer, it is pertinent!

Most people make their decision to try a bottle of rum based on the color of the rum, the shape of the bottle, or by label recognition. Before you take a drink, at least find out how much alcohol is in the bottle. This can be very important, believe me! It is possible to drink a couple glasses of aged, overproof rum before you realize that it contains enough alcohol to cook your dinner.

The label on Mount Gay's 154 proof rum, for example, is similar to the label on their Refined Eclipse, which is only 86 proof. Unless you read the label, it is possible to overlook the difference. In this case, there is a neck band, so it is hard to miss, but stranger things have happened.

Also look for the words *distilled by*. A label that

does not tell you who distilled the rum is a good clue that the rum probably was not distilled by the company whose name is on the label. Some labels only tell you who blended and bottled the rum. If a distillery does not tell you who distilled it, more than likely, they do not want you to know.

If the label does not tell you who distilled the contents, look at the bottle itself. It is not uncommon for there to be some kind of mark on the bottle. TDL, for example, stands for Trinidad Distillers Ltd. A bottle of rum from Jamaica will have the words Jamaica Liquor Bottle on the bottle. This may not tell you who actually distilled that rum, but it does give you a good clue to its origin.

All of this does not mean that the bottle of rum you are holding isn't good. If you like the rum and don't care who made it, where it was made, or how much alcohol is in it, well then drink it. Personally, I like to know more about the rum in my glass. After visiting the distilleries, I have found that there is nothing that a distillery deliberately forgets to tell you on the label or neck band.

Alcohol Content

On the rum labels in this book, there are five different ways to indicate the amount of alcohol in the spirit:

- % alcohol, or % alcohol by volume. In this book, % alcohol can be taken to mean % alcohol by volume. In fact, I have not encountered any measure of alcohol content based on weight.

- ° or degrees, used in the French islands to indicate % alcohol by volume. For example: 59° is 59% alcohol by volume.

- U.S. proof, which is exactly twice the % alcohol by volume. 86 U.S. proof is equal to 43% alcohol by volume.

- British proof is a little more complicated and, unfortunately, British proof is not always designated as such. By definition, a sample at 50 British proof weighs exactly 12/13 as much as an equal volume of distilled water at 10.6°C. Or, at 87.7 British proof, a sample contains 50% alcohol by volume.

If you are still confused, and I have no reason to believe you aren't, British proof can be converted to % alcohol by volume. Multiply the number given as British proof by 0.571. Or multiply the British proof by 1.142 to yield U.S. proof.

- Overproof is British proof over 100. To convert to % alcohol by volume, add 100 to the number given as overproof, and multiply by 0.571. For example: 40 overproof is converted by adding 100 and multiplying by 0.571: (100+40) x (.571)=79.94% alcohol by volume.

As the distilleries expand their markets to include the United States and Europe, more labels are including the amount of alcohol expressed as a percentage of volume.

In this book, I have used % alcohol by volume to describe the amount of alcohol contained in the products of the English-speaking islands. For convenience, I have used a degree symbol (59°) to describe the amount of alcohol in the rhum in the French islands. Since metric, imperial, and U.S. measurements are used in the islands, I have used the system practiced in each particular island.

Tasting

As when tasting other liquors, there is a time-honored protocol to be followed that will affect your response to the various spirits that you will sample.

First, look at the label. How strong is it? If you are expecting to taste a spirit that is about 43% alcohol, and what you put in your mouth is 55% or more alcohol, you are in for a surprise. Your taste buds will rebel in much the same way your eyes react to the sun when you walk out of a dark room in the middle of a bright day.

How old is the rum, or is there anything else the bottler wants you to know? If the rum was made from fresh sugar cane juice, for example, the label will tell you. It may also tell you if this is a spiced rum. All of the information you can attain from the label will help prepare you for actually tasting the spirit.

Next, pour a little into a glass. Hold the glass up to the light so you can look through it and judge the clearness or color of the rum. Now that you have a mental picture, swirl the liquid in the bottom of the glass. Stirring fills the empty space in the glass with the aroma of the rum and helps concentrate your senses on what you are about to do.

Take a deep breath, exhale, then raise the glass to your nose. Carefully, deliberately, and slowly inhale the vapors. If this is an aged, mature rum, you will be able to make a long, slow assessment of the delicate flavors in the aroma. On the other hand, if this is an unaged, strong rum, you will be able to remove your nose from the glass before you do permanent damage to your nasal passages.

If smelling the spirit was a pleasant experience, feel free to repeat it. The second or third assessment of a rum, by simply smelling it, may either confirm your first appraisal, or you may discover another subtle aroma that you missed the first time.

The distilleries will present their product either straight, with water, a little ice, or cane syrup. An overproof, unaged rum, for example, is a lot to put your taste buds through without at least a little water. I prefer to taste rums straight, at least the first time.

Now, sip the contents of the glass and savor the experience, if you can. Then, mentally compare your impressions of the spirit from smelling it and tasting it.

Plan to have something to eat before you sample these rums. Tasting a few rums before lunch can adversely affect your appreciation of the quality of these fine spirits.

Rums
OF THE World

I will not try to tell you which rum you will like best. As you taste them, note the characteristics of the rums, look for similarities and differences in the distillation equipment employed, the raw material that is fermented, and the time spent aging the rum. If, for example, you like white rhum from the French islands, you will see that nearly all of the white rhums made in the French islands are made from fresh cane juice in single-column continuous stills. None of these rhums are aged although some are allowed to rest for as much as six months. It is also worth noting that some of these rhums are distilled in copper stills and some are distilled in stainless steel stills.

You will quickly notice that just because the characteristics of the distillation and treatment prior to bottling are similar, the taste of various rums will differ widely. This is due in part to the quality or freshness of the cane or molasses used, the additives that may or may not be used in the fermentation process, the differences in the still itself, and how each still is operated. The time the raw alcohol is allowed to rest after distillation and the purity of the water used to dilute the rum before it is bottled are also factors that affect the taste of the finished product.

If the spirit is aged, the strength of the alcohol in the aging barrel and even the size of the barrel contributes to the taste and color of the bottled product. Since almost all of the distilleries use barrels of approximately forty gallons, I have not included aging barrel capacity except where that volume greatly differs from the norm. Information on the aging strength of the alcohol has been included when that information was made available.

If you visit the distilleries, you may discover that

some of the information provided below is inaccurate. Bear in mind that competition in the rum industry is high and some of this information is considered proprietary. Most of the information was acquired by actually visiting and seeing the distillery. In those cases where I was unable to visit the distillery, the information was compiled from material supplied by the distillery.

Even though I have tasted nearly every rum listed, it would be foolish for me to try to describe to you what every rum tastes like. Most of these rums are considered unique and defy description by a few simple adjectives. Instead, I encourage you to try new rums as they become available and to look for the characteristics that make certain rums attractive to you.

Yes, I do have a few favorite rums but my taste is colored by many factors such as the time of day, what I have or haven't eaten in the last few hours, and my mood. As much as I like some of these rums, I must also admit that I don't know of any rum that I would like to drink at the exclusion of all others. Nor do I know anyone who would be happy if they were only fed one food or one drink exclusively.

Finally it should be pointed out that really getting to know a new rum is a lot like getting to know a new lover. Sure your eyes may be taken by the appearance of the new encounter and when you get close enough to get a whiff of its fragrance you may feel your knees get weak. But to really know something requires more than just tasting it in your mouth and feeling it warm your body. No, to really get to know a new rum requires that you spend the night with it. I'm not suggesting you overindulge in your new acquaintance but don't hold back. In the morning, you will have a much better idea whether the rum that attracted your attention is really something you like or if it should be left alone.

U.S. Virgin Islands

While the Spanish were busy cultivating the much larger island of Puerto Rico to the west, Dutch and English planters found the soil and climate favorable on St. Croix. Though claimed by Spain, St. Croix did not have the gold that the Spaniards sought and was left unprotected, a situation that prompted the French to forcibly take possession of the largest of the Virgin Islands in the 1600s. Again, without close supervision from the homeland, the French governor acquired title to the whole island and then transferred his holdings to the Knights of Malta, presumably for a comfortable retirement and a small fortune. Not surprisingly, France was unhappy with the arrangement and took possession again in 1665.

In 1733, the Danish West India Company purchased St. Croix from France and built forts in Christiansted and Fredricksted for protection. The Danes also recognized the prosperity of the nearby Dutch free port of Statia and declared their Virgin Islands to have the same status, paving the way for the sugar and cotton plantations on St. Croix to compete with the English colonies twelve hundred miles to the northwest.

The Danish Virgin Islands flourished as free ports. By the end of the eighteenth century, there were 114 windmills and 14 animal-driven mills crushing cane. (Only Barbados was producing more sugar.) Today, from almost anywhere on the island, you can see the remains of the stone structures that supported the windmills. If you look closely around these ruins, you also can see the remains of some of the boiling houses used to cook the cane juice into sugar.

Free port status also stimulated the production of rum. The molasses that had been shipped to the forty New England rum distilleries was now being *distilled in the islands. Without the heavy burden of an export tax, rum production sped up. Since rum became a much more profitable cargo, thirsty ship captains were soon lying at anchor to load this valuable cargo.*

In 1776, while the attention of the navies in the Caribbean was tuned to news of the Revolutionary War being fought to the north, an unidentified schooner hoisted the stars and stripes. As the trading vessel gathered way, a salute was fired. The courtesy, returned by the fort at Fredricksted, was the first acknowledgment of the new nation that eventually bought these islands in 1917.

Virgin Islands Rum Distillery

Almost anyone who has been to the U.S. Virgin Islands has tasted Cruzan rum. By far the largest selling rum in the Virgin Islands, the character of Cruzan has earned this distillery a faithful following. The duty-free status of the U.S. Virgin Islands and the low transportation cost makes this one of the best rum values in the islands.

When I boarded the bus to visit the Virgin Islands Rum Distillery, I was anxious to find out for myself why this rum—the Virgin Island standard by which all others rums are measured—is so popular. The only operating distillery is just a few minutes walk south from Centerline Road on Highway 64, near the western end of the island. As I approached the distillery, the smell of fermenting molasses mixed with the scent of flowers. There was no doubt that this was going to be a very delightful morning.

The Nelthropp family has owned and operated this distillery for generations, interrupted only by

U.S. VIRGIN ISLANDS

prohibition in the United States (1920-1933). In the spring of 1994, the Cruzan Rum Distillery Company was acquired by Toddhunter International. President Donald Nelthropp, Sr. and the original staff continue to manage the distillery. Even though this is one of the largest production distilleries in the Eastern Caribbean, the feeling of a family operation permeates the atmosphere here.

Since there is no longer a sugar mill on St. Croix, there is not a local supply of molasses. The raw material arrives by ship from South and Central America. From the 1.5 million gallon storage facility at the southern port of the island, the thick, black liquid is trucked to the distillery. When it arrives, it contains 85% dissolved solids, called *85 brix* in the industry, more than half of which is sugar that can be fermented.

Before the molasses is fermented, it is diluted with well water to 16 brix, then boiled under pressure at 240°F for fifteen minutes for sterilization. Then, this solution is further diluted and the proprietary yeast culture is introduced. When the yeast begins to multiply, compressed air is injected at the bottom of the stainless steel vats. Aeration helps keep the carbon dioxide bubbles formed during fermentation from actually foaming over the top of the fermentation vats and reduces the amount of carbonic gas formed during distillation.

The terminology used at this distillery is unique, but easily followed once you understand the basics of the process. From the fermentation vat, the beer (fermented wash) is pumped to the first column called the beer still. In this column, the fusels, heads, and ethyl alcohols are separated from the other fermentation products.

The vapor collected from the top of the beer

still is condensed and piped to the next four columns. Aldehydes, esters, and other trace compounds are removed from the final product stream through various taps in the distillation columns. The final product stream is 94.5% alcohol by volume. Fusel oils, collected from the still, are sold to blenders in the states who use them for flavoring other liquors.

Presently, the still is capable of producing 18,000 proof gallons at 50% alcohol, per day. In combination with a new still under construction, production capability will soon be increased by nearly one third. In addition to the 450,000 cases of rum bottled annually for both the local and export markets, another 3,500,000 proof gallons (gallons at 50% alcohol by volume) of unaged rum are sold to be bottled under a variety of labels.

Although the purity of the rum produced at Cruzan is important, it is only the beginning of the story. All of the rum sold under the Cruzan label is aged at the distillery. Twenty-three thousand charred oak barrels of rum are maturing in the largest aging warehouses I have seen. Most of the rum aged here is light body rum, but a small amount of heavier rum is also aged for blending. To further the effects of aging in the heavier products, about two pounds of oak chips are added to the rum.

To maintain the quality of the rum produced, laboratory personnel perform quality control tests at several stages of production. A panel of human testers sign their names attesting to their personal inspection of everything that leaves the distillery.

U.S. VIRGIN ISLANDS

CRUZAN RUM DISTILLERY COMPANY, LTD.
ST. CROIX, U.S. VIRGIN ISLANDS

Fermentation: Molasses, less than twenty-four hours

Distillation Equipment: Four-column continuous still

Cruzan Dry Rums: Light-Dry and Dark-Dry

Bottled Strength: 40% alcohol by volume

Age: Blend of rums at least two years old

Notes: Light-Dry is carbon-filtered to remove the color attained during aging. Light and Dark-Dry are the only rums I have encountered with an age statement on the back label. (U.S. regulations require that the age statement on the label reflect the youngest rum in the blend.) These rums are the most popular of the Cruzan distillery.

Cruzan 151 White and Cruzan 151 Gold

Bottled Strength: 75.5% alcohol by volume

Notes: For those who prefer a stronger drink. 151 White is filtered to remove color. Used mostly in punches and cooking, these rums are flammable so beware—they have the potential to do more than light up your dessert!

Estate Diamond

Bottled Strength: 40% alcohol by volume

Age: Blend of four to ten-year-old rums

Notes: Estate Diamond is Cruzan's premium rum. If you have never tasted an expertly blended and aged rum, visit the distillery to taste this one. (U.S. law requires the age statement on a blended rum to represent the age of the youngest rum in the blend.)

Old St. Croix

Bottled Strength: 40% alcohol by volume

Notes: Blended in small quantities for the local market, this rum is similar in character to the Cruzan Dry Rums.

Cruzan Clipper Spiced Rum

Bottled Strength: 40% alcohol by volume

Notes: Blended with all natural spices and flavors. Good rich flavor in a spiced rum. Mixes well.

A. H. Riise

After a severe hurricane ravaged St. Thomas in 1837, Copenhagen granted an exclusive license to Albert Heinrich Riise to dispense retail drugs on the Danish island. Epidemics of cholera, yellow fever, and smallpox, followed by another devastating hurricane in 1867 and an earthquake three weeks later, tried the resources and commitment of the small company and its founder. But the A. H. Riise Apothecary proved itself, becoming known throughout the islands for quality and service.

In addition to running a thriving business, Albert Riise perfected a process to double-distill bay rum. Previously, bay rum had been made by simply crushing bay leaves in local rum and letting them "soak and settle." After Albert's retirement, his son Valdemar continued his father's work. He won top honors at the Chicago World Fair in 1893 for "the fragrance and purity of the product and the care taken in its manufacture." This gold medal crowned the honors already won at the Expositions in New Orleans in 1884 and 1885, and in Copenhagen and Antwerp in 1888.

In 1913, the Riise family business was sold to Olaf Poulsen, a pharmacist from Copenhagen. Four years later, the Virgin Islands were bought by the United States. In 1928, Isaac Paiewonsky purchased the Riise company. After World War II, his wife Charlotte and his sons Ralph and Isidor expanded the business and its products even further—becoming "the" place to shop in the islands. In 1961, Ralph Paiewonsky left the family business to become governor of the U.S. Virgin Islands.

Today, A. H. Riise Gifts and Liquor Store is run by Charlotte and Isaac's daughter, Avna Paiewonsky Cassinelli, and her sons, Sebastiano and Filippo.

A. H. RIISE CUSTOM RUMS
ST. THOMAS, U.S. VIRGIN ISLANDS

These custom rums are distilled by the Cruzan Rum Distillery Company, Ltd., and then blended by A. H. Riise. Both of these rums are bottled in beautifully-etched glass bottles.

A. H. Riise Custom Rums: 3 to 6 years old

Bottled Strength: 40% alcohol by volume

Age: A blend of three to six-year-old rums

Notes: This full-flavored blend of golden rums lends itself to being enjoyed straight.

A. H. Riise Custom Rums: 6 to 12 years old

Bottled Strength: 40% alcohol by volume

Age: A blend of six to twelve-year-old rums

Notes: Very smooth blend of very fine rums, rich color, and character. This is the oldest rum bottled in the Virgin Islands. A superb rum.

British Virgin Islands

Many pirates were born out of the severely brutal conditions of the seafaring life. Without navies large enough to enforce their rule, European kings and queens gave letters of marque that sanctioned ship captains to capture ships and cargo from other countries. Typically, ten to fifteen percent of the prizes captured by the privateers were given to the crown and the balance was divided between the ship owner and the crew.

This simple arrangement shifted the financial burden of outfitting and manning ships from the crown to the private sector. Resources that once had been committed to protecting merchant ships were now used for exploration or other things at home. By disrupting the trade of competing nations without committing any of the crown's assets to the task, privateering flourished.

Many famous naval heroes, including John Paul Jones, started their careers as merchant seamen and then turned privateer. Sir Francis Drake circumnavigated the globe essentially as a privateer. And more than once a privateer crew turned pirate after getting a letter of marque.

In the Caribbean, naval officers who were supposed to protect merchant shipments commonly took cargo aboard their own ships at inflated prices. The merchant's goods were delivered, the officers profited, and the pirates were left to attack shipments on other unprotected vessels. Privateer commissions were also given to attack pirates, but these were ineffective in eradicating piracy in the Caribbean. By not attacking navy ships, the pirates and the navy coexisted on a mutually profitable ocean.

The privateers, pirates, and smugglers who inhabited the islands left their mark from Thatch Island to Deadman's Chest, and windward up Sir Francis Drake Channel to Virgin Gorda.

Sopers Hole, on the west end of Tortola, was the largest pirate community in the British Virgin Islands. Out of sight from the commercial port of Road Town, Sopers Hole offered the renegades a well-protected, deep water refuge that could only be entered by sailing windward in shifting light winds. The cotton and sugar cane plantations traded fruit, vegetables, and rum to the pirates in return for other supplies that were in demand. The presence of the pirates also discouraged others from preying on the settlers.

Callwood Distillery

Dating back four hundred years, the Arundel Estate is the oldest, continuously operated distillery in the Eastern Caribbean. For the last two hundred years, the Callwood family has handed down the rum-making tradition in Cane Garden Bay from father to son. Michael Callwood, the present distiller, is not sure his son will want to carry on the tradition, but Mikey is still young.

The distillery, a few hundred yards west of the post office, is a working museum. As the last distillery operating in Tortola, it plays an important part in preserving the island heritage.

Every year between March and September, locally grown green sugar cane, only six months old, is pressed at the mill. When the distillery was part of a large estate, the mill was cattle-powered. Today, the previous work of several cattle is done by a small diesel engine. The crushed cane stalks are then burned to boil the cane juice.

After the juice has been boiled a few hours, it is put in barrels for about eighteen days to ferment naturally—without any added yeast. Sometimes the fermenting wine must be transferred to another barrel or be distilled due to leaks in the old barrels, some of which are older than anyone on Tortola.

When it is ready to distill, the fermented cane juice is poured into the copper pot still and the fire is lit. Coconut husks, scraps from local construction sites, and tree limbs are burnt to distill the fermented wine. Callwood uses a small fire to gently simmer the contents of the still pot. This slow process has two benefits. First, the amount of water boiled off with the alcohol is kept to a minimum. Second, the still pot will last much longer because it isn't exposed to as much heat. There are two pot stills to the left of the office. Attesting to the benefits of the slow process, the still that is no longer used was put out of service only a year ago; it dated back to slave days.

It takes all day to boil the alcohol from the still. The fragrant vapor is condensed in the cistern outside the office, since there is not a running water source. Inside the office, the fresh rum drips into a copper measure that sits in a small well in the floor. Large glass jugs, with rattan woven around them, hold the fresh rum to be later diluted and bottled. Before glass bottles were mass produced, handblown jugs like these were common.

Both white and dark rum are produced here. The white rum is not aged and is mostly drunk by local islanders. The dark rum, which is more popular with tourists, is aged three to four years in old oak barrels. After filling an assortment of recycled bottles, Mr. Callwood glues his labels to the bottles and sells them at the distillery and local retail stores in Tortola.

This is the only licensed distillery in the Eastern Caribbean that distills all of its rum in a single pot still. It is also one of the few distilleries in the English-speaking islands that makes rum directly from sugar cane juice. The long fermentation time, the single pot still, and the raw ingredients combine to make this rum unique.

ARUNDEL ESTATE, CALLWOOD DISTILLERY
CANE GARDEN BAY, TORTOLA, BRITISH VIRGIN ISLANDS
Fermentation: Fresh squeezed cane juice, approximately eighteen days
Distillation Equipment: Wood-fired, copper pot still

Arundel Cane Rum: White and Dark
Bottled Strength: 40% alcohol by volume
Age: White is unaged, Dark is aged three to four years in old barrels
Notes: The white rum is mostly drunk by local islanders; the dark rum is more popular with tourists.

Callwood Distillery is the oldest operating distillery in the Caribbean.

Tortola Spiced Rum

Since the closure of most of the distilleries in the British Virgin Islands, the business of importing and bottling rum has grown. Tortola Spiced Rum is spiced and labeled on the north side of the island.

Certainly this spiced rum does not claim to be a huge commercial success, but, since 1991, Styles Callwood has been blending rum from the Arundel Estate and the Virgin Islands Rum Distillery with fresh cloves, cinnamon, ginger, and cane syrup. In addition to blending rum, Styles also operates two taxis and manages his campground in Brewer's Bay.

When I first saw this rum, I assumed that this was St. Martin Spiced Rum. The likeness in the labels is striking, but this is a different blend. The similarities end when you open the bottle.

CALLWOOD DISTILLERY
BREWER'S BAY, TORTOLA, BRITISH VIRGIN ISLANDS

Tortola Spiced Rum
Bottled Strength: 40% alcohol by volume

Ingredients: Rum from the Arundel Estate and Virgin Islands Distillery, cane syrup, cloves, cinnamon, and ginger

Notes: A distinct blend of spices from Brewer's Bay on the north side of Tortola.

Pusser's

To compensate for the hardships of life on board naval ships in the sixteenth century, sailors were given a daily ration of beer. On the long passages to the West Indies, beer did not keep well and Royal Navy Pursers (commonly known as Pussers), in charge of provisions, bought rum from the island planters. To encourage the naval presence and deter the pirates that ravaged their merchant ships, the planters sold their spirits at bargain prices. West Indies rum quickly gained popularity with the sailors and, in 1687, the Royal Navy officially adopted a pint of rum as the daily ration.

Much stronger than the beer that it replaced, rum contributed to enough accidents and general disorder among the sailors that, on August 21, 1740, Admiral Edward Vernon ordered the ration to be diluted with two parts water prior to issue. The order also contained provisions for sugar and lime juice to be added to the daily allowance as a reward for good behavior, "that it be made more palatable to them." The diluted tot became known as grog by the sailors, in honor of Admiral Vernon who often wore a grogram coat. Over the next two hundred years, the ration continued to be reduced until July 31, 1970, when the last grog was drunk on board the ships of the Royal Navy.

After the abolition of the daily rum ration, stores of rum remained in warehouses in England and around the world. Contracts to buy rum, which had been in effect since 1810 when the preferred blend of West Indian dark rums was made a part of the official naval protocol, were canceled. Then, in 1979, Charles Tobias, an energetic adventurer who had just completed two circumnavigations, approached the Royal Navy with a plan that was looked upon with skepticism by most observers. Tobias offered to donate to the navy retirement fund if he would be allowed to blend the six Caribbean rums according to the naval tradition and market it as Pusser's Navy Rum. The Admiralty Board gave its approval and soon Pusser's Navy Rum was being bottled in Tortola.

In addition to blending and bottling rum, the spirited entrepreneur opened a small bar and restaurant. Today, Pusser's Co. Store is a landmark in the British Virgin Islands, in fact, four landmarks. If you are cruising the British Virgin Islands, you should certainly visit one of the com-

BRITISH VIRGIN ISLANDS

pany stores, decorated in nautical antiques and interesting memorabilia from the bygone era of wooden ships and iron men.

When the first plans to expand the successful restaurant, bar, and store concept were baffled by U.S. laws restricting the sale of liquor, the Pusser's Rum label was sold to Jim Beam Brands. They now market the product along with their other liquors. In 1994, the label on Pusser's was changed to appeal to a wider market. Fortunately, the blend of Caribbean rums hasn't changed.

PUSSER'S
JIM BEAM BRANDS OF THE UNITED STATES
Originally bottled in Tortola

Pusser's Red and Blue Label

Bottled Strength: Red Label-40% alcohol by volume, Blue Label-47.75% alcohol by volume

Notes: Blend of six aged rums from Guyana, Barbados, and Trinidad.

Originally Pusser's Blue Label was 95 British proof, which translates to over 100 US proof. Surprisingly, the higher proof Blue Label is smoother than the Red Label.

Foxy's

Jost Van Dyke, the most northwestern of the British Virgin Islands, is on almost every charter boat itinerary. It is a short, close reach from Sopers Hole, The Narrows to Sandy Key, or Little Jost, for a swim and a walk around the island. Then, take an easy sail back to Great Harbour for dinner or at least a few drinks at Foxy's. Another day in paradise!

Warning: The spirit of the people on this magical island is contagious and you may have more fun than you deserve.

The story of Foxy's is best told by Foxy himself on the back label of his rum bottle:

> *In 1968, Philicianno Callwood, better known as "Foxy," built a simple lean-to beach bar in Great Harbour on the tiny island of Jost Van Dyke in the British Virgin Islands.*
>
> *Known then for his spontaneous, witty lyrics and sense of fun to the few regular skippers frequenting his bar, "Foxy" has since become world renowned as an entertainer, entrepreneur, philosopher, community activist, world traveler, conservationist, musician, story teller, cultural historian, fisherman, comedian, and sailor—a new Renaissance Man of the nineties.*
>
> *Stemming from the hospitality of its legendary host, "Foxy's Tamarind Bar" is now internationally known as one of the most convivial watering holes for sailors throughout the Caribbean! It is a mecca for revelers on "Old Years Night" and the venue for the locally popular "Foxy's Wooden Boat Regatta" held annually in September.*
>
> *"Foxy's Fire Water"—a smoothly blended and aged gold rum—is the way for you to recreate the sense of warmth and camaraderie generated in this magical place. "Jus' one sip of dis island fire water, mahn, goin to put your spirit in de place where friends are met and memories made."*
>
> *75 cl   43% alcohol by volume*

BRITISH VIRGIN ISLANDS

FOXY'S.
JOST VAN DYKE, BRITISH VIRGIN ISLANDS

Foxy's Fire Water

Bottled Strength: 43% alcohol by volume

Notes: Blend of aged rums from Caroni (1975) Limited, Trinidad. Foxy's Firewater is a full flavored blend and slightly colored.

Silver Fox

Bottled Strength: 43% alcohol by volume

Notes: Blend of aged rums from Caroni (1975) Limited, Trinidad. Silver Fox has been filtered to remove the color from aging. Light bodied white rum with a good flavor.

In the 70s, while Foxy was busy singing and joking in Great Bay, things were a little more casual down the coast. White Bay lacked electricity to make fancy blender drinks, so intense work was undertaken to make a drink that would attract a few tourists to the Soggy Dollar Bar, where you had to swim ashore—White Bay also lacked a dock.

Start with two, three, or four good measures of Pusser's Rum and mix with pineapple juice, cream of coconut, and orange juice. Serve over ice and top with fresh ground Grenadian nutmeg. You will see a lot of imitations of the original Pusser's Painkiller in the islands, but to get the original, you will have to take a swim and see Raphael at the Soggy Dollar.

RUMS OF THE WORLD

Resort Blends

The British Virgin Islands are one of the most popular charter sailboat destinations in the world. Before you arrive, you can have your yacht fully provisioned by Fort Wine and Liquors. They will take care of all your liquor needs in advance, but you owe it to yourself to visit Fort Wine Gourmet in Road Town. At Fort Wine Gourmet, informed charter chefs find special things to make every meal something to remember, from prepared gourmet foods to the widest selection of exquisite cane spirits in the British Virgin Islands.

If you are staying at a guest house, you will probably see some of these private labels being sold here. From the Bitter End in Virgin Gorda to the Sandcastle on Jost Van Dyke, all of these rums are bottled at 43% alcohol by volume. These are aged blends from Trinidad that are labeled here. Each bears the name of one of the popular resorts where you may be staying.

PRIVATE LABEL RESORT BLENDS
Bottled Strength: 43% alcohol by volume
Notes: All of these resort rums are blends of golden aged rums up to three years old, from Trinidad Distillers Limited.

St. Martin/ St. Maarten

Since 1648, this tropical island has been administered by French and Dutch governments—resulting in a vibrant blend of culture. The success of the island is due in large part to its duty-free status. Alcohol, for example, can be imported, blended, and sold without the usual red tape associated with taxes. About ten years ago, the aging Potts distillery, the last to operate on this island, closed because it was too small to compete with untaxed imports from other islands. Today, a mélange of rums is imported, blended, and bottled here. Several entrepreneurs are taking different approaches to the business and attaining different results. The common ingredient in all of these enterprises is the pride they have in their products.

The research for this book began in earnest on St. Maarten, actually St. Martin. Not far from Marina Royale, a friend and I entered the shadows of a typical Antillean building. My friend stumbled over a large, black dog sleeping just inside the open doorway. The dog moved and I tripped over him, expecting him to bite me, or at least yelp. He yawned and resumed his nap, this time in the sun.

After a few moments, I adjusted to the dim surroundings and could see the dusty bar covered with gallon jars full of sliced fruit and rhum. On the floor behind the bar, five-gallon plastic pails held more fruit marinating in rhum. Raisins, star fruit, limes, orange slices, and spices that I couldn't identify filled more jars on the shelves. In the corner, under a stack of plastic pails, a barrel with a plastic hose hanging from the bung hole stood guard over more containers on the floor.

In his usual, friendly manner, my friend engaged the owner in conversation and, before we had finished our first drink, mentioned a book. Without hesitation, the old man looked at me through his thick glasses and said, "I don't want to know about no book. I don't want no book! Now drink that in your hand and get out." In the next seconds, he hurriedly exposed his fears of higher taxes on his building. Publicizing this small rum shop could lead to a higher tax assessment, which would destroy the laid-back business that gave him little more than a living and a place to drink. As things were, he was able to pay his bills without accumulating much.

Everywhere outside the small bar, the town had swollen up around him. The roads had been widened to accommodate throngs of people; the path that used to serve as a sidewalk was now part of the road. To pay for the growth, government tax assessors were busy raising revenues and forcing many of this man's neighbors out of business.

In an effort to salvage the situation and find out something about this man, who obviously knew a lot about rum, I asked where the best rum came from. Ignoring my friend, the old man smiled and replied without hesitation, "The best rhum comes from Guadeloupe and Martinique," although still obviously upset that any publicity could cause his taxes to be raised.

Over another drink, on the house, the old man talked about his early days on schooners between here and St. Thomas. "Stay on a starboard tack until you see Sombrero Light. If you tack before you see the light, you won't make St. Martin," he proclaimed.

Once the air had cleared, we tried a couple of other punches from the back shelf while the conversation shifted to fishing. Before we left, I thanked our host and confirmed again that I had no intention of naming him or his bar. Carefully, we stepped over the sleeping dog.

The first step out of the bar put us right in the path of traffic and blaring horns. As we retreated to the safety of the open door behind us, the dog rolled over and laughed, or maybe it was just a big yawn.

> *Although it was not in my research objectives to visit rum shops early in the morning, I did find myself walking by one or two while out to get a fresh baguette. The sound of laughter drew me inside where several fishermen, with their yellow coats and pant legs rolled up above their bare ankles, were drinking an early shot to ward off the dampness of a morning rain shower.*
>
> *All of the eyes in the dim bar turned to the tall stranger. Without asking for a drink, I was served. It wasn't bad, but the next time I drink a décollage (absinthe and rhum), I will make sure I have eaten breakfast.*

Busco

Derived from the name Columbus, Busco rhums are the work of Christian Carreau. He was the former owner of Champagne, an upscale spirits store in Marigot. During his years in the fine liquor business, M. Carreau became very familiar with the French West Indies distilleries and their rhum. In 1993, he began importing rhum from the Séverin distillery in Guadeloupe to blend in his Busco products. This white rhum is bottled as Busco Rhum Blanc Agricole. Four-year-old rhum from Séverin is also sold as Busco Rhum Vieux.

Busco is part of a growing trend in the spirit industry. Spirits produced on one island are exported, then blended and bottled on other islands under a variety of labels. These are not second-rate products. For example, this particular Séverin distillery rum is well respected in Guadeloupe.

CARREAU BLENDS
ST. MAARTEN

Busco Rhum Blanc Agricole de Plantation
Bottled Strength: 50% alcohol by volume
Notes: White rhum from the Sevérin distillery in Guadeloupe.

Busco Rhum Vieux
Bottled Strength: 43% alcohol by volume
Notes: Four-year-old rum from the Sevérin distillery in Guadeloupe.

ST. MARTIN/ST. MAARTEN

On the French Side

A number of wholesale liquor distributors, liquor stores, and well-stocked restaurant bars offer connoisseurs a chance to expand their horizons. The duty-free status also benefits the tourist who doesn't have the time to travel to the other islands.

Across the street from the north entrance to Marina Royale, Champagne is unquestionably one of the best purveyors of fine spirits in the islands. Giles Breion is very knowledgeable and caters to clients with refined tastes. Many of the bottled spirits you will find here are available nowhere else. Only the Bally Distillery visitors center in Martinique has a better selection of vintage Bally rhums. Considering the fact that all the bottles presented here are in perfect condition and worthy of the finest collections, the prices aren't unreasonable, especially when compared to the United States or Europe. Whether you are looking for collectible decanters or a bottle of the finest spirits, this is a good place to come.

Tucked away in the southeast corner of the Marina Royale complex, Krishna Stores is one of those places that you will be glad you found. This busy, little convenience store provisions charter boats in the marina and sells wholesale liquors to restaurants in the area. Bologne from Guadeloupe, Père Labat from Marie Galante, Cockspur from Barbados, Rhum Vieux St. James from Martinique, and others are displayed, but ask what else is available. I have no doubt you'll be surprised.

There aren't beautiful mahogany display cases, the aisles are crowded, and you may have to wait in line at the register. If you are in the marina, you'll probably make more than one trip to this bustling enterprise.

Among all the spirits imported here, Père Labat is the preferred choice of rhum in the adored ti punch served in the restaurants on this side of the island.

SugarBird Rum Factory

At the American West India Company in Philipsburg, I was introduced to even more spiced rum. A few years ago, Mike James and Mac Wingate-Gray came to St. Maarten from Florida and began looking for a marketable product. After an exhaustive search, they decided to make their own. Mac's Scottish ancestors had been making Scotch since the 1700s. After traveling the world in the English Army, he put his skills to work here with help from his friend. Mac's wife, Andrea, descended from a family of wine and spirits makers in Croatia, helps in all aspects of marketing and production.

The SugarBird Rum Factory blends fresh fruit, spices, and three Caribbean white rums to make six distinctive SugarBird Rums. These spiced rums differ from most others in the fact that they do not contain any of the fruit or spices in the bottle. Filtering not only helps insure the consistency of every bottle of SugarBird Rum, but reduces the amount of alcohol-soluble, essential oils leeched from the fruit and spices. When the fruit and spices are left in the bottle, these oils may continue to accumulate and, in some cases, may be found on top of spiced rums.

To be called rum, an alcohol must be at least 40% alcohol by volume. Liquors bottled at less than 40% alcohol by volume are considered

ST. MARTIN/ST. MAARTEN

liqueurs, most of which are bottled at about 24% alcohol by volume. All of the SugarBird rums are bottled at 40% alcohol by volume.

Considerable effort was spent developing the unique process to capture the natural flavors in each of these rums. Look for the SugarBird Tasting Center in Philipsburg where you can sample these unique rums and decide for yourself which is your favorite.

SUGARBIRD RUM FACTORY
PHILIPSBURG, ST. MAARTEN
Blends and bottles naturally flavored rum

SugarBird Orange Ginger
Bottled Strength: 40% alcohol by volume
Notes: Blend of three Caribbean rums, Caribbean orange, and Oriental ginger. This soft, gentle blend can be enjoyed before or after a meal, with or without ice.

SugarBird Lime Rum
Bottled Strength: 40% alcohol by volume
Notes: Blend of three Caribbean rums and fresh limes. Mix with ice for an easy-to-make daiquiri.

SugarBird Coconut Rum
Bottled Strength: 40% alcohol by volume
Notes: Blend of three Caribbean rums and coconut. Balanced taste of coconut and rum. Mix with half and half and a scoop of ice in a blender for a Sugarbird Piña Colada.

SugarBird Raspberry Rum
Bottled Strength: 40% alcohol by volume
Notes: Blend of three Caribbean white rums and fresh raspberries. Makes a difference in your favorite colada or daiquiri. Mix with pineapple juice for a refreshing tropical cocktail.

SugarBird Coffee Rum
Bottled Strength: 40% alcohol by volume
Notes: Blend of Caribbean white rum and select roasted coffee beans from Trinidad and Colombia.

SugarBird Dry Spice
Bottled Strength: 40% alcohol by volume
Notes: Blend of three Caribbean white rums, allspice, cove, cardamom, nutmeg, and cinnamon. Unlike many spiced rums, this does not include any added sugar cane syrup or sugar, hence the name Dry Spice.

On the Dutch Side

Caribbean Liquors is the local representative for Bally and Clément from Martinique, and several other rums that you can find in this book. Across the street is Sangs Food Store. You have to look around here because the inventory is not well organized, but take your time and you'll be rewarded. Afoos Supermarket, a few blocks away in Philipsburg, is also worth visiting. Look in the back corners of the shelves; you may find some nice rums here at bargain prices.

The Connoisseurs Shop in the La Palapa complex, just over the lagoon bridge near the airport, stocks many of the charter boats in the lagoon. The inventory is impressive and special orders are welcome. As more of the spirits in this book are imported—thanks to liberal laws on both sides of this island and more informed consumers—this is one of the places that you will find them.

Being an island, water is part of the experience of visiting St. Martin/St. Maarten. The Lagoon offers a unique opportunity to enjoy yourself aboard the *Alteza*. The large, wooden ship moored off La Palapa is a nice place to enjoy a rum punch at dusk. A lot of the men and women in the local sailing scene come here to unwind and relieve the stress of another day in paradise. To get to this floating bar, check the desk at the Mailbox in La Palapa Center.

There are also a number of watering holes where you will find everything from an "orgasm" to a "slippery nipple," and where "sex on the beach" may lead to a "brain hemorrhage." Enjoy yourself and don't forget—the best vacations are the ones you remember.

Blackbeard's

Few pirates of the Caribbean are as well known as Blackbeard. After serving on a privateer in the War of Spanish Succession, Englishman Edward Teach turned his sights to the warm Caribbean tradewinds. Within the next five years, he became legendary as a bloodthirsty, rum-drinking pirate who abused his crew and struck terror in the hearts of all who came in contact with him. Wearing his braided beard tied back over his ears, Teach resembled a giant devil with smoking incense in his hat, two cutlasses, and six muskets.

In return for stolen goods, the governor of North Carolina gave Blackbeard and his ship *Queen Anne's Revenge* necessary supplies and refuge. But, in 1718, Blackbeard met his demise at the hands of Lieutenant Robert Maynard. Legend maintains that even after he had been shot several times, had his head cut off, and was tied to the bowsprit of Maynard's sloop, Blackbeard swam twice around the boat.

In memory of this larger than life figure, Stephen Thompson's Sint Maarten Guavaberry Company blends and bottles three Blackbeard Five Star Rums. These white, dark, and gold rums

RUMS OF THE WORLD

are blended at 40% alcohol to capture the taste of the islands. Four more Blackbeard's rums are blended at 35% alcohol and include Coconut, Spiced, Pepper, and the most popular, Bois Bande rum. Blackbeard's rums can be tasted at the Sint Maarten Guavaberry Company on Front Street in Philipsburg.

SINT MAARTEN GUAVABERRY COMPANY
PHILIPSBURG, ST. MAARTEN
Blends and bottles Blackbeard Rums

Blackbeard Five Star White Rum
Bottled Strength: 40% alcohol by volume
Notes: Blend of molasses-based white rums from the Caribbean. One of the few blends of white rum I have encountered.

Blackbeard Five Star Gold Rum
Bottled Strength: 40% alcohol by volume
Notes: Blend of aged, molasses-based golden rums from the Caribbean. Very mixable blend of matured rums.

Blackbeard Five Star Dark Rum
Bottled Strength: 40% alcohol by volume
Notes: Blend of aged, molasses-based rums colored to attain the rich dark color. The added color of this rum doesn't overpower the flavor of the blend.

ST. MARTIN/ST. MAARTEN

Cariba Nativa

To complement their Blackbeard's rums, Gourmet Chocolate Fudge, Guavaberry Liqueurs, and colognes, the Sint Maarten Guavaberry Company also bottles five Caribbean rums under their Cariba Nativa label. These rums from Guadeloupe, Antigua, Barbados, the Virgin Islands, Trinidad, and Jamaica offer the tourist an opportunity to get to know rum from each of these islands.

As you should know by now, the rum from each of these islands is unique. All of these rums are molasses based, with the exception of the Guadeloupe rum which is made from fresh cane juice. Bottled at 40% alcohol by volume, each rum is aged on its island of origin except the clear spirits from Guadeloupe.

While you are in Philipsburg, look for the Antillean gingerbread house on the north side of Front Street. Here you can try all of these products, in addition to the Guavaberry Liqueurs, that made this a Sint Maarten landmark.

Even though Mr. Thompson's Blackbeard's Rum and Cariba Nativa rums were new to the market in 1995 and 1996 respectively, they have both gained respectable followings among local connoisseurs in spite of being introduced into the competitive tourist market.

RUMS OF THE WORLD

SINT MAARTEN GUAVABERRY COMPANY
PHILIPSBURG, SINT MAARTEN
Blends and bottles Cariba Nativa Rums

Cariba Nativa Trinidad Rum
Bottled Strength: 40% alcohol by volume

Notes: Aged rum from Trinidad. Made from fermented molasses.

Cariba Nativa Guadeloupe Rum
Bottled Strength: 40% alcohol by volume

Notes: White rum agricole from Guadeloupe; the only Cariba Nativa rum that is made from sugar cane juice.

Cariba Nativa Antigua Rum
Bottled Strength: 40% alcohol by volume

Notes: Aged rum from the Antigua Distillery Limited, made with fermented molasses.

Cariba Nativa Barbados Rum
Bottled Strength: 40% bottled strength

Notes: Aged rum from Barbados, representative of the Bajan taste for rum. Also made from fermented molasses.

Cariba Nativa Virgin Islands Rum
Bottled Strength: 40% alcohol by volume

Notes: Aged rum from the Virgin Islands Rum Distillery. Made from fermented molasses.

Cariba Nativa Jamaica Rum
Bottled Strength: 40% alcohol by volume

Notes: Very representative of the aged Jamaican light rums made from fermented molasses.

St. Bart's

Little, if any, rum was ever produced on this small island, named for the brother of Columbus. But hardly a rum drinker in the Caribbean has come through here without drinking some rum. (Some enterprising brokers here blend rum to make their product unique. This blending, however, is commonly done without even removing the bung.) Being a free port, this French island has prospered as a trading center.

In order for rum to be exported from Trinidad, for example, it must be shipped to another island, with clearance papers that document the cargo. If the spirit is not declared and the taxes paid, when the ship arrives at its destination, the cargo is confiscated, fines are levied, and sometimes the boat is seized. When a ship arrives in a free port, only port charges are levied, and cargo can be shipped without the taxes normally collected on the other islands.

Stories abound about rum coming here from Trinidad and Barbados to be reshipped, often on the same boat, back to the other islands. Since the customs officials in Trinidad and Barbados are commonly in contact with their counterparts on other islands, it isn't worth the risk to try to smuggle in goods from ports that are not duty-free.

Cane spirits are not the only commodity that has contributed to the prosperity of this island. The number of liquor warehouses on the waterfront is testimony to the demand for fine spirits in the islands—especially when they can be bought and sold without the taxes that so often discourage commerce.

As you enter Gustavia from the water, Segeco, on your starboard side, is the local distributor for Bologne, Clément, Simonnet, and Bally. Smoke and Booze, one block inland from the north side of the harbor, should also not be missed. You never know what you will find in the way of aged rhum from

Martinique and Guadeloupe.

While you are on the north side of the harbor, AMC et Cie Supermarket has a very impressive selection of rhum, some of which were distilled as long ago as 1949. Since most of the French distilleries have distributors here, you will be sure to find something that you didn't expect to see.

St. Kitts

Under some laws, a spirit is considered rum when it is distilled from fermented sugar cane juice, syrup, or molasses less than 95% alcohol by volume. If the spirit is distilled to a higher alcohol purity, it can be considered vodka or, if flavored with juniper berries, as gin. Sometimes a distillery will distill most of the alcohol to a high purity and then blend this with other alcohol that has been distilled to a lower alcoholic content.

It seems that about five years ago, Baron Edmond Rothschild built a distillery in St. Kitts to produce fine cane spirits. This is Cane Spirit Rothschild—you know Rothschild, the wine family. CSR, as it is known, is not rum because it is distilled to 95% alcohol by volume. Rothschild does plan to make rum in the near future. The small distillery, next to the sugar factory, has two small copper pot stills but there is a lot of work to be done to determine the label, packaging, and taste of the rum.

Ironically, there appears to be more rum made on this island, where no rum is officially produced, than on some of the other islands where rum is made. Here, hammond or culture is the drink of choice. This strong spirit is distilled from fermented molasses in small, illicit stills. On St. Kitts, the annual carnival celebration is called "culturama" after the drink culture which is part of their national pride.

All of the sugar cane grown on St. Kitts is processed at the government-owned sugar mill. But since so much of the island is covered with the sweet grass, some of the juice ends up in barrels, where it is fermented for three to five days and then distilled. It wasn't easy to ascertain many of the details that go into producing this spirit. It was, however, not hard to find this rum. Culture is usually sold shortly after it is distilled, and it is interesting to see how the flavor changes with time. As it rests, *even in a small bottle, some of the carbonic gas that remains in solution after distillation is released and the flavor improves.*

This strong rum, bottled straight from the still, is very unforgiving if you drink too much. CSR, on the other hand, guarantees you won't get a hangover. It has, however, been my experience that the only way to guarantee that you will not get a hangover from an alcohol is not to drink it. Good luck.

Culture or Hammond
Fermentation: Fresh sugar cane juice or cane syrup fermented for about three days.

Distillation Equipment: Steel drum pot still

Bottled Strength: 50-70% alcohol by volume

Notes: Very fragrant strong rum. This illicit rum is often flavored with local spices to make a more palatable drink.

Antigua

Only a few miles east of the northern Caribbean Islands, the Atlantic Ocean is over three miles deep. As the westerly equatorial current passes from this deep water to depths of only about a hundred feet on the banks between the islands, spectacular seas can build up, especially when the tradewinds are blowing at the usual 20-25 knots.

While I was waiting in St. Bart's for more favorable weather, the National Weather Service in Miami predicted easterly winds at 10-15 knots. A high pressure area that had been responsible for 15-25 knots of wind out of the southeast had moved slightly north. I expected the wind to back or shift counterclockwise to north of its present direction. At 13:00, I set sail for Guadeloupe with the outside chance that the wind would back even more, to north of east, and allow me to sail the seventy-two miles southeast to Antigua.

As the sun set behind St. Bart's, Tafia was on course to St. Johns, Antigua. The seas, built up from the southeast wind of the last three days, were beginning to dissipate and build from the new wind direction. When the moon finally rose above the loom of Antigua, Tafia was well along the rhumb line to St. Johns, despite sailing into the slightly confused seas. Few things in life are quite so gratifying as sailing under a bright moon, on course to the next island.

During the warm, moonlit night, I had only seen a northbound sailboat and an island freighter. Now, west of the southwestern point of Antigua, two dim, white lights appeared, one nearly above the other. As I approached the western coast of Antigua, I could make out a green light forward and below the white lights.

After consulting the log from my last visit here five years ago, I planned to enter Five Islands on a *bearing to the radio tower on top of one of the highest peaks on the island. As I approached the rocky shallows off Five Islands, the two white lights behind me separated. And the sky to the east, above the mountains of Antigua, showed the first signs of dawn as I dropped the anchor into this idyllic bay.*

A few hours later, when I anchored in St. John's to clear immigrations and customs, there was a large sailing ship made fast at the new cruise ship dock. The white range lights that I had seen earlier were high on the first two of four masts and the green navigation light was well forward on the upper deck cabin of the Bark Fantome.

Antigua Distillery Limited

The average elevation in Antigua is a few hundred feet. Only a few peaks rise above 1,000 feet, contributing to an annual rainfall of only 45 inches per year. Although this dry climate is conducive to a good vacation, it caused considerable hardship on the planters who settled here in 1623. When the rain did cooperate, however, the sugar cane that grew here was sweeter than that on neighboring islands. Muscovado sugar from Antigua was considered exceptional in the confectionery shops of England and the planters prospered.

Rum has been made in Antigua since sugar was introduced to the island from St. Kitts. At that time, rum was made in simple pot stills on the sugar estates. In 1932, a group of Portuguese traders founded the Antigua Distillery Limited using old distillation equipment that had been developed in the middle of the last century. Without much consideration from the ruling council, they were allowed to operate a distillery on a small piece of land known as Rat Island, just outside of St. John's. Today, the distillery stands next to the new, deep water dock. What was an undesirable island is now part of the expansion of St. John's, the capital city of the sister island nation of Antigua and Barbuda.

Since rum in the English-speaking islands has always been made from molasses, the businessmen acquired a sugar mill and several associated estates. This insured the supply of muscovado molasses, essential to the original Caballero Rum, which became known as Cavalier Muscovado Rum. The sugar business fell on hard times during World War II and, with the collapse of the Caribbean Island sugar economy in the years that followed, the sugar mill was closed. Today, the 1,800 acre Montpelier Estate produces a variety of other agricultural products.

At Antigua Distillery Limited, the distillation of rum does not claim to be based on some historical recipe. The owners realize that the connoisseur's taste for rum varies with geography and time. Rum produced in Guadeloupe, only 40 miles south of Antigua, does not have a large following here and, what was considered good rum here a hundred years ago, would not be salable in today's market.

Due to the economics of sugar production, sugar cane has not been grown commercially in Antigua since 1970. Molasses must be bought on the world market and imported for what is considered a fast fermentation process. After fermentation, the bulk of the rum is collected from the third column of the four-column still. Smaller quantities of lighter rum are also condensed from the fourth column. By law, a distillery in Antigua may only produce alcohol of less than 95% purity.

Depending from which column the rum was condensed, the raw output from the still is diluted to between 70% and 80% alcohol for aging.

A few years ago, the distillery was faced with the necessity of replacing its aging copper distillation column. John Dore and Company in England was contracted to provide the new, copper four-column still. Copper, it was agreed, had the advantage of producing a rum with a much improved flavor over the stainless steel alternative. This equipment would also produce rum closer to the previous product of the distillery.

Antigua's drier climate helped produce the high quality sugar grown here in the past. Today, the drier climate is credited with improving the aging process of the rum that sleeps on this island. With the greater evaporation losses, due to the more arid climate, comes a smoother, aged rum.

Committed to producing the best, aged rum possible, Antigua Distillery Limited uses 200 liter, charred oak barrels for aging its rums. Storing the barrels on their sides maximizes the contact between the barrel and the rum and the benefits of aging. (Some things have stood the test of time and remain unchanged.)

The bulk of the distribution of this distillery's rum is in the Caribbean. But distribution agreements have been made to market these products in Florida's ABC liquor stores. Soon, on the other side of the Atlantic, Cavalier Antigua Rum will be bottled in the United Kingdom to serve the expanding market there and in Europe. Antigua Distillery Limited is an aggressive company in terms of marketing, so look for new products which may include rums ten years old and older. The introduction of these products should put this small to medium distillery near the top of the connoisseur's list when looking for quality rums of the Eastern Caribbean.

Descendants of two of the entrepreneurs who founded this distillery operate liquor stores in St. John's. The Manuel Dias Liquor Store is on the corner of Long and Market Streets. Quin Farara's Liquor Stores are across the street at Long Street and Corn Alley and at the new Jolly Harbour Marina. Both of these friendly stores have extensive selections of imported liquor and all of Antigua Distillery Limited's products.

ANTIGUA DISTILLERY LIMITED
ST. JOHNS, ANTIGUA
Founded 1932
Fermentation: Molasses, with a fast fermentation of less than thirty-six hours
Distillation Equipment: Copper, four-column continuous still

Cavalier Antigua Rum: Light and Dark
Bottled Strength: Light–43% alcohol by volume, Dark–75.5% alcohol by volume
Age: Two years
Notes: Light and Dark refer to the color. The light rum has been carbon-filtered to remove the color while the dark rum has been slightly colored. Cavalier is commonly referred to as "Antigua" on the other islands.

Cavalier Five-Year-Old Rum
Bottled Strength: 43% alcohol by volume
Age: Five years
Notes: A blend of aged rum only bottled as dark rum. It is available everywhere in Antigua and on some of the other islands too.

RUMS OF THE WORLD

English Harbour Antigua Rum

Bottled Strength: 40% alcohol by volume

Notes: Blend of six-year-old rums from this distillery. Introduced a few years ago, English Harbour is the premium bottled rum of Antigua Distillery Limited. There are plans to sell a three-year-old, blended rum under the English Harbour label in the export market.

Every year on the last Sunday in May, hundreds of yachts are attracted to the clear water and warm climate of Antigua. Started as a week of friendly racing between the charter seasons in the Caribbean, New England or the Mediterranean, Antigua Sailing Week is now a world-famous event.

Whether you come to race or just watch, you won't be bored—unless you don't enjoy great tropical beach parties on a grand scale.

Bolans

This quiet village near the west coast of Antigua is well known by the local rum drinkers. After rowing ashore to the beach near the Valley Church, just south of the new Jolly Harbour Marina, I walked north to Bolans.

Across the street from the two petrol pumps, Bushy is the postmaster, storekeeper, and dispenser of fine, blended rum. John "Bushy" Angelo Barreto came to Antigua in 1956 from Madeira. Since that time, he has lived above the biggest business in town. Downstairs, on the right side of the building that houses the post office and a small general store, is the liquor counter.

Rum, known locally as Bolans, is bought from Antigua Distillery Limited at a high proof and diluted nearly in half by this cheery man. Depending on availability, Bushy bottles different rums with different labels. The bottle I bought for EC $6 didn't have a label, but neither did any of the other bottles on the shelf. If you are in the market for a crate of rum, John will gladly oblige. Don't be surprised if the bottles are different, recycling rum bottles is a matter of course in the islands.

It was well after noon by the time I had procured a bottle of the only rum available that day, Bushy's Best Matured Rum. I had been invited to join the Tot Club in English Harbour for the nightly ritual, so I was unable to spend as much time here as I would have liked. The next time I come to Antigua, I'll certainly come back to the Bolans Post Office and, maybe, I will have a letter to send home.

RUMS OF THE WORLD

BUSHY BARRETO'S BLENDS
BOLANS VILLAGE, ANTIGUA

Bushy's Best Matured Rum

Bottled Strength: about 40% alcohol by volume

Notes: Blended rum from the Antigua Distillery Limited; its age varies. Very popular on the west coast of Antigua, with a distinctly different taste from the Cavalier Rums bottled by the distillery.

The Tot Club

After a hurricane wreaked havoc on the English fleet in Barbados in 1780, the repair and outfitting center was moved to Antigua. In 1784, Horatio Viscount Nelson arrived in English Harbour and became the Commander of the English fleet in the Leeward Islands. English Harbour became known as Nelson's Dockyard.

In those days, copper was used to sheath the bottom of wooden ships to protect them from worms and other growths that quickly attach themselves to anything in this warm, tropical water. Hundreds of English seamen were living here while their ships were repaired. The well-protected, deep port was a throng of activity where everything needed to supply the wooden ships could be found, including stores of rum for the daily ration.

The original Copper and Lumber Store that served Nelson's ships is now an elegant hotel, restaurant, and bar steeped in antiques and history. About twelve years ago, an English seaman, retired from twenty-one years in the Royal Navy, arrived and revived a tradition that was last celebrated on August 31, 1970.

Traditionally, a daily tot was served before lunch. Today, the dedicated members of the Tot Club meet every night at 18:00 hours to propose the daily toast and honor the Queen.

Membership in the Tot Club is restricted. Only those willing to participate at least four nights a week are considered worthy of the group. All of the members either own their own yachts or are directly involved in the local sailing industry. Tot Club founder Mike Rose used to charter his beautiful yacht *Paladin*. My host at the evening ceremony, Hamish Burgess-Simpson, manages the locally based Sun Yacht Charters

Usually the Tot Club meets at the gentlemen's bar at the Copper and Lumber Store Hotel, but during the off season, in June and July, the group meets by previous arrangement at other watering holes in the area. Onlookers at the nightly ceremony are welcome. Respect for the tot is greatly appreciated by those who have revived this Royal Navy tradition.

On most nights, Mike Rose acts as master of ceremonies. Alan Jeyes, the owner of the hotel and one of the original members, tends bar for the proceeding. Each member and invited guest are served one-half gill (one-eighth of an imperial pint) of Pusser's Blue Label Navy Rum. A glass of ice water is also served to cleanse the palate and to act as a fire engine afterward.

Although Pusser's Blue Label Navy Rum is the preferred drink, it is not always available. To drink this quantity of most other rums in one drink is difficult, if not impossible. The smoothness of Pusser's Blue Label has earned it a very faithful following among the Tot Club members in English Harbour.

As the white-bearded gentleman makes sure

all is ready, a quiet reverence permeates the group that includes the members, a few wives, girlfriends, and respectful onlookers. Guests are introduced, then the order to cleanse the palate is given. After drinking some of the ice water, silence fills the high-ceiled bar. In unison, the toast of the day is given. All of the toasts end with: "The Queen, God Bless Her!" And the tot is drunk in one.

The toasts were originally given by the Royal Navy officers and reflected shipboard life in the West Indies. Two of the traditional toasts have been altered by the Tot Club to reflect the modern atmosphere of the ritual:

Sunday:
Absent friends and those at sea.

Monday:
Our ships at sea.

Tuesday:
Our friends. Originally, "Our men."
(The Tot Club has changed this as none of them have a crew as such.)

Wednesday:
Ourselves, as no one else is likely to concern themselves with our welfare.

Thursday:
A bloody war and a quick promotion.
Originally a very West Indian-oriented toast, "A bloody war and a sickly season." Either, would lead to a quick promotion.

Friday:
A willing foe and sea room.

Saturday:
Sweethearts and wives.
May they never meet.

ANTIGUA

Royal Navy sailors were known as "limeys," named after the juice that was a part of their diet to ward off scurvy. To the civilians in English Harbour, the limeys appeared to be on vacation while they were in port. Commonly associated with drinking what was most available—rum—and doing what most sailors did in their free time—chase the opposite sex—"liming" became a reference to goofing off and just enjoying oneself. When you are invited to "lime," go ahead and indulge yourself.

Guadeloupe

Just as the languages vary from island to island, so do the tastes for food and drink. When you read the label on a bottle of rhum, look for the words agricole, industriel, or traditionnel. This will tell you whether the rhum was made from cane juice or molasses.

To be called rhum agricole, the spirit must be made from fresh sugar cane juice as opposed to molasses or cane syrup. Rhum agricole can be loosely divided into two categories—aperitifs and digestives. When you visit the distilleries, notice how these rhums are presented to you to be tasted.

Aperitifs are drunk before a meal and are commonly served as a punch of rhum blanc, or white rhum. Most distilleries will mix a little cane syrup with a small slice of lime, then add rhum blanc, and sometimes a little water. This is also the drink you will be served when you order a rhum punch in a restaurant or bar. It is worth noting that the distilleries suggest different proportions for mixing this simple drink called ti punch. Although it takes some time and patience to learn to make a good ti punch, I encourage you to try. After several months of intensive research, mixing, and drinking French rhum, I was surprised how properly mixing this cocktail can make or break the enjoyment of white rhum agricole.

Digestives, easily recognized by their darker color, are consumed after a meal. These mature rhums can be enjoyed straight, with a little cane syrup or with a small amount of water. All of the distilleries will let you sample the rhum blanc, or unaged white rhum, but they are much prouder of their aged products.

It is easier to acquire a taste for these aged rhums. After tasting the white rhums, I am sure you will be surprised how the taste of these spirits *changes with age. Many people liken these aged rhums, known as* rhum vieux, *or old rhum, to fine cognac. In fact, much of the process apparatus employed in the manufacture of rhum is made by the cognac distillation equipment manufacturers in France. Even though the fermentation and raw ingredients are very different, the distillation of cognac and rhum is quite similar.*

Paille *refers to straw-colored rhum, which has been aged less than three years—usually one year to eighteen months. Less expensive than rhum vieux, rhum paille is smoother than rhum blanc and makes a good ti punch.*

I encountered only a few examples of rhum industriel, and will refer to them as either rhum industriel *or* rhum traditionnel. *These spirits are made from fermented molasses and are, therefore, less expensive to produce. Most of the rhum industriel made in the French West Indies is exported to Europe to be bottled under a variety of labels.*

The aging time for rhum vieux varies anywhere from three or four to more than twenty years. According to French law, rhum vieux must be aged at least three years in barrels of no more than 650 liter capacity. Rhum that has been put in the barrel before the first of July is considered one-year-old on that date. All of the distilleries use barrels that have been previously used for whiskey or cognac. Because smaller barrels enhance the benefits of aging, none of the barrels used are more than about 250 liters.

You will see a difference in the color of the aged rhums. Part of the difference is from the barrels and part is due to caramel coloring. None of the distilleries want to be known for adding significant color to their rhum, but there is universal agreement that many of the rhums are colored. Compare the different colors, ages, aromas, and tastes for yourself.

Rhum Marsolle

In my quest to discover all of the rhums distilled in the Eastern Caribbean, I found a rhum that is only sold as rhum blanc. Rhum Marsolle is actually a blend of white rhums from the Montebello and Séverin distilleries. Introduced during Christmas of 1992, this rhum won the Médaille d'Or at the Concours Général Agricole de Paris in 1993.

The Marsolle family has been involved in the rhum business in Guadeloupe for many generations. The fine result of their experience is this award-winning white rhum agricole.

CLAUDE MARSOLLE & CIE
POINTE-À-PITRE, GUADELOUPE

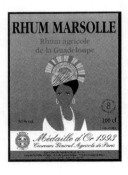

Rhum Marsolle

Bottled Strength: 50% alcohol by volume

Notes: Blend of white rhum agricole from the Montebello and Séverin distilleries. Although Rhum Marsolle is blended from these two white rhums of Guadeloupe, it is quite different from either of its parts.

Bologne

As the oldest distillery in Guadeloupe, Bologne reveals the colorful history of the lives of its people, including the conflicts they endured after sugar was introduced in the early seventeenth century.

In the sixteenth century, the Protestant de Bologne family, originally from France, emigrated from Holland to the Spanish-controlled colony of Brazil. While Spain was preoccupied with the quest for gold in the new world, the Dutch refugees prospered by cultivating sugar cane and selling the sugar in Europe.

In 1640, Portugal won her independence from Spain. Together, Portugal and Brazil then declared war on the Dutch planters in Brazil. The immigrants were forced to leave once again. After being refused permission to land in Catholic-dominated Martinique, a convoy of several boats and twelve hundred refugees arrived in Guadeloupe early in 1654. The prosperous de Bologne family brought gold, silver, slaves, and equipment from their sugar factory with them.

By 1664, Louis de Bologne and his two sons, Guillaume and Pierre, had begun to rebuild their sugar trade in the southwest region of Guadeloupe. For one hundred years, the de Bologne family business was successful. But in 1764, Joseph Samuel de Bologne was unable to pay his debts and the property was sold.

Thirteen years later, the estate, which consisted of the cane mill, sugar factory, distillery, a beautiful brick master's house, a separate kitchen, cages for fowl, and a jail had changed hands three more times.

Two years later, the French Revolution (1789-

1802) was declared in Paris—an event that changed the lives of everyone from the slaves in the colonies to the king himself. When the decree of the abolition of slavery was signed on the 4th of February 1794, large numbers of newly freed slaves joined the troops and went to war or simply disappeared. Eight years later, slavery was reinstated, but the fighting had destroyed the estates and their ability to produce sugar.

The Bologne house and sugar factory changed hands again before Jean-Antoine Ame-Noël bought the sugar factory on the May 26, 1830. A black man, "free by birth," originally from Bouillante, Jean-Antoine was a free mason, fisherman, corsair, speculator, and coffee grower in Bouillante. Until that time, no black man had owned a sugar factory of such significance as the Bologne factory.

The estate now consisted of more than one principal house, a better cane mill, four boilers, filters for making sugar, and a four-stone mill to grind manioc. The cane mill and the stone aqueduct, which brought water from the river, can still be seen at the distillery.

The definitive abolition of slavery, in 1848, accentuated the economic problems of the planters prompting Jean-Antoine to organize a société agriculturale with sixty cultivateurs. The profits from this arrangement were shared equally between the owners of the land, the equipment, and the labor.

In 1850, Jean-Antoine was buried in a small garden next to the distillery in the midst of his 140 hectare estate. Francois Joseph Ame-Nöel inherited his uncle's fortune but, despite his best efforts, the sugar industry continued to decline. In 1874, he was unable to pay his debts and the property was auctioned to settle the account.

In 1873, the Le Dentu and Cie corporation built the Usine de la Basse-Terre, a central sugar factory. This marked a turning point in the evolution of the sugar industry. Modern machinery, which tripled the efficiency of the sugar crystallization process, was imported. Even a railroad was built to transport the cane to the factory. A million francs were raised by selling bonds to finance the operation and, in 1875, the Bologne house was allotted to M. Emile Le Dentu for his own use.

When the Usine de la Basse-Terre was unable to repay the huge debts it had incurred, the properties were again fragmented by auction in 1887. On November 3, 1930, the house and grounds were purchased by M. Louis Sargenton-Callard. Since that time, the property has not changed hands. Today, Suzanne Sargenton-Callard is responsible for the distillery operation at Bologne.

From Deshaies, it's an interesting bus ride to Baillif, just north of Basse-Terre. Start early, the 8:00 bus to Basse-Terre stops just north of the jetty, near the vegetable stand. You can get a cup of coffee and a croissant in one of the sidewalk cafes while you wait. Just south of the Basse-Terre airport, the Bologne distillery is easily spotted on your left up the steep, stone road in the cane fields.

When the production of sugar became unprofitable at the end of the nineteenth century, Bologne began specializing in making white rhum agricole. The process begins by hand-cutting mature cane from the fields around the distillery and other farms in Guadeloupe. After the cane is weighed and crushed to extract the juice, or *vesou*, the filtered juice is pumped to one of the eight 50,000 liter fermentation vats. During the twenty-four to forty-eight hour fermentation, the heat generated in these tall tanks promotes natural circulation. The circulation, the large surface area, and the shade from the sheet metal building dissipates the heat and reduces the possibility of the wine spoiling due to high temperatures.

After fermentation, the *grappe*, or cane wine, is distilled in one of the two identical, copper distillation columns. The beautifully crafted copper piping and polished columns that make up these stills are truly works of art.

Bologne is unique in that the rhum is distilled to only 55° to 60°, allowing more of the flavor of the cane juice to come through. This practice requires careful quality control of the cane, the fermentation process, and the trained fingers of the distiller, or *maître rhumier*. Cane cut from a burned field, for instance, would negatively affect the taste of the finished product.

After careful distillation, the clear raw rhum, or *rhum distillerie coulage*, rests in large oak casks up to six months while the flavor improves. After resting, the rhum is blended with pure, spring water to 50°, filtered, and then stored in stainless steel tanks prior to bottling.

Bologne produces 1,400,000 liters of rhum between November and August, then bottles it throughout the year. In order to minimize production and inventory costs, only one liter bottles of white rhum are bottled here at 50°.

A lot number, including a date, is stamped on each label during bottling. The finished product doesn't vary much, but the rhum bottled just before the end of the year would have been allowed to rest the longest and would, therefore, be the smoothest. Close examination of the bottled product reveals the slight color attained during the time spent in the oak casks.

Tours at Bologne are from 9:00 A.M. to 1:00 P.M. daily during the season. Come taste for yourself what a difference the low distillation purity and staling in oak vats can make on the most popular white rhum in Guadeloupe.

BOLOGNE DISTILLERY
BASSE-TERRE, GUADELOUPE
Founded 1664
Fermentation: Fresh squeezed sugar cane juice between twenty-four and forty-eight hours
Distillation Equipment: Two copper, single-column continuous stills

Rhum Bologne
Bottled Strength: 50% alcohol by volume
Age: After distillation, this rhum rests in large oak casks for up to six months.
Notes: Produced between November and August, the rhum bottled near the end of the year rests the longest and is therefore slightly smoother—look for the lot number on the label. Its unique taste is due to its low distillation purity and oak vat staling. The only product of this distillery, Rhum Bologne is the most popular white rum in Guadaloupe.

Séverin

The spectacular view of northern Guadeloupe from this distillery is one of the great vistas in the Caribbean. Between the northern coast of Basse-Terre and the mountain ridge that runs along almost the whole length of the island, fertile cane fields stretch from the ocean to the steep mountains. Clouds moving in from the east against the mountains turn to showers over these fertile fields and add dimension to a scene that must be experienced to be appreciated.

When the northern coast road east of Sainte Marie crosses the Rivière Goyaves, head south. About a kilometer down this road, one of the last sugar mills in Guadeloupe is on your left and the sweet smell of molasses fills the air. A few hundred meters past the sugar mill is a sign to the Domain de Séverin pointing to the right.

Entering the Séverin estate is like entering one of the finest resorts on the island; flowering tropical plants and fruit trees are everywhere. A restaurant, above the distillery, serves lunch with a grand view stretching to the ocean.

Started by the Marsolle family in 1929, this distillery is fairly new compared to some of the others in Guadeloupe. From the fields around the estate, one-year-old cane is cut by hand, tied in bundles, and loaded onto small trailers. After the cane is weighed, it is manually unloaded onto a conveyor, where an electric-powered machete shreds it before it's fed twice through the old three-roller mill. The original water wheel, the centerpiece of the distillery, uses water that flows down the mountain to power the cane mill. A manually cleaned screen removes the pulp from the juice so that it can be put back into the mill to be pressed again. This filtering is usually done mechanically by a roll of metal screen, but here most of the work is done by hand.

From the cane mill, an electric pump moves the juice to the stainless steel fermenting vats. In the hot tropical sun, the fermenting tanks actually overflow with foam produced during the forty-eight hour fermentation. When fermentation is complete, the wine is distilled in a new, stainless steel distillation column. A few years ago, the original copper column was replaced because it was beyond economical repair; the years of separating the alcohol from the wine had taken its toll.

After distillation, the rhum is diluted to 50° and bottled as Séverin Rhum Blanc, or put in 250 liter barrels to age. After at least six years, the mature rhum is bottled as Séverin Rhum Vieux at 45°. Neck bands on the bottles of rhum vieux indicate the year the rhum was distilled. This rhum is generally bottled before the rhum season in order for more barrels to be available for the next season's production.

The aging warehouse at the distillery is not open to the public, but all of the Séverin rhums are available in the visitors center. A variety of rhum punches, made from passion fruit, guava, and other fruits grown on the estate, are also available here.

Even though this is a small distillery, seventeen employees produce 210,000 liters of rhum between January and July each year. In a small building next to the distillery, large baskets of small, *very* hot, green peppers are prepared, by hand, to make hot sauce. I have mistakenly eaten these small peppers, an experience that changed the way I look at Caribbean hot peppers. If you like hot sauces, these peppers will satisfy even the hottest taste.

The Domain de Séverin is a very pleasant estate to visit. It is possible to see, up close, how the cane is processed, fermented, and distilled. Guided tours at this popular tourist attraction are every half hour from about 10:00 A.M. until early afternoon.

DOMAIN DE SÉVERIN DISTILLERY
SAINTE ROSE, GUADELOUPE

Founded 1929

Fermentation: Freshly squeezed sugar cane juice fermented for forty-eight hours

Distillation Equipment: Stainless steel, single-column continuous still

Séverin Rhum Blanc

Bottled Strength: 50% alcohol by volume

Age: Aged in barrels, the number of years are identified by neck bands on the bottles

Notes: This rhum won the Médaille d'Or at the Concours Général Agricole de Paris in 1992. It is also used in many of the fruit punches made at the distillery.

Séverin Rhum Vieux

Bottled Strength: 45% alcohol by volume

Age: At least six years

Notes: Look at the year on the bottle to determine when the rhum was distilled. The distillery does not maintain a large inventory of aged rhum, so the age of the rhum vieux is approximately the number of years since distillation.

As you travel the roads in Guadeloupe, you will see cane stalks that have fallen off the trailers that carry the cane to the distilleries and sugar mills. If the cane stalk is long and has been cut on an angle, it was probably cut by hand. Machine-cut cane is cut perpendicular to the stalk into short pieces about forty centimeters long.

Simonnet

Since I had walked many miles in the last few days, I boarded the bus in Pointe-à-Pitre for Pris d'Eau, hoping the route would take me close to the distillery. The smell of molasses and sugar being processed on the right and the fermenting wash and aging warehouse on the left will signal your arrival. I soon found out that of all the distilleries and sugar mills I have visited, this is the first place where the road actually goes between the buildings.

In 1928, the sugar factory, or *sucrerie* as it is called in Guadeloupe, was built by M. Remonique. Since then, the French government acquired control of the sugar factory and the distillery. In 1967, the distillery was sold to a corporation headed by Charles Simonnet and has remained physically connected to the mill. The pipes you see over the road carry fresh cane juice, molasses, and steam from the sugar mill to the distillery.

During the early months of the year, when cane is being harvested, some of the juice from the sugar mill is fermented for the production of rhum agricole. In the later months, molasses is fermented for the production of rhum industriel. After fermenting twenty-four hours, the wine is fed to a unique still.

In this specially built configuration, the vapor from the first column is not condensed. Instead, a large duct carries the vapor to the bottom of the second column. Had the still been built as one straight column, it would have been much taller than the building and would have faced other problems, including wind loads from tropical storms and hurricanes that occasionally hit the island. The effective, taller column allows the molasses-based rhum industriel to be distilled to a higher purity than is possible in a shorter, single column.

In the aging warehouse, over three thousand barrels, some as small as 190 liters, are stored on their sides in steel racks. In July and August, all of the barrels are topped off with similar rhum from the same year in the French tradition called *houillage*. An average temperature of 27°C in the aging warehouse causes losses from ten to fifteen percent annually.

Ventilators are being installed in the roof to reduce the temperature and, hopefully, reduce the evaporation in the aging barrels. Controlling evaporation during aging is a recurring problem in these warm tropical islands. All of the distilleries credit these losses with an improvement in aging but want to control the loss of the product, which becomes more valuable every year.

About ninety percent of the two million liters of rhum distilled here annually is exported to France to be bottled under the Charles Simonnet label or sold to other bottlers. Bulk alcohol is also sold to a company in Pointe-à-Pitre that blends and bottles rhum and sweet, fruit-flavored syrups under the Madras label. Madras exports most of its products to France, but they are also available on the island.

Tours of this facility are held only on Wednesdays. They are an enjoyable way to see some of the countryside and a unique distillery.

GUADELOUPE

GRAND RHUMS CHARLES SIMONNET DISTILLERY
PRIS D'EAU, GUADELOUPE

Founded 1967

Fermentation: Sugar cane from the sugar mill is fermented twenty-four hours for rhum agricole. Molasses is fermented twenty-four hours for rhum industriel.

Distillation Equipment: Stainless steel, two-column continuous still

Rhum Charles Simonnet
Bottled Strength: 50 and 55% alcohol by volume
Age: Unaged
Notes: This white rhum agricole is shipped to France to be bottled under the Charles Simonnet label.

Charles Simonnet Rhum Vieux
Bottled Strength: 45% alcohol by volume
Age: At least four years
Notes: The labels for the agricole rhums bottled here are similar but easily distinguishable by the color of the rhum in the bottle.

Fajou Rhum Blanc Assemblage
Bottled Strength: 50% alcohol by volume
Age: Unaged
Notes: This is a blend of rhum industriel and rhum agricole. It is also slightly cheaper than rhum agricole.

Mon Repos

Although the label on Mon Repos rhum shows an address of Capesterre, the distillery is actually just south of St. Anne. A sign on the eastern coast road of Basse-Terre points to Neuf Chateau. A few hundred meters west on this road takes you up through the cane fields of the estate, where the smokestack of the distillery can be seen. Several tall palm trees mark the entrance to the estate.

In 1995, this family-owned distillery celebrated its hundredth anniversary. On the foundation of the original distillery house is a three-roller cane mill that had been in service in Martinique until 1968. Behind the cane mill, timbers that supported the old distillation column still stand, blackened by years of exposure to the heat and smoke of the boiler. Some of the old piping also remains, attached to part of the old condenser.

One look at the distiller's desk, next to where the old distillation column stood, will tell you that there have been a lot of long, hot days worked here. Even though the days can be long, they all stop at sunset since there are no electric lights at the distillery shed. The whole operation runs on steam generated by burning the bagasse after the cane is crushed. Mon Repos is one of the few distilleries that does not employ electric pumps.

Between December and May, the year-old cane is harvested from the estate fields. After the cane is crushed, the fresh juice is fermented for two days in one of the six 1,500-liter fermentation tanks. Without pumps to circulate and cool the fermenting wash, the fermenting wine can get too hot, when the weather is very warm. If the fermentation is interrupted, the wine must be discarded.

About eleven years ago, the old copper distillation column was replaced with a new, stainless steel column capable of producing 6,000 liters of rhum per day. Since it takes about ten liters of fermented juice to yield one liter of rhum, the distillery is limited by the volume of fermented wine available at one time. After experience showed that the stainless steel column did not produce the same flavor rhum as the old copper column that it had replaced, the trays inside the column were reworked to include sections of copper.

The raw rhum condensed from the still varies, but is condensed at about 72% alcohol by volume. To improve the taste of the fresh rhum, it is stored for two or three months in large oak casks before being transferred to stainless steel tanks for storage prior to bottling.

Traditionally, the first rhum of the season is tasted at Christmas dinner. Before the holiday dinner is celebrated, some of the aged rhum reserve from the warehouse behind the estate house is used.

Rhum from the Mon Repos distillery is bottled under two labels. The red Mon Repos label you will find in Guadeloupe. For export, the Rhum Longueteau label is used. All of the rhum, however, is bottled here at the estate.

In addition to one liter bottles of rhum blanc, smaller 25 cl bottles with plastic caps are also used. According to M. Longueteau, if you drink one of these small bottles of rhum blanc every day, you will live a long and healthy life.

Along with its rhum distillation, the estate grows bananas. After World War II, refrigerated ships began to transport bananas from here to the European market. This small family operation now plants half the estate with bananas and the other half with sugar cane. Banana growers in the French West Indies enjoy slightly more favorable market conditions in France than their counterparts in the English-speaking islands, where competition from Central and South America is driving them out of business.

There is no organized tour at this distillery, but some of the guides in Guadeloupe come here as part of their island tour. All of the visitors who find this small estate will be rewarded. Francois Longueteau is justly proud of the rhum he and his father produce at this century-old distillery and is eager to show you why they consider Mon Repos to be "the best rhum in the world." Try to see this distillery before noon because most of the work in the islands goes on during the morning.

MON REPOS DISTILLERY
CAPESTERRE, GUADELOUPE
Founded 1895
Fermentation: Freshly squeezed sugar cane juice fermented for two days
Distillation Equipment: Stainless steel and copper, single-column continuous still

Mon Repos Rhum Blanc
Bottled Strength: 50% alcohol by volume
Age: Unaged, stored in large oak casks for a few months
Notes: This rhum is also sold under the Longueteau label.

Mon Repos Rhum Vieux
Bottled Strength: 50% alcohol by volume
Age: Seven years
Notes: This is one of the few aged rums bottled at 50% alcohol by volume in the French Islands.

Montebello

The Carrere Distillery, more commonly known as Montebello, is just a little south of Petit Bourg. Take the new highway south. At the roundabout, follow the signs west to the distillery. When the road forks, stay to the right. The cane fields that once surrounded this distillery have yielded to development and, now, as you approach the distillery, the tall fermentation tanks seem almost out of place. In recent years, this distillery has expanded to occupy almost all of the available space on the property.

With twenty-five employees, this is not a small distillery, but all of the fermentation, distillation, aging, and bottling is done under the close supervision of the Marsolle family. Attention to the details of making rhum is only one of the reasons for the success of this operation.

The estate has only fifteen hectares of cane today, so most of the year-old cane is bought from farmers in the Petit Bourg area. Once the sugar content of the cane has been determined, it is weighed, and then processed to extract the juice. In the tall fermentation tanks, yeast is added to the fresh juice to quicken the fermentation process. Using equipment developed in Brazil, active yeast is separated from the fermenting wine. This recovered yeast is used to ferment the next batch of juice and, in turn, some of the yeast from that batch will be used in the future.

Like the other distilleries in the area, the fresh cane juice is fermented for about two days, depending on the temperature of the fermenting wine. The optimum temperature for the yeast to multiply and change the sugar into alcohol is 42°C, but this is hard to control in the open tanks which sit in the sun. To provide some cooling in the tropical heat, water is dripped on the outside of the tanks.

Once fermentation is complete, the 12% alcohol wine is distilled in the two-column copper still to about 85% alcohol by volume. This is one of the highest distillation purities of any of the distilleries in Guadeloupe. Due to the sugar content of the cane and the yeast used for fermentation, Montebello produces only about sixty liters of rhum per ton of cane.

Once distilled, all of the rhum is allowed to rest in a stainless steel tank for one month. If the rhum will be bottled as Montebello Rhum Blanc, it is put in oak barrels for at least a week before bottling. This labor-intensive procedure enhances the character of the rhum, which is then bottled at 50° and 55°. All of the production is bottled here at the distillery. The majority of the rhum is bottled in one-liter bottles, but 70 cl, 50 cl, and even 25 cl bottles are also used.

After aging at least four years, Montebello Rhum Vieux is bottled at 42°, a slightly lower alcohol content than most of the other distilleries. Presently, Montebello is bottling four, five, and eight-year-old rhum. A neckband on the bottles of rhum vieux indicate the year the rhum was distilled. Since this is bottled according to demand, the age of the rhum can be approximated. Montebello is planning to sell a ten-year-old rhum in the future. One of the considerations is the bottle; a ten-year-old rhum deserves a very distinctive bottle. And the label for this rhum should, likewise, reflect the special contents.

Under the quota system instituted after World War I, Montebello is allowed to sell 350,000 liters of pure alcohol annually. Currently, the distillery falls short of that quota, with most of the production exported to France.

As part of the quota system, rhum sales are controlled; production is not. A distillery may increase its stock of rhum for aging or for sale in the future. This appears simple, but to properly store large quantities of rhum is an expensive task that requires considerable planning. The availability of barrels for aging is only one consideration; properly ventilated space is another. The capital required to produce a product and then warehouse it for some years presents even more challenges.

In spite of the difficulties encountered operating a distillery under this artificially controlled system, quotas are accepted as an integral part of this business at all of the distilleries.

Look for this distillery to begin visitor tours in the future. Although this is not the biggest distillery in Guadeloupe, the pride of Alain Marsolle and his sons is evident in every bottle of Montebello rhum.

DISTILLERIE MONTEBELLO
PETIT BOURG, GUADELOUPE
Fermentation: Fresh cane juice fermented for two days
Distillation Equipment: Two-column copper still

Montebello Rhum Blanc
Bottled Strength: 50 and 55% alcohol by volume
Age: Unaged, stored in small barrels for at least a week before bottling
Notes: Made in one of the few two-column stills in the French islands.

Montebello Rhum Vieux
Bottled Strength: 42% alcohol by volume
Age: At least four years
Notes: Check neck band to see when this rum was distilled. Probably bottled within the last six months. Look for a ten-year-old rum from this distillery.

Damoiseau

In contrast to the water-powered cane mills on the mountainous island of Basse-Terre, windmill foundations dot the low-lying countryside of Grand-Terre. Each of these foundations represents the remains of a small sugar mill, most of which included a still.

The hollow foundation of one of these windmills that faced the easterly trade winds stands next to the new visitors center at the Distillerie Bellevue. Before the end of the last century, when the demand for sugar was high, steam power replaced this windmill in order to increase production in the lucrative market. Then, in 1942, Roger Damoiseau bought the distillery. Today, his grandsons, Jean Luc and Evre Damoiseau, operate the only distillery on the island. In and around the visitors center, a collection of sugar mill and distillery equipment from the last hundred years gives the visitor a glimpse of the development of this operation.

Some of the cane processed here is still cut by hand from the surrounding fields, just as it has been for centuries. The rest of the raw sugar cane is trucked in from all over the island. The small farmer, unloading his harvest next to large semi-trailers of machine-cut cane, offers quite a contrast at the modernized facility.

Once pressed, the cane juice is fermented for thirty-six hours prior to being distilled to about 72° in the single, copper and stainless steel distillation column. Stainless steel is used in the lower sections of the column to help reduce the maintenance associated with a copper column. The top of the column is made of copper to reduce the sulfur compounds that are formed when the fermented wine is distilled.

After distillation, the rhum is either diluted to 50° for bottling or put in oak barrels for aging in the sheet-metal building that also houses the bottling operation. Damoiseau is one of the few distilleries in Guadeloupe that bottles rhum paille—rhum that has been aged less than the three years required to be called rhum vieux.

Damoiseau Rhum Paille is aged one year and is predictably smoother than the unaged rhum blanc. Rhum paille is also slightly more expensive than the more popular rhum blanc. In addition to the usual one liter and 70 cl bottles, rhum blanc is available in hand-painted bottles that are popular souvenirs.

Depending on demand and availability, Damoiseau Rhum Vieux is aged five or six years before it is bottled at 45°. Damoiseau also bottles a rare fifteen-year-old rhum. If you like the more mature rhums from the French West Indies, this aged spirit may suit your taste.

To complement the rhum agricole produced here, the distillery also bottles a large selection of rhum punches. Orange, passion fruit, coconut, planters, and Kimbe Rand (claimed to be an aphrodisiac) are only some of the punches available at the visitors center and gift shop.

Most distilleries in the French West Indies distill alcohol less than half the year, during the cane cutting season. Here, when sugar cane is out of season, molasses from a sugar factory is trucked to the distillery to be fermented. Since bagasse from the cane is not available, fuel oil is burned to generate the steam for distillation. All of this alcohol, called rhum industriel, is shipped in bulk tanks to France for blending and bottling under other labels. But in Guadeloupe, all of the rhum sold under the Damoiseau label is rhum agricole.

Damoiseau is one of the larger production distilleries in Guadeloupe and a popular tourist destination. Combined with lunch at one of the oceanside restaurants in Le Moule, this is a nice way to spend a day and experience some of the history of the island. Come prepared to relax and enjoy yourself. Both Jean Luc and Evre Damoiseau want to make this a memorable experience for everyone who takes the time to visit their distillery on the eastern side of Guadeloupe's butterfly islands.

DAMOISEAU DISTILLERY
GRAND-TERRE, GUADELOUPE

Fermentation: Freshly squeezed sugar cane juice fermented for thirty-six hours

Distillation Equipment: Copper and stainless steel, single-column continuous still. Damoiseau also distills rhum industriel from molasses for export to France.

Damoiseau Rhum Blanc
Bottled Strength: 50 and 55% alcohol by volume
Age: Unaged
Notes: Very representative of rhum agricole distilled in Guadeloupe.

Damoiseau Rhum Paille
Bottled Strength: 50% alcohol by volume
Age: One year
Notes: Predictably smoother than rhum blanc, this is the only distillery in Guadeloupe presently making rhum paille.

Damoiseau Rhum Vieux
Bottled Strength: 45% alcohol by volume
Age: Five or six years
Notes: Damoiseau also bottles a rare fifteen-year-old rhum vieux and very limited quantities of rhum as much as forty years old.

Marie Galante

In spite of its small size, Marie Galante has maintained its self-sufficiency by depending as little as possible on the importation of food from the bigger islands and becoming an established exporter of sugar and rhum. At the time I sailed to this picturesque island, there were only three distilleries in operation. Two more distilleries, which had been in operation only a few years ago, had closed due to the cost of maintaining and operating them on a small island. The future of the small distillery is threatened, but judging by the interest of tourists visiting the distilleries on this island, there will be an increasing demand for these distilleries as tourist attractions.

Marie Galante, with its highest elevation only 130 meters, is a drier island than Guadeloupe and receives only about 150 centimeters of rainfall annually. About ninety-five percent of the sugar cane produced on this island goes to the sugar mill just south of St. Louis on the northwest coast, where it is processed and shipped to foreign markets. The remaining five percent is consumed by the three distilleries on this beautiful island.

Rhum in Marie Galante is made from fresh cane juice, similar to Guadeloupe, but on a much smaller scale. Marie Galante has the right by law to produce rhum that is 59% alcohol by volume. 59° is the trademark of Marie Galante, making the rhum from this island unique in the French rhum market.

Marie Galante holds many travelers in awe. The island lifestyle is of one that most people dream and few can believe actually exists. This is one of the few places where a team of oxen pulling a wooden cart is a common sight, especially around the distilleries. Time has been kind to this small island, where life in the sun moves at a more comfortable pace.

Public transportation is best before noon, so plan your trips in the morning and enjoy the beach or just relax in the afternoon. But above all, try to spend at least a few days on this enchanted island. I never tire of the hospitality of the people, the beautiful vistas, or the chance to relax in what many travelers consider to be paradise.

Père Labat

Southeast of Saint Louis, Distillerie Poisson is on the public minibus route from Saint Louis to Grand Bourg. As you walk under the canopy of trees that shade the remains of the old wooden estate house on your left, you enter the grounds of the best-known distillery in Marie Galante.

Under an old tree is a collection of equipment from the past. Some of these pumps and cane mills have only recently been retired. Judging from the scale of this machinery, this has been a small operation for a long time.

The original stone building was built in 1860 for the production of sugar. In 1934, a single-cylinder steam engine was installed to power the cane mill and increase production in the sugar factory. The production of rhum agricole and the production of sugar begin the same way—crushing the cane. As the price of sugar fell and the cost of labor rose, many small sugar factories were sold or became distilleries.

While visiting Marie Galante, I was served a delightful cocktail. I hope you enjoy it as much as I did. Squeeze the juice from two passion fruit into a glass, add a measure of 59° rhum blanc, a little sugar, and stir with ice. Bon boisson.

The distillation of rhum began in 1940 with a copper pot still. This copper pot is still in place at the distillery, though it's no longer being used. Fifteen years later, a copper distillation column was commissioned. Today, there are two identical columns, each capable of distilling 200 liters of rhum per hour.

The original stone foundation and the walls of the sugar factory house the cane mill, fermentation vats, and distillation columns. A diesel generator makes electricity to power the cane mill and bottling operation, reducing the labor required to run the small distillery. Electricity also provides better control of the cane mill. Steam for the distillation process is generated by burning the bagasse from the cane-crushing operation.

Below the heavy cast rollers of the cane mill, a polished copper trough in the floor carries the sweet juice from the mill to a sump where it is filtered, and then pumped to the fermentation tanks. Before being used for the distillation of rhum, this trough fed the sugar pots that cooked the fresh juice to thicken it to make sugar.

Fermentation is a three-day cycle. On the first day, one of the eight steel fermentation vats is filled with cane juice and a second vat is filled to a level of about thirty centimeters. The second day, the second vat is filled, and a third vat is filled to a level of about thirty centimeters. The third day, the first vat of fermenting wine is distilled. Then, that vat is cleaned and the process is repeated.

Once distilled in the single copper column, the rhum that will become white rhum is stored in large wooden casks until it is bottled. The rhum that will become rhum vieux is put directly into oak barrels for storage. In August of each year, the barrels are topped off to replace the angels' share.

The distillery is in operation from January through May or June, depending on the sugar cane crop, present demand for rhum, and the availability of space to age rhum for the future. Like the other distilleries on this island, rhum is bottled according to demand throughout the year. This is the Distillerie Poisson, but all of the rhum produced here is known as Père Labat.

Presently owned by Rameau Heritiers, Distillerie Poisson produces about 100,000 liters of rhum at 50° annually and markets it only in Guadeloupe, Marie Galante, St. Martin, and France.

Although there is no organized tour at the distillery, several people arrived and were shown around by M. E. Renault, the manager. The staff necessary to provide a tour are not presently available; however, I expect that in the near future visitors will be encouraged as tourism continues to grow and becomes more of an important part of the island's development.

While waiting to speak to the only person here that spoke English, four French military men, on exercise in Marie Galante, appeared in their camouflaged four-wheel drive vehicle—berets and all. Looking like soldiers on a mission, they got in line with the tourists to sample the rhum. Later, these men appeared at another distillery, recognized me, shook my hand, and offered me a ride back to town. Cheers.

DISTILLERIE POISSON
GRAND BOURG, MARIE GALANTE

Founded 1860: Distillation of rhum began in 1940
Fermentation: Freshly squeezed sugar cane juice fermented for three days
Distillation Equipment: Two copper single-column continuous stills

Rhum du Père Labat
Bottled Strength: 50 and 59% alcohol by volume
Age: Stored in large oak vats before bottling
Notes: The most popular white rhum distilled in Marie Galante. (Remember that it is probably stronger than other rhums you are used to drinking.)

Rhum Paille du Père Labat
Bottled Strength: 50% alcohol by volume
Age: Two years
Notes: For export to Europe only; not available to the local market. This straw-colored rhum is the only rhum paille from Marie Galante.

Rhum Vieux du Père Labat
Bottled Strength: 45% alcohol by volume
Age: Five years
Notes: Bottled in small quantities at the distillery.

Bielle

No matter how you get to Guadeloupe, you will want to take the ferry to Marie Galante. When you arrive in Grand Bourg, you are a short, scenic ride from Distillerie Bielle in the south central part of the island. The minibus depot is a little south of the center of town.

The two-story estate house, adjacent to the distillery, was built by the great uncle of the present occupants, Dominique Thiéry and his family. M. Thiéry came to Marie Galante twenty years ago and learned the family business. While M. Thiéry operates the distillery, his wife oversees the pottery works, where fired pottery is made to contain the finer rhums from this distillery.

In his precious spare time, Dominique has built several attractive guest cottages on the south coast beach for those who come to this unique island for more than the day. Fortunately for the traveler who knows how to relax, Marie Galante is not yet the full-scale resort destination of the other French islands and retains a very personal character.

Around the distillery grounds are the remains of generations of steam-powered pumps and other cane-processing equipment that are no longer used. Originally steam-powered, the cane mill is now powered by a diesel truck engine and gear box. Electric pumps have replaced the old steam ones due to the high cost of maintaining the pumps and the large boiler required to drive them. Now the boiler, fired by burning the bagasse, is only used to produce steam for the distillation process.

Surrounded by sugar cane fields, Bielle buys cane from a number of local farmers. Ox-drawn carts arrive at the distillery loaded with cane from the fields, which were once part of a much larger estate. From February through April, the best time for harvesting cane, a ton of fresh-cut cane yields 90 liters of rhum. In the fall and summer, yields fall off to as little as 65 liters per ton of fresh cane.

After the cane is crushed, it is fermented in steel vats for forty-eight hours. Once fermentation is complete, the cane wine is fed to the copper distillation column. Hurricane Hugo almost toppled this old column, but fortunately the column got wedged between the frame of the building and other fallen debris.

The distiller's artistry takes place, up a ladder, on a landing in front of the copper-framed sight glass. By adjusting the flow rate of the steam, which enters the column at the bottom, and the flow of the fermented wine into the top of the ten-meter column, the distiller separates the alcohol from the waste products of fermentation. (For generations, there has always been a hog being fattened with distillery waste and food scraps).

Above the sight glass and control landing, up another ladder, is the condensation tank, which takes the vapor from the distillation column and condenses it into rhum. Bees, which pollinate many of the tropical plants on the island, are attracted to the tank and the sweet rhum.

Bielle presently bottles seven, eight, and ten-year-old rhums that have been aged in oak casks at the distillery. Bielle also bottles a large assortment of orange and other citrus punches. One of the most popular products is an eight-year-old rhum bottled in a ceramic decanter, which is also produced on the premises. The ceramic work is in keeping with the history of the distillery and a treasure to keep long after the rhum has been enjoyed. This decanter is also available at the pottery boutique, along with other attractive works from the kiln.

In order to meet the demand for his products in Marie Galante, Martinique, and France, M. Thiéry distills year round, producing about 60,000 liters of rhum annually.

Most business is conducted here in the morning, so it is recommended that you plan your visit before noon. Transportation is also easier to find earlier in the day. Although very little English is spoken here, signs in English will make your visit to Distillery Bielle a memorable and pleasant one.

DISTILLERIE BIELLE
MARIE GALANTE
Fermentation: Freshly squeezed sugar cane juice fermented for two days
Distillation Equipment: Copper, single-column continuous still

Bielle Rhum Blanc
Bottled Strength: 50 and 59% alcohol by volume
Age: Unaged, stored in large vats before bottling
Notes: This rhum agricole is also used to make a variety of fruit-based liqueurs.

Bielle Rhum Vieux
Bottled Strength: 45% alcohol by volume
Age: Six to ten years
Notes: This special rhum is bottled in a ceramic container produced at the distillery.

Bielle Hors-d'Age
Bottled Strength: 42% alcohol by volume
Age: At least eight years
Notes: Sold in an elegant 50 cl bottle, this rhum is a classic example of an aged French rhum and certainly worth the effort to find.

Magalda

The label on this rhum shows the address as 97140 Capesterre. From Grand Bourg, I took a bus to Capesterre and was instructed to take a bus to Etang Noir. When a bus with Etang Noir painted on the side arrived, I asked the driver, "Etang Noir?"

"Oui," he replied, and off we went—back to Grand Bourg. When almost everyone had gotten off the bus, a young man from Dominica spoke to me in English. After consultation with the driver, it was explained that the bus goes to Etang Noir only after 10:00 A.M. It would be another five minutes before the bus would take the route advertised, back to Etang Noir. After another trip around the town square, we headed to the higher elevation of the southern part of the island. Before we actually reached Etang Noir, the driver directed me down a dirt road to the distillery.

The first thing a visitor to Distillerie Bellevue sees is the stone windmill tower, built about the time the estate was founded in 1821. Next to the windmill tower is the still house. After the turn of the century, a steam engine replaced the windmill and the original still house was enlarged to enclose the new mechanical mill and boiler.

After the addition of a boiler to make steam for the new cane mill, the original copper pot still was replaced with a small diameter continuous distillation column. To accommodate the tall copper column, a well was dug in the floor instead of cutting a hole in the roof. This left much of the original plumbing intact and simplified the installation of the new equipment. Over the years, as sections of the still have been replaced, the column has been regenerated.

Behind the copper column, where wooden vats once stood, six steel fermentation tanks now sit on the old stone foundations. Before the tall column was installed, the fermented wine flowed from the raised vats to the pot still by gravity.

Throughout the year, this small family distillery crushes cane from the farms around the estate, then ferments it for two days. Usually early in the week, the boiler is fired, the fermented wine is pumped to the column, and the distillation process begins. On a wooden platform above two large oak barrels, the raw rhum is condensed and drips, at first, into the sight glass. Overhead, copper pipes lead to the control area where the distiller manipulates the steam to the column and the flow of spirit through the sight glass.

Most mornings, local men arrive on motorcycles carrying an assortment of containers. From bottles stored under a table on the north side of the estate house, their containers are filled with clear rhum.

Just north of the still house is the locked aging house, where the rhum vieux is aged five to six years. Like the original still house, this building has been expanded over the years to accommodate the slow growth of the distillery. In front of the estate house, the rhums from this distillery can be sampled. T-shirts from the distillery and honey produced on the estate are also available.

There is not always a guide available, but tourists are encouraged to look around at the equipment where the distiller practices his magic. Even without a guide or a translator, it's possible to follow the evolution of this sugar estate through the last one hundred and seventy years.

MAGALDA
CAPESTERRE, MARIE GALANTE
Fermentation: Freshly squeezed sugar cane juice fermented for two days
Distillation Equipment: Copper, single-column continuous still

Magalda Rhum Blanc
Bottled Strength: 50 and 59% alcohol by volume
Age: Unaged white rhum
Notes: White rhum is also used to make fruit-based liqueurs at the distillery.

Magalda Rhum Vieux
Bottled Strength: 50% alcohol by volume
Age: Five to six years
Notes: Full-flavored rhum aged at the distillery.

Dominica

Just after sunrise on April 12, 1782, sixty-six French and English ships engaged in the last sea battle of the War of American Independence. Admiral Rodney sailed north from the lee of Dominica and engaged French Admiral de Grasse, an ally of the colonies, on the opposite tack. As the wind shifted toward the southeast, the British gained a significant advantage over their adversaries, who could no longer maintain their conventional line of naval combat. Sailing through the disorganized enemy, Rodney inflicted heavy damage and havoc. By sunset, five French ships had been captured.

The successful tactic of sailing through the enemy, as opposed to fighting in lines, was adopted in the Royal Navy Fighting Instructions and changed the architecture of future battles.

In spite of the fact that the sea surrounding Dominica was controlled by foreign naval powers, the island itself was the last stronghold of the fierce Carib Indians. In the middle of the eighteenth century, the French and English agreed to let the Indians control the rugged island. But the planters of both countries, still drawn to the fertile soil and abundant rainfall, continued to cultivate land near the coast. Predictably, the fighting continued.

Situated between Guadeloupe to the north and Martinique to the south, Dominica is a rich blend of its French and English history. The distillation of rum in Dominica began with the French colonization of the island. The French emperors of the seventeenth century considered the spirit made from sugar cane grown in this rich, volcanic soil to be unique. Today, none of the rum bottled on this island is exported. Belfast, the larger of the distilleries, bottles rum made from molasses, while Shillingford Estates Ltd. makes rum from fresh sugar cane juice.

Dominica grows a lot of the fruit and vegetables that are sold on the other Caribbean islands. The market in Roseau is always bustling early in the day, but don't miss the smaller market in Portsmouth on Saturday morning. Anything that is in season is on sale on the crowded streets. Flowers, hand-woven baskets, fresh bread, fish, and even fresh fried crabcakes are available. Most West Indian markets start early, but here, if you aren't ashore by 7:00 A.M., you have already missed a lot of the day's bargains.

As the cruise ship dock in this sleepy town becomes more active, Portsmouth will change, but, until then, don't miss this typically West Indian town.

SHILLINGFORD ESTATES LTD.
DOMINICA

Founded seventeenth century
Fermentation: Freshly squeezed sugar cane juice fermented for five days
Distillation Equipment: Stainless steel, single-column continuous still

Soca Rum
Bottled Strength: 50% alcohol by volume
Age: Unaged
Notes: This is one of the few rums made in the English-speaking islands from freshly squeezed sugar cane, similar to West Coast Rum being introduced this year.

Macoucherie

When I cleared immigration in Portsmouth, I was told the Macoucherie Estate, locally referred to as the sugar factory, was on a river south of the new radio tower. Sailing south from Portsmouth, I steered *Tafia* close to the western coast of Dominica and tried to identify the numerous small settlements on the chart.

After a few hours, the small river, a mile or so south of Nero, made itself known. Even though the distillery chimney was out of sight, there was no doubt that the flowering sugar cane and coconut palm, heavy with fruit, was part of an estate. A little further south, a small cove offered some protection from the swell so *Tafia* was anchored close to shore, in front of the Castaways hotel.

Rowing with the current and swell was easy in anticipation of seeing a distillery of such renown in the Caribbean. As I approached the sandbar that guards the shallow river, I tried to time my entrance between the breaking waves. When the stern of my small boat rose, I pulled harder on the oars but wasn't able to stay upright in the foaming water.

I certainly wasn't the first sailor to capsize the ship's tender while trying to get to this distillery, but I didn't mind at all. The cool, fresh water was refreshing in the hot August afternoon. Gathering my oars, another wave broke into my capsized dinghy.

As I rowed upstream against the slow river current, it was hard to believe that I had not been transported back in time. Everything around me seemed to be from another age. When the river became too shallow to row, I dragged the light dinghy up the beach and covered it with palm fronds to hide it from any curious passersby. A little further up the riverbed, a bridge passed overhead, and the first signs of the distillery were visible.

I was lucky to meet Mr. Ken George, the distiller, just as he was preparing to leave for the day. Most of the day's work had been completed, but three men were still busy crushing cane in the water-powered mill. After being crushed three times, the spent cane is used for fertilizer on the estate, since there are plenty of coconut husks and pieces of wood to burn in the boiler firebox.

The fresh juice is fermented for five days. To keep the mixture of juice and yeast from getting too hot, cool water from the river passes through a coil in each of the fermentation tanks. Next, Mr. George showed me the sight glass, adjacent to the still. Even late in the afternoon, the single copper distillation column was still quite warm from the day's work.

The distiller's job is a hot one as he must control the distillation from the small room that houses the still. But it is also a rewarding job, with a lot of responsibility to both the distillery and the government customs regulations. In addition to performing the distillation, the distiller must also account for all of the rum before it is placed in the bonded storage on the first floor of the still house.

MACOUCHERIE ESTATE
DOMINICA
Fermentation: Fresh juice fermented for five days
Distillation Equipment: Single copper distillation column

Macoucherie Rum
Bottled Strength: 40% alcohol by volume
Age: One and a half years
Notes: Aging makes this a nice rhum similar to rhum agricole from the French islands.

DOMINICA

Macoucherie Elixir of Bois Bandé

Bottled Strength: 40% alcohol by volume

Age: One and a half years

Ingredients: Blend of rum, Bois Bandé tree bark, and spices

Notes: Spiced with the bark of the Bois Bandé tree. Reputed to be an aphrodisiac, this liquor was hailed as a wonder drink by all of the men gathered under the almond tree at the Portsmouth town jetty. The women's unanimous consensus was that Macoucherie did not improve the sexual abilities of men or women. With a clearly split verdict, you will have to decide for yourself.

Belfast Estate Limited

While in Dominica, I anchored *Tafia* in Prince Rupert Bay, off the northern town of Portsmouth. From here, it is an hour or so minibus ride from the town dock to Belfast Estate, just north of the Canefield Airport in the Coconut Complex. On the west side of the road, you will see part of an old water wheel that powered a sugar cane press many years ago. Just down the hill, on the same side of the road, inside a white building, was the barrel-making operation and old distilling area of the estate. If you happen to be walking by this building and the window is open, it is certainly worth looking inside.

You can see where the coopers assembled barrels for aging rum when the distillery was in operation. Typically, barrels are broken down for shipment and then reassembled at the distillery. While researching this book, I did not encounter any distillery that still makes its own barrels. The laws in the United States allow whiskey barrels to be used only once, after which they are often sold to rum distilleries in the Eastern Caribbean if they are in good shape. Barrels also come from Canada and Europe, where they are not reused.

A couple of years ago, the still pot and copper distillation column were shut down at Belfast, but R. A. J. Astaphan, the manager, has plans to use them again in the future. Currently, Belfast blends rum from Guyana, Trinidad, and Barbados, and bottles it under the Belfast label.

All of the products from Belfast are widely available in Dominica, but none of the rum from either Belfast or Shillingford is currently available outside this island. In spite of the fact that the labels state that these rums are distilled and bottled by Belfast Estate Limited, in Dominica it is no secret that these are imported and have been for some time.

In addition to the bottled rums, Belfast also sells cask rum. This strong, white rum is about 100 proof and sold to the local retail outlets. On Saturday morning in Portsmouth several of the local rum shops were busy tapping the 40-gallon barrels. It isn't uncommon to spill a little rum while pouring the contents of the heavy barrel out of the bung hole into a smaller container. No one seems to mind, and, after a round of rum, all is forgotten.

Cask rum is also sold to the numerous smaller shops and spiced with a variety of local spices. It is always interesting to taste one of these spiced rums and then try to determine what has been used in the spice. A clue is sometimes present in the bottle. Cinnamon sticks, for, example, are easily identified, but other spices are much harder to see. Spicing the cask rum also helps take the edge off this strong liquor.

DOMINICA

BELFAST ESTATE LIMITED
DOMINICA

Blends rums from Trinidad and bottles it under the Belfast label

Red Cap
Bottled Strength: 43% alcohol by volume

Age: Unaged

Notes: Raw rum makes this the strongest tasting rum from the Belfast Estate.

D Special Rum
Bottled Strength: 43% alcohol by volume

Age: A few months in oak barrels

Notes: Even a few months makes this a smoother rum than Red Cap.

At one time, much of the Rose's Lime Juice sold around the world was shipped in barrels from Roseau. Dominica is still the largest exporter of limes and lime juice in these islands.

Martinique

The first successful settlers arrived in Martinique in the middle of the seventeenth century, bringing cane sprouts from St. Kitts where sugar had already been established as a valuable crop. After an epidemic threatened the success of the new colony, thirty-year-old Jean-Baptiste Labat, a Dominican priest from Paris, was dispatched to the French West Indies.

On January 28, 1694, Père Labat arrived at St. Pierre on board the French ship La Loire after surviving an eight hour battle engagement with the English ship The Chester. He brought with him the latest advances in distillation technology to be used in the production of alcohol at the Charity Hospital of Monks. His arrival marked a change in the production of alcohol in the French islands. Even three hundred years later, many surviving traditions are still credited to Père Labat.

As in the other French islands, you will find clear rhum agricole and dark rhum vieux in Martinique. You will also see other classifications that are not as common on the other islands. Millésimé is a designation some of the distilleries use on the labels of vintage rhum. Millésimé 1979, for example, describes an aged rhum that was distilled in 1979. Hors d' Age is usually a blend of several rhums that has aged longer than the normal rhum vieux and costs slightly more than the unblended rhum vieux. Très Vieux literally means very old, generally ten to fifteen years. Très Vieux rhums may be more expensive than Hors d' Age, depending on the age of the blend. Currently, there are no standard criteria for these designations, so they vary according to the distiller.

Martinique has more distilleries than any of the other Eastern Caribbean islands. Plan on seeing at least one; it could easily be the highlight of your *vacation. Several distilleries sell alcohol to blenders and bottlers in France where the rhum is bottled as Martinique rhum. Look for the words "Appellation d'Origine Contrôlée Martinique." This is your assurance that the rhum is made from sugar cane juice and meets strict quality control standards. All rhum agricole bottled after May 31, 1997 in Martinique must carry these words on the label.*

DePaz

Following the signs along the beach from St. Pierre to DePaz takes the pedestrian slightly out of the way on the one-way streets that are typical of the French coastal towns. Don't despair —the walk up the hill is worth it.

As you approach the DePaz distillery, the grade of the road increases slightly and the beauty of the mountainside unfolds around you. The well-kept grounds around the distillery and estate house frame a very impressive sight. The round visitors center on your left is a good place to catch your breath before you begin the self-guided tour of the distillery. The architecture of this structure is based on the design of an ancient, animal-powered cane mill.

In 1917, Victor DePaz amused his contemporaries by being the first planter to move back to the site of the devastation resulting from the eruption of Mt. Pelée fifteen years earlier. He planted sugar cane on the fertile slopes of the mountain, which had been enriched by the eruption. The crop flourished and still produces one of the highest yields of cane in the Caribbean. In 1929, a second eruption occurred, but this time the eruption directed its force upward and the distillery, as well as the town of St. Pierre, was spared.

When the DePaz family came here from St.

Kitts at the end of the seventeenth century, sugar was the primary crop. When sugar became less profitable, the DePaz plantation focused on other commodities. Today, sugar cane covers 120 hectares of the estate, but no sugar is produced. All of the cane is squeezed to make DePaz rhum.

The distillery is housed in a modern, sheet-metal building. Its open design offers workers and visitors the most comfortable accommodations possible in this tropical climate. The metal construction also reduces the risk of fire, a constant threat in the flammable alcohol business. Even though an alcohol fire can be extinguished with water, the damage even a small fire would cause could easily shut down the operation for a long time. Since this distillery only produces rhum from February through May, any lost time would cause considerable problems. But the biggest risk is that the rhum aging warehouse, where the future profits of the distillery are matured, might catch fire—a catastrophe few distilleries could survive.

During the distilling season, eight to ten thousand tons of fresh cane are harvested from around the distillery. Recently, mechanical cane-cutting equipment has been employed, but due to the rough terrain, some of the cane must still be cut by hand.

At a rate of ten tons per hour, the cane is crushed by the steam-powered mill. Then, the sweet juice is fermented in twelve 30,000 liter fermentation tanks for thirty to thirty-six hours. To maintain the fermenting wine below the critical temperature of 30°C, water from the Roxelane River drips on the outside of the fermentation tanks.

The fermentation tanks and most of the process piping at this distillery are stainless steel.

This helps facilitate sterilization of the equipment between distillations, reducing unwanted bacteria. Quality control and cleanliness are important ingredients for this rhum agricole.

Once the wine reaches 4.5% alcohol by volume, it is fed to the distillation column where the alcohol is concentrated to 68-70% by volume. Typical of the distilleries in Martinique, DePaz employs a single-column distillation process. To keep up with the demand for DePaz rhum, two identical columns stand next to each other. The distillation columns appear to be stainless steel, but both contain copper plates or trays inside. The large, water-cooled condensers for both stills are also copper.

After distillation, the rhum, which will be bottled as rhum blanc, is allowed to rest for a few months in stainless steel tanks. This is referred to as staling and improves the taste of the fresh rhum in much the same way as a good stew is better the second day. The remainder of the production is put in burnt-oak casks for aging. Once a year, the barrels are topped off with rhum from the same production year, since the slightly porous oak barrels allow some of the alcohol to be lost to the "angels." Replacing the angels' share is not unique to DePaz, but is an essential part of their tradition.

Although DePaz produces 1,000,000 liters of rhum annually, the local market for this rhum is not as large as some of the other rhums from Martinique. DePaz does, however, enjoy a large market in France, which has contributed to the prosperity of the distillery.

If you are walking on your return to St. Pierre, turn left down the walkway through the ruins of the old fort and cathedral of what was Old St.

Pierre, before the eruption of Mt. Pelée. This shortens the trip and leads to the museum of the old city above the waterfront.

From the water, as you approach St. Pierre, the lights over the stadium, just north of town, form a range that leads to DePaz. When you are between the northern and southern sets of lights, the big stone house and the smokestack at the distillery can easily be seen on the side of Mt. Pelée.

DISTILLERIE DEPAZ
ST. PIERRE, MARTINIQUE
Founded 1917
Fermentation: Freshly squeezed sugar cane juice fermented for thirty to thirty-six hours
Distillation Equipment: Two copper and stainless steel, single-column stills

Rhum Blanc DePaz
Bottled Strength: 50 and 55% alcohol by volume
Age: Unaged
Notes: Stored in stainless steel tanks prior to bottling.

Rhum Paille DePaz
Bottled strength: 50% alcohol by volume
Age: Two years in small oak casks
Notes: A good example of how aging affects the taste and color of rhum. Although smoother than Rhum Blanc, it still maintains the character of rhum agricole. Not as dark or mellow as Rhum Vieux DePaz, but certainly worth trying. Makes a very good ti punch.

MARTINIQUE

Rhum Vieux DePaz

Bottled Strength: 45% alcohol by volume

Age: Four years

Notes: Most of this rhum is exported to France. Good value in an aged rhum from Martinique. Popular for good reason—should not be missed.

Rhum Vieux Plantation Millésimé DePaz

Bottled Strength: 45% alcohol by volume

Age: Four years

Notes: These special production years are available only in limited quantities. Some available years include: 1979 for FR 118, 1950 for FR 540, or a rare 1929 rhum for FR 1,250.

Rhum Vieux DePaz Reserve

Bottled Strength: 45% alcohol by volume

Age: Blend of fine rhums aged four years and more

Notes: Affordable blend of fine rhums, only available at the distillery.

J. Bally

Known since 1924 by its square bottle, cork closure, and distinctive label, J. Bally rhum has enjoyed a most successful history.

Not far from the center of Carbet, just follow the signs to the old J. Bally distillery. It is east from the coast road, up the hill along the river which, at one time, was the source of water for the distillery. The visitors center and gift shop is in what was the still house for many years. The wooden frame that supported the original copper distillation column remains. Near the ceiling, you can see the old condensing tank and some of the original copper piping. A short film in French describes the rhum making process. For a small fee, the estate gardens can be toured too.

The distillation column has been moved to Distillerie Simon, where Bally Rhum is now distilled. Today, only the aging warehouse and bottling operation are located at the Bally estate in Carbet.

Even though you can't see the distillery in operation, you have come to the right place to sample a very impressive collection of Bally rhum. The congenial staff will show you the different rhums, from the white rhum to the dark aged rhums, some of which have been in the bottle more than half a century. Bally also bottles rhum paille that is reported to be three years old and rhum vieux that is aged six years.

Although a bottle of J. Bally rhum from 1924 costs FR 3200, only the time that the rhum was aged in oak barrels, before it was bottled, will have an effect on the rhum. Before you buy a vintage rhum, find out how long the rhum was aged before it was bottled. If you can't find out, maybe you should buy something else, unless you want an expensive souvenir.

J. BALLY
CARBET, MARTINIQUE
Founded 1924
Bally rhums have been distilled at the Simon distillery on the east coast of the island since 1978. Aging and bottling is still done at the old distillery site in Carbet.
Fermentation: Freshly squeezed sugar cane juice fermented for twenty-four hours
Distillation Equipment: Copper, single-column continuous still

MARTINIQUE

J. Bally Rhum Blanc
Bottled Strength: 50 and 55% alcohol by volume
Age: Unaged, stored in stainless steel tanks prior to bottling
Notes: Popular rhum blanc in a distinctive square bottle.

J. Bally Rhum Paille
Bottled Strength: 50% alcohol by volume
Age: Two years
Notes: Harder to find than the other Bally rhums, but worth looking for.

J. Bally Rhum Vieux
Bottled Strength: 45% alcohol by volume
Age: Six years
Notes: Aged rhum available from as far back as 1924.

Neisson

Distillerie Carbet Neisson is much like it was seventy-five years ago when the Neisson family began planting cane on Morne Vert. From St. Pierre, take the public bus south along the coast about eight kilometers and get off south of the town of Carbet. When the main road curves to the east, a sign points the way to Distillerie Carbet Neisson. A short walk leads to an unpaved road to the right. When you cross the Rivière du Carbet, the distillery is visible to the right, across a field of cane.

This is not a big distillery with an air-conditioned visitors center and multimedia presentation, but it's certainly worth your time—especially if you are in the area during the short rhum season, March through June.

The conveyor in front of the mill was quiet the first time I was here in August. A few men were busy maintaining the equipment, and I was lucky to find a man who spoke enough English to help me understand what went on here during the rhum season. On my second visit in June of '94, as I walked through the cane fields, I was elated to see smoke coming from the stack behind the sheet-metal building that houses the boiler, steam engine, and cane mill.

Humming with activity, the distillery was producing rhum while cane was being crushed for juice to be distilled later that week—the final distillation of the season. This is a great opportunity to see an old, single-cylinder steam engine crushing cane at about 100 rpm. At the same time, next to the copper distillation column, fresh rhum fills the sight glass.

The rhum making process is similar to the other distilleries in the area, except here fermentation is allowed to continue for three days before the wine is distilled. Seven years ago, the single-copper distillation column was replaced with a new one. The old column, weakened by years of distilling, had begun to leak too much.

Leaks reduce the amount of rhum condensed and increase the danger of fire—flammable alcohol is the most abundant product of distillation. The new column, like the old one, is made of many sections held together with clamps on the outside so that it can be disassembled for cleaning and maintenance.

The expected life of the distillation column is a function of the temperature at which it is operated, the maintenance schedule, and the quality of construction. Some columns, more than fifty years old, are still in use, but the maintenance required increases as the columns age.

After distillation, the rhum is stored in large oak vats prior to bottling, or aged in smaller oak barrels. Before the introduction of stainless steel storage tanks, all of the distilleries used oak vats or barrels to store their products. The large vats require considerable maintenance and are prone to leaks, especially if they are not kept full. Barrels, on the other hand, require more labor to fill and empty.

In contrast to some of the other more elaborate visitors centers, the products of this distillery may be tasted in the small business office, west of the production area, which also serves as a retail outlet. The friendly staff doesn't speak English, but are very helpful and will make your visit something to remember.

Even before I visited this distillery, I had seen the distinctive square bottles of Neisson in the stores, both full on the shelves and empty in the front of the stores, waiting to be recycled. At the distillery, large wicker baskets of bottles are washed prior to being refilled. A high percentage of these unique bottles are recycled locally, more than any other rhum bottle in Martinique. In the restaurants and bars in Carbet, the rectangular bottles, sitting next to pitchers of water and smaller bottles of cane syrup, are a common sight.

DISTILLERIE CARBET NEISSON
CARBET, MARTINIQUE
Founded circa 1919
Fermentation: Freshly squeezed sugar cane juice fermented for three days
Distillation Equipment: Copper, single-column continuous still

Rhum Blanc Neisson
Bottled Strength: 50 and 55% alcohol by volume
Age: Unaged, stored in wooden vats until bottled
Notes: Distinctive taste has attracted a very loyal following.

Rhum Vieux Neisson
Bottled Strength: 45% alcohol by volume
Age: Blend of rhums aged up to fourteen years at the distillery
Notes: Slightly darker than the other aged rhums from Martinique. Small production capacity makes this harder to find except in the local area where it is the most popular rhum.

Distillerie J. M

To reach J. M from St. Pierre, you must cross the northern mountains of Martinique. As soon as you leave sea level at St. Pierre, you begin to climb until you reach Morne Rouge. The scenery behind you is spectacular. The cool mountain air is a pleasant change from the warm coast and, more than likely, a little rain will fall as you make your way along the winding road of the mountain pass. As you descend from the mountains near Ajoupa Bouillon, flowers of every description line the road, and you will see why Martinique is known as the "flower island."

As the terrain levels off, pineapple fields give way to bananas and the Atlantic Ocean is on the horizon. Just past Basse Pointe, on the way to Macouba, a well-marked road to the left directs you to Rhumerie J. M at Fonds-Preville. The distillery first appears as a cluster of metal roofs in a valley surrounded by tall bamboo. You will see that Rhumerie J. M is a distillery that takes a lot of pride in the past and has retained most of the process equipment that was installed earlier this century.

In 1790, the stream that flows through the valley supplied a water wheel with the power to crush the cane at Jean-Marie Martin's sugar factory. After sugar cane from the estate was pressed, the juice was introduced to six cast-iron, round-bottom sugar pots. The sweet juice was cooked and, as it thickened and reduced in volume, it was ladled to the next progressively smaller pot.

The names of the pots are indicative of their sizes: Le Grande, La Proper, La Lessive, Le Flambeau, Du Feu, and La Batterie. The last pot held the heavy black syrup from which sugar would be filtered. What was left after filtering was known as *melasse*, or molasses. From this, rhum, or *tafia* was made.

When the price of sugar fell, rhum was made directly from the cane juice and became the main product of the distillery. Since the bagasse was no longer needed to cook the sugar, it was available to make steam, and the water wheel was replaced by a more reliable steam engine.

In April and May of each year, sugar cane is harvested from the estate cane fields. Once the cane is weighed, it is crushed in the steam-powered cane mill. These single-cylinder steam engines, found in many of the distilleries of the French islands, are quite impressive with their associated controls and linkages.

The juice takes two days to ferment, after which it is distilled in a two-column copper still to about 80% alcohol. This is the only two-column still operating in Martinique. To cool the freshly distilled rhum, water from the river flows in a gutter on the floor next to the copper still.

Once distilled, the rhum blanc is allowed to rest in a stainless steel tank for about six months, while the rhum paille is put in small, oak barrels from France for one year. The fact that the rhum paille is put in 200-liter oak barrels, instead of large vats of 20,000-liter capacity or more, accounts for the yellow "straw" color of this rhum.

Most of this distillery's annual production of 200,000 liters is consumed in Martinique, but small quantities are shipped to France. A few bottles of this rare spirit may be found in St. Martin at Grands Vin de France. As the consumption of aged rhum from the French West Indies continues to grow, there is no doubt that J. M will continue to gain recognition.

The distillery welcomes visitors from 9:00 A.M. to 5:00 P.M. daily, except Sunday. This is the northernmost of the distilleries in Martinique, and the tranquillity of the stone distillery buildings makes an enjoyable stop on your island tour.

DISTILLERIE J. M
MACOUBA, MARTINIQUE
Founded 1790
Fermentation: Freshly squeezed sugar cane juice fermented for two days
Distillation Equipment: Copper, two-column continuous still

Rhum Blanc J. M
Bottled Strength: 55% alcohol by volume
Age: Unaged, stored in stainless steel tanks for six months prior to bottling
Notes: Higher distillation purity from the two-column still yields a lighter rhum than many of the other rhum agricoles from Martinique.

Rhum Paille J. M
Bottled Strength: 55% alcohol by volume
Age: One year in 200-liter oak barrels
Notes: This rhum paille is bottled at 55% alcohol by volume instead of the usual 50% alcohol by volume.

Rhum Vieux J. M
Bottled Strength: 50% alcohol by volume
Age: Ten years, one of the oldest aged rhums from Martinique
Notes: Certainly the pride of the distillery and comparable to a fine cognac. Very rich taste and color. This aged rhum is only sold at the distillery.

Saint James

By the time colonists established a settlement on Martinique, sugar was the most valuable crop in the Caribbean. Soon, ships loaded with sugar and molasses to be made into rum were sailing to North American distilleries from the Saint James Sugar Factory in St. Pierre.

In 1765, Saint James began making alcohol from the sugar production by-products. Until only two years before, it had been illegal to export rhum from the colonies to France. The sugar company continued to expand until the eruption of Mt. Pelée destroyed the factory and distillery. Since then, Saint James has relocated to the eastern side of the island.

Opened to the public in 1981, the Saint James museum, on the west side of the main road in Sainte Marie, is housed in the mansion previously associated with the Sainte Marie Sugar Factory. On the museum grounds, a collection of machinery documents the development of the equipment used in the sugar industry over the last three hundred years.

Inside the cool shade of this picturesque mansion are smaller displays of equipment and photos of the sugar and distillery industry in Martinique. A beautiful bar on the ground floor offers samples of the rhums made here. Entrance to the museum is free and time well spent even if the distillery tour, which starts here, is closed.

The distillery, next to the museum, is a large operation that operates nearly year round. Most of the cane processed here is grown on the Saint James Company's land; the remaining twenty percent is bought from local farmers. At the distillery, the cane is shredded, then crushed in one of the four three-cylinder cane mills. To improve the efficiency of the juice extraction, water is added in the crushing stage of the process. The resulting cane fiber is burned in a large boiler that generates steam to power the machinery in the factory.

During the cane season, the four cane mills, capable of processing sixty tons of cane an hour, yield more juice than can be fermented. Most of the fresh juice is pumped directly from the cane mill to the fermentation tanks. The rest is filtered, then concentrated by vacuum to a syrup for storage. Basically, this is the first step of sugar production, but the sugar is not crystallized as it would be in the more refined process. At a later date, this syrup is diluted to its original consistency before being pumped to the fermentation tanks.

After twenty-four to thirty-six hours of fermentation, all of the sugar is transformed into alcohol. The fermented juice, or *vin*, is then distilled in one of the six single-column stills. Leaving the columns at 75°, all of the raw, clear rhum is transferred to one of the twenty 68,000-liter stainless steel tanks and allowed to rest for six months. While the rhum is resting, the carbonic gas formed during fermentation is released and other molecular changes take place. The rhum dismisses some of the tastes acquired during distillation and becomes a more consistent and pleasing drink.

After resting, the rhum, which will be bottled as white rhum, or *Grappe Blanche*, is diluted with distilled water to reduce the alcohol content to 50° or 55°. If it is to be bottled as Imperial Blanc Saint James, treated water is used to dilute the rhum.

Another portion of the production is put in one of the 35,000-liter wooden vats, or *tuns*, for eighteen months. Here, the rhum attains a slight yellow color and some components in the rhum exchange chemical compounds with the wood, forming complex esters that also add to the flavor. This rhum, bottled at 50° and 55°, is sold as Rhum Paille Saint James.

Finally, the last part of the production is put in 200-liter oak barrels, where it is allowed to sleep for three years. After three years, the Rhum Vieux Saint James, bottled at 42% alcohol by volume, has a rich, brown color and a mature aroma and taste.

Also bottled at the distillery are Rhum Saint James Hors D'Age, a blend of several aged rhums, and Rhum Ambre Saint James, a two-year-old rhum bottled at 45% alcohol by volume.

All of the Saint James rhums described above are bottled in elegant, square bottles from Marseilles. Plantations Saint James Martinique is embossed on the side of these distinctive bottles that make nice souvenirs of a popular Martinique rhum.

In addition to the rhum distilled in the single-column stills, a pot still, resembling the one depicted on the label, is used to make small amounts of Coeur de Chauffe. Although originally heated by a wood fire, this pot still is steam-fired to reduce the fire hazard in the alcohol plant. This rhum is also made from pure sugar cane juice and is bottled at 60% alcohol by volume. I have only seen this rare rhum at the distillery.

This is one of the few distilleries in Martinique that utilizes its equipment after June, generally the end of the cane-cutting season. The six stills represent the second-largest distilling capacity on the island, and are employed to make alcohol made from molasses. Unavailable in Martinique, this product is sold to other bottlers in France and elsewhere.

DISTILLERIE SAINT JAMES
SAINTE MARIE, MARTINIQUE
Founded 1765
Fermentation: Freshly squeezed sugar cane juice fermented for twenty-four to thirty-six hours
Distillation Equipment: Four three-cylinder cane mills

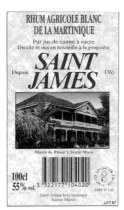

Grappe Blanche Saint James

Bottled Strength: 50 and 55% alcohol by volume

Age: Unaged, stored in stainless steel tanks for six months before bottling

Notes: Diluted with distilled water, comparable to rhum blanc agricole.

Imperial Blanc Saint James

Bottled Strength: 50 and 55% alcohol by volume

Age: Unaged, stored in stainless steel tanks for six months before bottling

Notes: Diluted with treated water.

Rhum Paille Saint James

Bottled Strength: 50 and 55% alcohol by volume

Age: Eighteen months in 35,000-liter oak vats

Notes: Slight yellow color, flavored by time spent in large oak vats.

Rhum Ambre Saint James

Bottled Strength: 45% alcohol by volume

Age: Two years

Notes: Less expensive than rhum vieux, but with a slightly less wood flavor.

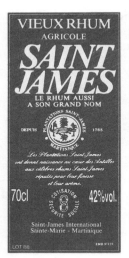

Rhum Vieux Saint James

Bottled Strength: 42% alcohol by volume

Age: Three years in large oak vats

Notes: One of the most popular rhums from Saint James, bottled at slightly less than the usual 45% alcohol by volume.

Rhum Saint James Hors D'Age

Bottled Strength: 45% alcohol by volume

Age: Blend of aged rhums

Notes: Blend of several rhums aged for more than three years—one of the best rhums from Saint James.

Coeur de Chauffe

Bottled Strength: 60% alcohol by volume

Age: Unaged

Notes: Distilled in a traditional pot still, this rhum is available exclusively at the distillery. Only small quantities of this rhum are produced.

G. Hardy

The eastern coast of Martinique holds many surprises. North of Trinité, the island rises abruptly from the Atlantic Ocean, with black beaches attesting to the volcanic activity of the past. South of Trinité, coral reefs protect the much lighter colored beaches. East of Trinité, fishermen mend their nets and traps along the picturesque shores of the peninsula.

Livestock graze on the remains of the recently harvested cane fields, and time moves at a slightly slower pace than on the rest of the island. On the north side of this mesmerizing peninsula, just past the village of Tartane, is a distillery that has witnessed more than a century and a half of changes to the island of Martinique, and, yet, retains much of the tradition of the past.

Along the road to Tartane, signs depict a water wheel and the name G. Hardy Distillery. There is no water wheel here today but, in the quiet shade on the right side of the road, a rusting, sheet-metal shed houses a complex copper still. Only an electric light hanging from a rusty truss reminds the visitor that this is still the twentieth century.

Until recently, cane from the surrounding countryside was harvested by hand each year between February and May bringing the distillery to life. When I visited this distillery, plans were under way to renovate the building. I certainly hope the copper still and other steam equipment can be preserved, and that I am able to see it in operation next year during the cane-harvesting season.

Although this is not the only distillery I visited that was no longer producing, it is a rare opportunity to see a complete still with the distiller's original art intact. All of the process equipment and piping is copper and has taken on a dark green patina over the years.

Small stills like this one are no longer being built due to the cost of manufacture, the craftsmanship required to maintain them, and the moderately low production capacity. Modern continuous stills generally employ more than one column, have stainless steel process piping, and are capable of producing much more rhum than this small, complex still.

Another factor contributing to the decline of small distilleries is labor. This distillery employed six people year round and an additional twenty-five during the rhum distilling season, making this a very labor-intensive operation.

Today, white rhum is bought from another distiller in the area, stored in barrels, and then bottled as rhum blanc or after eighteen months, as rhum paille. When I visited G. Hardy, rhum blanc was being bottled to meet the local demand. Distribution of G. Hardy rhum is primarily in Martinique, although small quantities are exported to France.

The rhum vieux, which is available in the distillery boutique, was produced here. This aged rhum has been in oak barrels since 1975, when the distillery was still in production. Although it is rare for a distillery to age rhum this long, the price of FR 150 did indicate that this was special. I was impressed by the color, aroma, and smoothness of this rhum, and only wish that I could afford to drink rhum of this character all the time.

Even though this distillery was not operating at the time this book was printed, visitors are encouraged. I expect the distillery to begin producing rhum again soon. The G. Hardy label is well respected among rhum drinkers in Martinique, and the owners of this unique distillery are dedicated to their business.

When your travels bring you this way, don't miss this distillery—a tribute to the dedication of the dying breed of small distillers in the Caribbean. The beach at Tartane is a nice place to have lunch, and bring your bathing suit for a memorable day on the east coast of Martinique.

DISTILLERIE G. HARDY
TARTANE, MARTINIQUE
No longer distilling, the distillery is presently buying rhum agricole to be bottled here.

Rhum Blanc G. Hardy
Bottled Strength: 50% alcohol by volume
Age: Unaged
Notes: Popular locally.

Rhum Paille G. Hardy
Bottled Strength: 50% alcohol by volume
Age: Stored eighteen months in oak barrels at the distillery
Notes: Slightly more color than some of the other rhum paille from Martinique. Mixes well.

RUMS OF THE WORLD

Rhum Vieux G. Hardy
Bottled Strength: 46% alcohol by volume
Age: Aged since 1975, when the distillery was in operation, this rhum is reported to be eighteen years old
Notes: Dark, rich color; a favorite of Martinique.

Try it.

After spending a little time in the French West Indies, you will certainly pick up a few words and phrases that will make your travels easier and more rewarding. One of the simplest gestures that will endear you to the people of these islands is the simple greeting, "Bonjour." Pronounced something like "Bozur." Don't be shy. Try it, and you will see a difference in the attitude of the people you meet. Don't worry about the pronunciation, it will come. Even if you don't say it exactly right, you will be rewarded for trying.

I started by trying to understand the French rhum labels. Since this book is about rum and rhum, you should already understand at least a few words on the bottles. For instance:

Rhum agricole means made from pure sugar cane juice, or issu du pur jus de canne à sucre. *Another common phrase you will see is* vielli en fûts de chêne—*aged in oak barrels.* 10 ans d'age *means aged ten years. You will also see* mis en bouteille à la distillerie—*bottled at the distillery. Or* mis en bouteille à la Martinique—*bottled in Martinique.*

Another common symbol that you will see looks like two links of a chain with the words

> *COTISATION SECURITE SOCIALE around the links. This is similar to a tax stamp and is required for exported products.*
>
> *When you visit the distilleries, you will notice that many English and French words have the same origin and spelling. Distillation and fermentation are obvious examples. Now, if you pronounce the "a" as "ah," and soften the "tion" to sound more like "shion," you will sound like a tourist but you have tried, and that is what is important.*
>
> *Paille sounds like pie. Accent on the long "e." Rhum Vieux is easier; just say "rhum view," and you will be understood.*
>
> *Don't be shy. Before you know it, you will be speaking a few words of French and enjoying yourself even more. Sometimes when I was having trouble, I would try what I thought was my worst French accent and to my surprise I would be understood.* Bonne chance! *(Good luck!)*

Simon

Originally built as a sugar factory in 1900, Distillerie Simon, south of Le Francois on the east coast of Martinique, is an interesting mixture of the past, present, and future. Built when the price of sugar was high enough to justify the construction of a new facility near the Clément sugar factory, Distillerie Simon has been fortunate to survive the turbulent conditions of the past. Today, the large cane mill is used to process cane solely for the production of rhum agricole. Although there is no rhum sold in Martinique under the Simon label, this distillery makes rhum for two well-known companies on the island.

In 1978, the copper distillation column at the J. Bally distillery in Carbet was moved here. Distillerie Simon now ferments fresh cane juice to be distilled in the old Bally distillation column, to the mutual benefit of both Bally and Simon. In 1988, another agreement was reached with the Clément distillery. Although the Clément distillation column was not moved to Simon, Clément now buys all of its rhum from Simon. The old distillery at Clément remains intact and can be seen as part of the museum of the Clément plantation.

Sugar cane for the production of this rhum comes from two sources. A group of twenty small farmers in the local Francois area bring hand-cut cane to the distillery. From the Lamentin area, near Fort de France, machine-cut cane is trucked to the distillery. Once crushed, the fresh juice is fermented only one day and then distilled in one of the three columns, depending on where the rhum will be shipped after production.

Since storage capacity is limited here, all of the rhum is put into 20,000-liter bulk tanks to be shipped to the aging and bottling facilities at Bally and Clément. In addition to making rhum for these well-known bottlers, Simon also produces another 800,000 liters of rhum agricole for shipment to France, where it is bottled as cocktails and rhum punch under other labels.

At Distillerie Simon, only rhum blanc, or unaged white rhum is produced. Behind the distillery itself, several *foudres*, or large oak casks, have warped from not being used and, what was once a warehouse for aging rhum, is now used for equipment storage. This facility is not open to the public, but is very much a part of the rhum business in Martinique.

Clément

Located on the site of a sugar refinery built in 1770, the Habitation Clément was purchased by Homère Clément in 1887 and remained in operation until 1988. Today, the habitation, which includes the land and the buildings, is a museum. It was the site of meetings between Presidents George Bush and Francois Mitterrand in 1991.

Educated in Paris, Homère Clément became a doctor and then returned to Martinique to become the mayor of Francois. On February 8, 1900, a confrontation between striking workers at the Francois sugar factory and the military led to the death of ten strikers. Clément intervened, called a cease-fire, and was able, with the respect of the strikers, to negotiate and maintain a peaceful settlement.

The following year, he was elected to the Martinique Parliament. In 1902, after the eruption of Mount Pelée, he became the island's parliamentary representative in Paris. A popular politician, he was often considered the uncrowned king of Martinique.

Rhum is no longer produced here, but the Clément distillery remains complete and can be seen at the estate. Other exhibits document the slave trade between the New World, Africa, and Europe. A display of cooper tools, in a 30,000-liter wooden cask, shows what remarkable work went into the construction and maintenance of these large vessels. Close your eyes and you can smell the rhum that was stored in this cask until 1990.

At the visitors center, a short film documents the history of Clément, and you can sample the fine rhums that are aged and bottled here. There is a small fee to enter the Clément property, but come to relax amidst the beautiful gardens of one of the great estates of the last century.

CLÉMENT
LE FRANCOIS, MARTINIQUE
Founded 1770

Since 1988, Clément rhums have been distilled at the Simon distillery, a few kilometers away. Aging and bottling is still done at the Habitation Clément.

Fermentation: Freshly squeezed sugar cane juice fermented for twenty-four hours

Distillation Equipment: Copper, single-column continuous still

Clément Rhum Blanc
Bottled Strength: 50, 55, and 62% alcohol by volume
Age: Unaged, stored in oak vats prior to bottling
Notes: Rhum Blanc is used to make a complete line of citrus-based rhum punches and liqueurs.

Clément Rhum Vieux
Bottled Strength: 44% alcohol by volume
Age: Six, ten, and fifteen years
Notes: These are the rhums that made Clément famous around the world. Rhum Vieux from many years, including 1952, 1970, and 1990, are available at the habitation.

Le Galion

Before Martinique was colonized by the French, Spanish galleons docked at protected Galion Bay to take on fresh water. By the end of the eighteenth century, sugar cane dominated the landscape. The Le Galion plantation, owned by the prominent DuBuc family, included land from Trinité to Tartane and Galion.

In 1861, Eugène Eustache borrowed 1.2 million francs to finance the purchase of equipment for the Galion Sugar Factory. With a domain of 2,344 hectare around the Baie du Galion, Eustache grew all of the cane necessary to feed his sugar factory. The prosperity of the sugar industry was unparalleled, here and on the other islands. Advances in equipment increased both the quantity and quality of production. New factories took on huge debts in order to participate in record profits. During the second half of the nineteenth century, twenty-one sugar factories were operating on the island.

Speculation on the world market and advances in the sugar beet industry led to overproduction and a predictable collapse. While the industry was suffering a hangover from the boom party, a severe hurricane ravaged the island in 1891, followed by a drought in 1895, and the destruction in St. Pierre in 1902. Only a third of the sugar factories survived to participate in the next boom.

World War I brought with it a huge increase in the demand for alcohol to be used in explosives. To support the war effort, sugar cane was processed directly into high-purity alcohol, instead of sugar and molasses. Following the closure of the competition and the subsequent collapse of the industry's manufacturing capacity, Galion's profits multiplied.

After the war, France was faced with trying to salvage the industry that had served her. The sugar beet industry, destroyed during the war, contributed to an increased demand for sugar from cane. But the island's main industry was immersed in politics, and quotas were instituted for the production of alcohol and sugar. In the 1920s, the production of sugar and alcohol finally stabilized. While many more small distilleries closed due to competition, others managed to prosper in the artificially controlled market. Quotas are still part of the rhum and sugar businesses and are credited with saving some distilleries and destroying others.

While Europe and the United States concentrated their resources on problems at home during the world depression of the 1930s, the island economies were again particularly hard hit. Between 1930 and 1937, the number of small distilleries fell from 155 to 120, and then to only 25 in 1939.

Since World War II, several mergers and acquisitions have resulted in the Société Anonyme d'Economie Mixte, which now controls Le Galion, the only sugar factory operating in Martinique. In addition to sugar, nearly three million liters of rhum industriel are produced here annually.

Two of the Le Galion products are available in Martinique, but the bulk of the production is exported to France. Unfortunately, there is not a public tour at the Le Galion distillery at this time. It may, however, be possible to see the sugar processing operation during the cane season in the future.

DISTILLERIE DU GALION
GALION, MARTINIQUE
Founded in 1861
Associated with the Galion sugar factory, this distillery makes rhum traditionnel, or rhum from molasses. This is the only rhum made from molasses marketed in Martinique.

Fermentation: Molasses fermented for twenty-four hours

Distillation Equipment: Copper, single-column continuous still

Rhum Traditionnel Le Galion
Bottled Strength: 50 and 55% alcohol by volume
Age: Unaged
Notes: Least expensive rhum in Martinique.

Grand Arome Le Galion
Bottled Strength: 40% alcohol by volume
Age: Aged in oak barrels prior to bottling
Notes: Distilled from a wash of molasses and the vinasse from a previous distillation that has fermented for ten days. This is a unique alcohol. Most of the production is exported to France.

La Favorite

Heading east from the congestion of Fort de France toward Gondleau, and past Chateauboeuf, takes you through the area known as La Favorite. When you cross the river, you can see the distillery smokestack. A sign on the main road points the way to La Favorite.

The distillery is housed in a brick building dating from 1842 when this was a sugar factory. Like all but two of the distilleries in Martinique, La Favorite only produces rhum agricole.

From the second floor of the still house, above the cane mill, you can see most of the process equipment in this large rhum factory. Directly in front of you, a large, steam-powered cylinder is the muscle of the cane mill. To your right, smaller steam engines power conveyor belts to move the bagasse to the boilers, while other steam-powered pumps move the fermented juice to the distillation columns.

Because the amount of cane being fed between the heavy rollers varies, the rollers must be able to move up and down to prevent damage to the mill. To apply the pressure necessary to crush the cane, in addition to the weight of the rollers, hydraulic cylinders are fitted to the bearing on both ends of the rollers. Steel hydraulic lines, on top of the mill, connect these cylinders to hand-powered pumps that can be seen below the observation platform. Heavy weights, next to the pumps, balance the hydraulic force being applied to the rollers. To prevent damage to the mill, the force on the rollers is maintained by raising the weights. In most cane mills, the pressure on the rollers is maintained by an electrically driven hydraulic pump.

Like most of the other distilleries in Martinique, fermentation is completed in less than forty-eight hours. Then, the fermented wine, or *vin*, is fed to the distillation columns. The distillery has expanded over the years, and now has two distillation columns—one is all copper and the other is stainless steel and copper. The condensers for both columns are copper, as well as most of the process piping. Two boilers produce enough steam to power the expanded operation.

The raw rhum is distilled to 70% alcohol, then allowed to rest for two months in large oak casks, or *foudres de chêne*. The rhum paille is allowed to mellow here another year. What will become rhum vieux is put in oak barrels to age in the warehouse.

One of the problems facing all of the distilleries is the scarcity of coopers, or skilled labor to assemble and maintain the barrels. Since the cooper at this distillery retired, it has been difficult to maintain enough barrels to age the volume of rhum that this distillery must keep on hand in order to meet demand and remain profitable.

After watching several barrels being assembled and trying myself, I have come to appreciate how difficult this task can be. In the past, each stave was fit to the one next to it with hand tools, much like building a wooden ship. Today, even though the staves are made by machine and are somewhat interchangeable, it takes considerable skill to assemble a barrel that won't leak for five years or more.

La Favorite is another example of a distillery taking over the production of other nearby distilleries. As the need to replace expensive equipment arises, sometimes it is more economical to contract another distillery for production than to take on new debt. Distilleries, which at one time were competing for the market, are now cooperating for survival. About eight years ago, the St. Etienne distillery, located only a few kilometers from La Favorite, closed. Now this label is distilled and bottled at La Favorite.

Most consumers are very loyal to their label. Even though the rhum may not be produced at that distillery anymore, if the consumer market can be maintained by producing rhum under a particular label at another distillery, this is sometimes a profitable alternative to closing a distillery and then losing the market for that label. Sometimes these changes in production location go completely unnoticed in the marketplace.

La Favorite encourages tourism during the cane season while the distillery is operating. I tried to interview people at some of the distilleries when they were not in production. The distilleries are a lot quieter when the machinery is not in operation and people had more time to help me understand their operations without the inevitable interruptions that occur during production.

DISTILLERIE LA FAVORITE
FORT DE FRANCE, MARTINIQUE
Founded 1842
Fermentation: Freshly squeezed sugar cane juice fermented for forty-eight hours
Distillation Equipment: Two copper, single-column continuous stills

La Favorite Rhum Blanc
Bottled Strength: 50 and 55% alcohol by volume
Age: Unaged
Notes: Rhum blanc is also bottled under the Courville label at the distillery.

MARTINIQUE

La Favorite Rhum Vieux
Bottled Strength: 45% alcohol by volume
Age: Four years
Notes: Also sold under the Courville label.

La Favorite Cuvée spéciale de la Flibuste
Bottled Strength: 40% alcohol by volume
Age: Thirty-three years
Notes: The premium rhum of La Favorite and the oldest rhum commercially sold in Martinique. A very special rhum.

Saint-Etienne Rhum Blanc and Rhum Vieux
Bottled Strength: 50 and 45% alcohol by volume
Age: Unaged and eight years
Notes: Unlike the La Favorite labels.

On each of the islands, I visited a number of small bars. One hot afternoon, while waiting for a bus in Macouba, on the north coast of Martinique, I found Chez Paulette. Across the street and a little north of the post office, Chez Paulette offers cool drinks and some relief from the tropical sun.

Besides a variety of pastries and drinks, Chez Paulette has one of the better selections of rhum that I have encountered in a small shop. Most of the small shops have three or four different brands of rhum. Here, I was surprised to find at least seven different rhums and plenty of discussion as to which is the best rhum in Martinique—and why. Even if you don't understand French, you will enjoy the hospitality of the proprietor and her customers at this well-stocked bar.

Dillon

About a mile east of the cruise ship docks in Fort de France, behind the largest supermarket in the Eastern Caribbean, is the Dillon distillery. It can be easily reached even if you are only going to be in Martinique a few hours.

In 1670, this was the site of the Girardin sugar refinery. During the American War of Independence, French Colonel Arthur Dillon, while carrying out his orders from France, bought the property and established a sizable plantation. In a classic turn of events, Colonel Dillon fell out of favor and ended up on the gallows in 1794.

The story of Dillon, his relations with Napoleon, and, more importantly in Martinique, with Napoleon's wife Josephine, is told at the distillery's air-conditioned visitors center. An interesting film, in French, illustrates the production of rhum and can be viewed before seeing the distillery itself.

In the last fifty years, Fort de France has expanded to the doorstep of this distillery and the cane fields that surrounded this estate are gone. Now, sugar cane is bought from 120 growers around the area. Some is still cut by hand, but, with the increasing cost of labor, each year more of this backbreaking labor is done by machine. Between February and June, about 16,000 tons of cane are processed, depending on the production requirements and the sugar content of the cane.

The large cane mill, installed in 1934, shows how little the technology of crushing cane has changed in the last sixty years. Improvements in lubrication of the bearings and better techniques to filter the fresh juice have enabled mills like this one to remain in service for many years.

Dark-Dry Cruzan
**St. Croix,
U.S. Virgin Islands**

One of the most popular Cruzan distillery rums; a blend of rums aged for at least two years.

Arundel Cane Rum
**Garden Bay, Tortola,
British Virgin Islands**

Available in both white and dark, this rum is from the oldest operating distillery in the Caribbean.

Pusser's Blue Label
**Jim Beam Brands,
United States**

Name derived from the Royal Navy Pursers who drank rum as part of their daily ration.

Foxy's Fire Water
**Jost Van Dyke,
British Virgin Islands**

Full-flavored blend of rum easily found and enjoyed at the popular Foxy's Tamarind Bar.

Busco Rhum Blanc
St. Maarten

An imported rum from Guadeloupe that is blended and bottled by Carreau Blends.

SugarBird Rum
**Philipsburg,
St. Maarten**

Naturally flavored rums including orange ginger, lime, coconut, raspberry, coffee, and dry spice varieties.

Cavalier Five-Year-Old Rum
St. Johns, Antigua

Available not only in Antigua but other islands as well, this blend of aged rums is bottled as a dark rum.

Bushy's Best Matured Rum
Bolans Village, Antigua

This rum is bought from Antigua Distillery Limited and then bottled by Bushy himself. Labels and bottles may vary depending on what is on hand.

Rhum Marsolle
Pointe-à-Pitre, Guadeloupe

A blended result of two distilleries' rums, Montebello and Séverin, that is unique from either of its parts.

Rhum Bologne
Basse-Terre, Guadeloupe

The most popular white rum in Guadeloupe; includes a lot number and date on each bottle.

Séverin Rhum Blanc
Sainte Rose, Guadeloupe

Winner of the Medaille d'Or at the Concours Général Agricole de Paris in 1992.

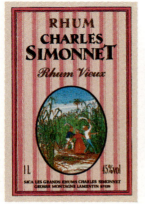

Rhum Charles Simonnet
Pris d'Eau, Guadeloupe

Distilled in Guadeloupe, this rum is then shipped to France for bottling or sold to other bottlers.

Mon Repos Rhum Blanc
Capesterre, Guadeloupe

Made at the century-old Mon Repos distillery, the owners proudly label it "the best rhum in the world."

Montebello Rhum Blanc
Petit Bourg, Guadeloupe

From one of the few operating two-column stills in the French islands.

Damoiseau Rhum Vieux
Grand-Terre, Guadeloupe

An aged rhum agricole, this spirit will suit those who prefer a mature French West Indies rhum.

Rhum Vieux du Père Labat
Grand Bourg, Marie Galante

Aged for five years and then bottled in small quantities at the distillery.

Bielle Rhum Blanc
Marie Galante

Unaged, this rhum agricole is often used to make a variety of fruit-based liqueurs.

Magalda Rhum Blanc
Capesterre, Marie Galante

Unaged, this white rhum is used in making fruit-based liqueurs at the distillery.

Macoucherie Rum
Dominica

Aged for a year and a half, this is a nice rhum similar to the rhum agricoles from the French islands.

Red Cap
Dominica

Named for its red-colored cap, this raw rum has a very strong taste.

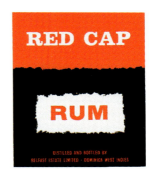

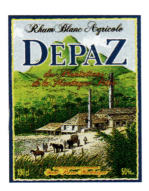

Rhum Blanc DePaz
St. Pierre, Martinique

One of several DePaz rums, this rum is stored in stainless steel tanks prior to being bottled.

J. Bally Rhum Vieux
Carbet, Martinique

The available stock of this particular rhum vieux dates back to 1924, the year the distillery was founded.

Rhum Blanc Neisson
Carbet, Martinique

Sold in a distinctive square bottle, this rhum has attracted quite a loyal following.

Rhum Blanc J. M
Macouba, Martinique

Due to its high distilling purity, this rhum is much lighter than many other rhum agricoles.

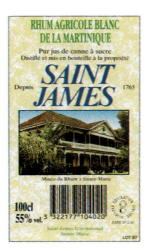

Grappe Blanche Saint James
Sainte Marie, Martinique

Diluted with distilled water, this rhum is similar to rhum blanc agricole.

Rhum Blanc G. Hardy
Tartane, Martinique

Very popular in the local markets; this rhum agricole is bought from another distillery and then bottled under the G. Hardy label.

Clément Rhum Vieux
Le Francois, Martinique

World-famous aged rums; distilled at the Simon distillery, then bottled and aged at Habitation Clément.

Grande Arome Le Galion
Galion, Martinique

A unique alcohol distilled from a molasses wash and previously distilled vinasse.

La Favorite Rhum Blanc
Fort de France, Martinique

Also bottled under the Courville label, this rhum blanc agricole is available aged.

Très Vieux Rhum Dillon
Fort de France, Martinique

Aged for fifteen years, this rhum is hard to find except at the distillery.

Rhum Blanc La Mauny
Rivière Pilote, Martinique

A product of the largest distiller on the island, La Mauny is available at three proofs—50, 55, and 62% alcohol by volume.

Rhum Blanc Trois Rivières
Sainte Luce, Martinique

Bottled at 40, 50, and 55% alcohol by volume, only the 40% alcohol by volume is exported.

Buccaneer Rum
Castries, St. Lucia

Not as dark as most heavy rums, Buccaneer is popular in cocktails and fruit-based punches.

Sunset Very Strong Rum
Georgetown, St. Vincent

A local favorite, this rum is HOT. Bring your own container to take ten or more gallons home with you.

Jack Iron
Carriacou

Straight from the barrel, this 80% alcohol by volume rum is nicknamed the "King" in Carriacou.

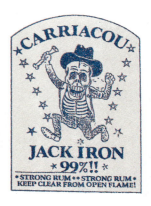

Royale Grenadian Rum (Rivers)
St. Andrews, Grenada

Available right from the still, this rum is less than a week old when bottled.

Spicy Jack
Grenada

Similar to Carriacou's Jack Iron with less alcohol. Small spices are also added.

Westerhall Plantation Rum
Grenada

Premium rum of Westerhall; the distillery's most popular product among tourists.

Clarke's Court Pure White Rum
Woodlands, Grenada

Most popular white rum in Grenada; many spiced rums are made from this strong rum.

Rhum Runner Rhum Punch
Bottled on board the tour boat *Rhum Runner*

Rum punch blended from Clarke's Court Pure White Rum, lime juice, nutmeg, bitters, raw cane sugar, and spring water.

Tradition Yellow Label
Grenada

Another blended spice rum with Clarke's Court Pure White Rum, spices, barks, nuts, herbs, roots, and sea extracts.

Mount Gay Premium White Rum
St. Michael, Barbados

Aged for two years, this light-bodied white rum is filtered to remove its color.

Cockspur Old Gold Reserve
Fontabelle, Barbados

This rum is bought from the West Indies Rum Refinery Ltd. and then blended at Hanschell Inniss Limited.

Old Brigand
Bridgetown, Barbados

Made in both a White and Black blend, these rums are bottled at different proofs for export.

Doorly's Macaw
Bridgetown, Barbados

Bottled as a White and Dark. Macaw Dark, a colored rum, is commonly used in rum punches.

Vat 19
Trinidad

A widely recognized label in the Eastern Caribbean; natural aging color is adjusted with caramel.

Caroni Special Old Cask Rum
Trinidad

Known as a "red rum" due to coloring; the premium rum blended by Caroni Ltd.

Knockemdown Rum
West Palm Beach, Florida

The Conch Republic's premium rum; unfiltered rum that maintains its color, taste, and aroma.

Inside the mill house, nearly a half-million liters of juice can be fermented in the twenty-two stainless steel fermentation vats. Fermentation is strictly controlled and completed in forty-eight hours. Collars, installed around the top of the vats, drip water down the outside of the vats to keep the fermenting wine from getting too hot and killing the yeast.

Like most of the distilleries in Martinique, Dillon employs a single-column distillation process. The older of the two columns in operation today was imported from France in 1920 to replace a pot still that had been in operation since 1869. As the demand for alcohol increased, a second copper column was imported. Now, both copper columns distill alcohol at 70° from the fermented cane juice.

After distillation, all of the rhum at Dillon is put into oak barrels for three months. The white rhum is then diluted, filtered, and bottled at 50, 55, or 62°. The 62° rhum is used mostly for cooking and is not exported.

Small quantities of rhum paille are bottled after one year, but the pride of Dillon are the aged rhums. Over 2,000 barrels of rhum are aging in the warehouse. To facilitate handling, the barrels are stored on pallets. Like many of the distilleries in Martinique, once a year, Dillon weighs the barrels to determine the volume that has been lost during the last twelve months. Then, rhum from the same year is added to the barrels to make up for losses attributed to the angels. This ritual, called *houillage*, helps keep the barrels full and increases the contact between the rhum and the oak in the barrels.

Several aged rhums are bottled at Dillon. The youngest is a six-year-old rhum that sells for FR 58. The 15-year-old très vieux, or very old, sells for FR

72. Since at least eight percent of the rhum in a barrel is lost annually, only small quantities of the oldest rhums are produced. The oldest rhum bottled here is a twenty-year-old rhum that sells for FR 155. Some of these products are available elsewhere, but if you go to the distillery, you can see the widest selection of Dillon products available.

Most of the annual production of 1.5 million liters of rhum is exported to France, but some is shipped to the United States. When you taste one of these fine old rhums, you will understand that patience is rewarded.

DISTILLERIE DILLON
FORT DE FRANCE, MARTINIQUE
Founded circa 1775
Fermentation: Freshly squeezed sugar cane juice fermented for less than forty-eight hours
Distillation Equipment: Two copper, single-column continuous stills

Rhum Blanc Dillon
Bottled Strength: 50, 55, and 62% alcohol by volume
Age: Unaged, stored in oak barrels for three months prior to bottling
Notes: Well-known rhum in Martinique, mixes well.

Rhum Paille Dillon
Bottled Strength: 50% alcohol by volume
Age: One year
Notes: Bottled in small quantities depending on demand and production.

MARTINIQUE

Rhum Vieux Dillon
Bottled Strength: 45% alcohol by volume
Age: Six years
Notes: Notice the longer aging time of this rhum vieux.

Très Vieux Rhum Dillon
Bottled Strength: 45% alcohol by volume
Age: Fifteen years
Notes: This rhum is hard to find except at the distillery.

C.O.D.E.R.U.M.

All of the distilleries in the French West Indies are members of what is known as C.O.D.E.R.U.M. This is an organization for the defense of the market of French West Indies rhum producers. Among the issues faced by this organization are quotas for the sale of French Caribbean rhum in France and standards for bottling and labeling.

The labeling requirements are not the same as in the other islands and, although I did find a few rhums that were not made where the label said they were made, I did not find any label that claimed to be rhum agricole that was not. Some distilleries use the Appellation d' Origine, *or Mark of Origin, as a mark of authenticity but, at this time, there are no strict standards for the use of this term.*

When you open a bottle of French rhum, you may notice that the glass is thicker than that found in bottles on the other islands. Due in part to strict trade laws, all of these bottles are imported from Europe—most other bottles are manufactured in Trinidad. Presently, the majority of the bottles are one liter or 75 cl. New laws in France, however, are replacing the 75 cl bottle with a 70 cl bottle.

La Mauny

You probably recognize the La Mauny name from your travels in the French islands, the Pacific, or maybe Africa, Germany, or Japan. Started in 1749, this is the largest distillery in the French West Indies and the largest distiller of rhum agricole in the Caribbean.

The distillery is actually a good walk north of Rivière Pilote. Unless you have a car, best wear your walking shoes. It is possible to get to the distillery by minibus, but even if you don't get a ride, it is an interesting walk along the river through some beautiful land. Breadfruit, banana, and avocado trees flourish and flowers of every description bloom around you. When you reach the cockfighting pit on the east side of the road, you are almost there.

The visitors' tasting center is on your right as you approach the bottling operation and business offices—the first buildings you will see. But the tours start from the reception area near the distillery itself, a short walk further uphill, past the remains of the old distillery.

Each year, between February and June, La Mauny plantation grows about 10,000 tons of cane on 120 hectares of cultivated land. Another 18,000 tons of cane is bought from local farmers. All of the cane is still cut by hand because the mountainous terrain is too rugged for the big mechanical equipment. Four crushing machines operate twenty-four hours a day during the rhum season so that the cane can be processed immediately.

To increase the efficiency of the juice-extraction process, a controlled amount of water is sprayed on the mills while the cane is being crushed. At most distilleries, the juice is transferred to a fermentation vat, the sugar content of the juice is measured, and then more water is added to adjust the sugar content. Here, the sugar content is evaluated as the juice is pumped to the fermentation vats, and the water is automatically controlled to make further adjustments unnecessary.

Two steam boilers produce enough steam to drive the crushing operation, the three distillation columns, and produce 1,000 kw of electrical power! An operation of this size doesn't have to rely on outside energy when there is so much bagasse to burn.

Thirty-six 30,000-liter tanks stand at one end of the production area to ferment the fresh cane juice. After fermenting for twenty-four hours, the 4° wine is distilled to 70° in one of the three copper distillation columns, then stored in stainless steel tanks. To help the distiller maintain quality control, samples are taken at various stages in the fermentation and distillation process and analyzed in a gas chromatograph.

La Mauny produces 35,000 liters of rhum per day, more than the annual production of some of the smaller distilleries in this book.

Rhum that will be bottled as rhum blanc is allowed to rest three months in 50,000-liter oak casks before it is diluted, filtered, and then bottled at 50° or 55°. Some of this white rhum is also bottled at 62° for the local market.

For aging, used 250-liter oak barrels from France or Kentucky are scraped and then burnt again before they are filled with 62° rhum. This is one of the few distilleries that burns the barrels again after they are assembled.

After the tour, an extensive collection of La Mauny products can be sampled at the rhum boutique and tasting bar.

DISTILLERIE LA MAUNY
RIVIÈRE PILOTE, MARTINIQUE
Founded 1749
Fermentation: Freshly squeezed sugar cane juice fermented for twenty-four hours
Distillation Equipment: Three copper, single-column continuous stills

Rhum Blanc La Mauny
Bottled Strength: 50, 55, and 62% alcohol by volume

Age: Unaged, stored for three months in 50,000-liter oak vats

Notes: Produced by the largest distiller on the island.

Rhum Vieux La Mauny
Bottled Strength: 45% alcohol by volume

Age: Five years

Notes: This is one of the few distilleries that burns their barrels after each use to enhance the aging process.

MARTINIQUE

Rhum Vieux Agricole Hors D'Age
Bottled Strength: 43% alcohol by volume
Age: Ten years
Notes: One of the oldest rhums produced in quantity; worth waiting the ten years.

Trois Rivières

About eight kilometers west of Sainte Luce lies the Trois Rivières estate. It was originally part of a 5,000-hectare land grant to Nicholas Fouquet during the reign of Louis XIV in 1661. While amassing great wealth, Fouquet also attracted the jealousy of the king. Accused of misappropriation of public funds in 1664, all of his assets were confiscated. In 1680, he died in prison at the age of sixty-five.

Today, a new south coast freeway borders the 600-hectare distillery property. Access to the distillery is available from the freeway exit to the west. Heading south from this exit, the old coast road is at a dead-end intersection. Among the trees is a small sign on a fence pointing the way to the right. Follow the old country road past Pizza Panoramique. When this shaded, country road curves to the right, you are almost on the freeway again and at Trois Rivières.

Only 120 hectares of the estate property are presently cultivated with sugar cane and account for eighty percent of the production requirements of the distillery. The remainder of the cane is grown by small, independent farmers on land that was once part of the original land grant.

Each year, between the 15th of January and the 15th of June, the cane is harvested and then crushed in a three-roller cane mill. Incorporated in the mill are pumps which move the fresh juice to fourteen stainless steel, 33,000 liter fermentation vats. Old stone foundations elevate the vats, allowing them to be emptied by gravity and reducing the need for additional pumps, energy, and maintenance requirements.

By adding yeast to accelerate the process, fermentation is accomplished in only twenty-four hours. After fermentation, the 4% alcohol wine is distilled in one of the two single-column stills. Each year more than 1,000,000 liters of rhum at 65-72% alcohol by volume are distilled, then shipped in bulk tanks to the warehouse at Fort de France, where they are stocked and divided into six categories to be bottled or aged.

The aging warehouse is like a cathedral. Barrels form its pillars and the smell of incense is replaced by the scent of tannin and aging rhum. Over two million liters of rhum, contained in ten thousand barrels, are sleeping to maturity within the moss-covered walls of the old building. Like all of the distilleries in this book, once-used whiskey and bourbon barrels are used here for aging rhum. Although the barrels are made of oak, the bungs are poplar—a wood that is better suited for sealing the barrels.

In 1976, Martini and Rossi acquired three companies: Les Rhumeries Duquesne (Martinique); La Société des Grands Rhums Duquesnes (S.G.R.D.) in Bordeaux, France; and Trois Rivières, which had been producing both rhum industriel and rhum agricole under the name M. Aubrèy until 1975. As a result of this acquisition, Duquesne-Trois-Rivières was formed.

The name, Trois Rivières, comes from the geography of the estate. The Duquesne name was shared by Ange and Augustin-Marie Duquesne, who both distinguished themselves in the histories of France and Martinique. Ange Duquesne (1702-1778) was an important Canadian army leader. In 1754, he signed a peace treaty with the Iroquois Indians at Fort Duquesne. The fort was later renamed Pittsburgh. Augustin-Marie was born in 1765 and became Captain of the Port in Martinique before cruising the Atlantic Ocean on the privateer, *La Fortuneand*.

Prior to the acquisition, Rhums Duquesne were made at Rivière-Salée and belonged to the Marraud-Desgrottes family. In 1953, there was an aging cellar large enough for storing part of the production in reserve for aging. Some of the exceptional aged rhum from that cellar is still being marketed.

In another part of the Fort de France complex, the rhum is bottled under two labels. Even though the two rhums come from the same plant, the distinction between the two products and the marketing objectives for the labels are quite apparent. Duquesne rhums are primarily marketed in France, where eighty percent of the rhum bearing the Duquesne label is sold. Trois Rivières is marketed more locally, with about eighty percent of the rum being sold in Martinique.

The production of Duquesne rhum amounts to 450,000 bottles of rhum blanc and rhum vieux, in addition to bulk shipments for bottling in Europe. The production of Trois Rivières is about 440,000 bottles, with the majority being rhum vieux. Trois Rivières prides itself on the large number of fine aged rhums available.

In spite of the fact that the rhum is not aged at

the distillery, most of the Duquesne and Trois Rivières rhums are available in the distillery boutique. A large oak cask, used for aging rhum in the past, now serves as a unique rhum boutique. Among the selection of rhums, I found a ten-year-old Duquesne Très Vieux Rhum for only FR 65. Even though the bottle was only 70 cl, it is unusual to find a ten-year-old bottle of rhum at this price. Look for the neck band that gives the age of these special rhums. There is also Trois Rivières Rhum available from 1969, 1975, 1979, 1980, and 1982. But, these rhums are not aged ten years.

The aging and bottling warehouse in Fort de France is closed to the public, but there is a distillery tour at Trois Rivières. The signs are in French, but even if you don't understand the language, you will enjoy seeing the historic buildings and the beautiful landscape around the distillery. The fine rhums produced here can be sampled in the shade of the reception area where the tours begin.

This is the only distillery that I found to be particularly hard to get to by public transportation. If you are prepared, this can be a nice outing, but take along some water. From the distillery, it is a good walk to Sainte Luce, where the buses or taxis will pick up tourists. Don't let me discourage you from coming here if you don't have a car. You will enjoy your visit.

DISTILLERIE TROIS RIVIÈRES
SAINTE LUCE, MARTINIQUE
Founded 1661
Fermentation: Freshly squeezed sugar cane juice fermented for twenty-four hours
Distillation Equipment: Two stainless steel continuous stills

MARTINIQUE

Rhum Blanc Trois Rivières

Bottled Strength: 50 and 55% alcohol by volume

Age: Unaged, stored in oak vats prior to bottling

Notes: This is also bottled at 40% alcohol by volume for the export market.

Rhum Vieux Trois Rivières

Bottled Strength: 45% alcohol by volume

Age: Five years

Notes: Rhum Vieux is available from many years including 1969, 1975, 1980, and 1992.

Rhum Blanc Duquesne

Bottled Strength: 50 and 55% alcohol by volume

Age: Unaged

Notes: This rhum is primarily marketed in France.

Duquesne Très Vieux Rhum

Bottled Strength: 45% alcohol by volume

Age: Ten years

Notes: Look for this rare value in aged French rhums.

Many of the distilleries in this book were important to the history and development of the islands. Trois Rivières is of particular interest. In 1805, when England and France were at war, British Admiral Hood stationed a contingent of men on a strategic pinnacle island southwest of here. The rock was declared an English sloop of war, the H.M.S. Diamond Rock.

The English valiantly manned their H.M.S. Diamond Rock *for eighteen months and successfully slowed maritime traffic along the south coast of Martinique, an area where the westward current and coastal shoals require careful navigation.*

Frustrated by their lack of success at driving the English from their precarious position on Diamond Rock, the French let barrels of rhum from this distillery float down the river and out to sea. From here, the tide and current did the rest. After a few hours, the westerly current had taken the barrels of rhum to the feet of the war-weary English sailors. The next day, the H.M.S. Diamond Rock *was captured without much resistance.*

In a truly heroic spirit, the French recognized the value of such dedicated military men and allowed the captured troops to return to England, instead of spending the rest of the war in prison camps.

St. Lucia

St. Lucia, like its neighbors to the south, emerged from its status as a British colony to that of an independent nation in the last twenty years. As political and economic changes swept the islands of the Caribbean, the ability of small distilleries to remain profitable has been tested. The last twenty years have seen the consolidation of the two distilleries on this island as the exportation of sugar was replaced by bananas in the early 1960s.

Although Castries is avoided by many tourists and yachts are commonly told that they are not welcome, you would have to agree that Castries is a vibrant city. Most West Indian cities turn out for the market on Saturday morning, but Castries blossoms every day. From seven o'clock in the morning until well into the afternoon, vendors are set up under colorful umbrellas selling whatever is in season.

The daily catch of fish is brought up from the seawall by young men to take its place between people selling coconuts, mangoes, avocados, tomatoes, and many other locally grown fruits, vegetables, and spices. When you get hungry, fried fish steaks and chicken with a spicy sauce are served with a warm smile sure to please. Unlike many of the straw markets in the Caribbean (where most handmade articles are imported), the baskets for sale are made by the people who live here.

While exploring this explosion of color, aroma, and sound, you may end up behind the commercial dock. The distribution warehouse for bulk rum is behind the petrol station on Manoel Street. This is a busy place where you can see barrels of rum being readied for shipment to hotels around the island. I always have to stop and admire the oak barrels and the writing on their heads, which tells the volume in a particular barrel and its lot number.

While in St. Lucia, I tried a few of the spiced rums and was very surprised at how smooth and pleasant "spice" can be. Generally, these spiced rums sit for a few weeks, take on the flavor of the spices, and lose the raw alcohol taste of the rum. But the pleasant taste belies the amount of alcohol in these flavorful concoctions. It is important to remember that these spiced rums are made with overproof rum and contain a lot more alcohol than your normal cocktail. More than once I have had to resist the temptation of having another of these tasty drinks at the risk of not being able to continue the day's research.

St. Lucia Distillers Limited

The Barnard family had been making rum at their Dennery Factory Company for three generations before a joint venture merged the resources of the Geest Distillery and the Dennery Factory Company. The new company was formed to better respond to the changing business environment in St. Lucia and the Caribbean. When the island economy shifted from sugar cane to bananas, the Dennery Factory Company was faced with the increased costs and logistics of importing molasses, essential to the production of rum in the English-speaking islands.

Today, St. Lucia Distillers is located on the site of the old Geest Distillery. It was once a part of the Sugar Manufacturers mill in Roseau, just south of Marigot, on the west coast of St. Lucia. The abandoned mill and remaining equipment are reminders of the difficult years following the change of the agricultural base from sugar to bananas.

Since 1972, the joint venture that kept the Barnard family's distillery interests alive has evolved in many ways. The equipment from the two aging distilleries was replaced in the second half of the last decade with a new two-column still. In 1987, East Caribbean Distilleries Limited was formed and another joint venture with Duncan, Gilbey and Matheson International Limited led to the diversification of other spirits that could be produced with the modern still. The introduction of gin, vodka, and brandy not only opened new markets for products distilled and bottled in St. Lucia, but also opened the door to the exportation of bulk alcohol to Europe and Africa.

More recently, under another agreement between the Martinique-based company of G and P Dormoy and the newly formed West Indies Liqueur Company, popular La Belle Creole liqueurs are being produced and bottled in St. Lucia. This is the only cooperative agreement I am aware of in the alcohol business between the French West Indies and their English-speaking neighbors. Considering the fundamental differences between the business climates in the French and the English-speaking islands, this is a milestone in cooperation for the mutual benefit of the islands.

Although changes are under way to make the La Belle Creole product labels more attractive by adding embossing and slight color adjustments, you will certainly recognize these products on the shelf. These liqueurs are popular in Martinique and are gaining a respectable following in the other islands.

As chairman of St. Lucia Distillers, Laurie Barnard has overcome many obstacles in order to succeed in what he considers a small distillery. A commitment to quality control, as well as a diversity of production and distribution, is serving this company well. However, to remain competitive in the growing market, many decisions must be made that will affect the distillery in the future. As new products are introduced, there must also be an investment in production equipment and provisions to make that product consistent.

St. Lucia Distillers Limited has the largest product line of any distillery of its size. I expect some of these rums will be discontinued in the future, but look for new products as the directors continue to diversify their strong market base. Presently, St. Lucia Distillers bottles a variety of rum products, from white fresh rum to aged and blended products.

While you are here, take time to contact your hotel activities center, St. Lucia Reps at 452-3762 for tour information, or visit the new visitors center in Castries, where all of these products are available.

ST. LUCIA DISTILLERS LIMITED
CASTRIES, ST. LUCIA
Founded 1972
Fermentation: Molasses fermented for less than forty-eight hours
Distillation Equipment: Stainless steel, two-column continuous still

Denros Strong Rum
Bottled Strength: 80% alcohol by volume
Age: Unaged
Notes: Local rum shops buy this rum in five-gallon containers to be spiced with a variety of fruits and spices. These are known appropriately as "spice." This rum is also distributed to many hotels and resorts in St. Lucia in barrels.

ST. LUCIA

Bounty Rum
Bottled Strength: 40% alcohol by volume

Age: Unaged

Notes: The most popular white rum in St. Lucia, also bottled as an amber rum.

Bounty Crystal White Rum
Bottled Strength: 40% alcohol by volume

Age: Unaged

Notes: Dry white rum for cocktails or drinking on the rocks.

Buccaneer Rum
Bottled Strength: 43% alcohol by volume

Age: Unaged

Notes: Buccaneer has a heavier taste than Bounty Rum. Although it is not as dark as some other heavy rums, it is popular in cocktails and fruit-based punches.

Ron D'Oro Superior
Bottled Strength: 43% alcohol by volume

Notes: Primarily exported to England and Europe. This blended rum complements the other St. Lucia dark rums.

Le Marquis Rhum

Bottled Strength: 50 and 55% alcohol by volume
Age: Unaged
Notes: The newest rum from the distillery, blended to imitate the taste of rhum agricole.

Kweyol Spice Rum

Bottled Strength: 40% alcohol by volume
Notes: Spiced with Bois Bande, this is another new addition to the rums from St. Lucia Distillers.

Old Fort Reserve Rum

Bottled Strength: 43% alcohol by volume
Age: Aged in oak barrels at the distillery
Notes: Not an ordinary rum, blended to be the smoothest of the St. Lucia rums. Available in most of the larger outlets on the island, it's worth trying while you're in St. Lucia. The premium rum from St. Lucia Distillers Ltd.

---

*A*nother rum in St. Lucia is labeled Lucian Rum. The label is an artist's concept of a red sun to the east of the Pitons with water in the foreground. Since the label on this bottle does not say where the rum was distilled, I was baffled until I looked on the bottle for a clue. Embossed on the bottom of the bottle are the words, "Jamaica Liquor Bottle." This is a product of Jamaica, but the label doesn't tell you where the rum was distilled or bottled. I expect the importer to change the label to include the country of origin. When I saw the bottle, I was reminded of an ancient mariner's rhyme:

    Red sky at night, sailors' delight.
    Red sky at dawn, sailors be warned.

St. Vincent and the Grenadines

When you visit St. Vincent and the Grenadines, you will certainly want to take a ferry from Bequia to Kingstown (not Kingston, that's in Jamaica). The ferries leave at six-thirty in the morning. The one with the most people on it is the faster of the two. The day I went, we came in at least two boat lengths ahead of the slower ferry and didn't have to wait to disembark from the seven-mile trip. The fare is EC $5 to Kingstown and EC $10 return to Admiralty Bay, Bequia. Beer is available at the bar aboard the ferry.

Once you make your way off the bustling dock, minibuses are a ten-minute walk through the old stone storefronts along the historic waterfront. Just past the new market on your left is the minibus area. Destinations on the windward side of the island are on the east side of the area, and destinations on the leeward side of the island are on the west. St. Vincent Distillers Ltd. in Georgetown is a little north of the middle of the windward side of the island. When I asked how much the fare was to Georgetown, I was told, "Don't worry, get in!" The minibus ride itself is spectacular.

I had sailed within a few miles of this coast on my way from St. Lucia to Bequia a few days earlier in hopes of catching a fish. While trying to bring in a tuna, I had gotten much closer to the island and was not prepared for its beauty. Below the road, steep cliffs meet the pounding surf. Above, the virility of this volcanic island appears boundless. As you ride around hairpin turns on a wet road, you have to remind yourself that the driver has made this trip so many times that he could almost do it in his sleep. For only EC $4, sit back and enjoy the experience.

St. Vincent Distillers Limited

A little beyond the tunnel is Georgetown, and just past the center of town is St. Vincent Distillers Ltd. About sixty-five years ago, Bentinck Estate Ltd. built a distillery here to make use of the readily available molasses from the sugar mill next door.

In 1963, the distillery became St. Vincent Distillers Ltd. In the same year, the fields that had been planted with sugar cane were turned to bananas and the sugar mill shut down. Not only could sugar be produced from sugar beets and other sources with less labor and energy, transportation routes had developed so that sugar could be imported at a lower cost than it could be produced locally. When the sugar mill closed, molasses for the distillery had to be imported from Guyana.

In 1983, a new crop of sugar cane was planted, and hopes were restored for an inexpensive, domestic source of molasses. The sugar mill, which had been all but torn down, was refurbished with equipment from Trinidad, while the new crop of cane was beginning to cover the mountainside. With the promise of cheaper raw material and renewed economic optimism, new distillation equipment was ordered from John Dore and Company in England.

On June 11, 1985, the first rum from the new distillery was produced. Unfortunately, the sugar mill next door had already closed and bananas were once again taking over the landscape. Today, the bananas, which have provided the fuel for the economy over the last thirty years, are threatened by foreign competition. Rum is beginning to emerge as a viable source of foreign trade, even though molasses must be imported.

Fitz-Stephen Pitt, the distiller, learned his trade at this distillery. He is responsible for mixing the wash of molasses, water, and yeast and then fermenting it in the 5,000-gallon steel vats over two to three days. Tubes in the ten fermentation vats carry cool spring water and maintain the proper temperature without the need for any additional energy source and without polluting the river water.

Once fermentation is complete, the brix, as the fermented wash is known here, is fed to the two-column stainless steel still. The first column, or the distillation column, produces alcohol at about 72% by volume. This is redistilled in the rectifying column to 89% alcohol. This alcohol is condensed and leaves the distillation area at room temperature. The steam for the process is produced by a diesel-fired boiler since there is no waste bagasse to burn.

Although there was not a set tour at the time I visited here, I was shown great hospitality. St. Vincent and the Grenadines are truly to be experienced, but be sure to get your rum early on Friday or you may have to drink some imported spirit. And that would be a shame.

Back in Admiralty Bay, on board *Second Wind*, we found Captain Bligh to be very agreeable. Then, we added some Very Strong Rum to the sweet Rum Punch and, predictably, suffered the first noticeable malady of this cruise.

RUMS OF THE WORLD

ST. VINCENT DISTILLERS LIMITED
GEORGETOWN, ST. VINCENT
Founded 1963
Fermentation: Molasses fermented for two to three days
Distillation Equipment: Stainless steel, two-column continuous still

Sunset Very Strong Rum
Bottled Strength: 84.5% alcohol by volume
Notes: Favored by the local taste, this HOT rum is available on Tuesday and Friday mornings. Bring your own container if you're in the market for ten or more gallons of this rum.

Captain Bligh
Bottled Strength: 40% alcohol by volume
Age: Aged up to ten years in oak casks at only 54% alcohol by volume
Notes: This rum is hard to find before the weekend. Second in the Caribbean Week Rum Testing Competition in both 1991 and 1992.

Sunset Red
Bottled Strength: 40% alcohol by volume
Notes: Similar to Captain Bligh with an added essence. Winner of the 1993 Caribbean Week Rum Testing Competition.

Carriacou

While *Tafia was anchored off Windward, a fishing boat was careened to repair the bottom. Once the repairs were complete, the ballast stone reloaded, and a little paint brushed on the deck, the boat was almost ready to resume fishing. The next morning, the four-man crew assembled on deck to apply the finishing touches. After the youngest crew member anointed the bow and the fish hold to ensure a good catch, he handed the bottle to the eldest man. In silence, the crew watched as he poured a little Jack Iron on the tiller so the boat would always find her way safely back home.*

By now, it was too late to go fishing. So they sat down on the rough deck, waved me over to join them, and drank to their good fortune—a long life in Carriacou.

Two cups were used, one for Jack Iron and one for water. After the first person drank a little rum, then some water, he crossed his forearms and handed the two cups to the next person. Without crossing his hands, the recipient took both cups so that the rum and the water stayed in the correct position. Rum in the left hand and water in the right.

A few months later, I met the crew of Margeta *on the south coast of Grenada. It had been raining all day and the crew was fixing an awning on the foredeck when I rowed over to see if they had any fish for sale.*

Soon we were playing cards and quenching our thirst. A couple of limes were cut and squeezed into a plastic pail, a little sugar was added along with a good splash of rum and some water. Swirling the pail mixed the drink and dissolved the brown sugar. Without glasses, it was easy to spill a few drops on your chest as you tipped the pail, but there was no doubt—these men certainly know how to mix a good afternoon cocktail.

Jack Iron

In Carriacou, Jack Iron is not just rum. Jack Iron is King! "Jack Iron is made in Carriacou. Well, no, it comes from Trinidad and St. Bart's. It's made in Trinidad, but it's more expensive there. It's made in Trinidad by people from Carriacou." Although the words of the story hardly vary, the facts usually do. Never mind the disparity—this is the truth!

Near a boat under construction on the beach, I found an empty Jack Iron barrel. Among the markings on the barrel head were 1993 (date the barrel was filled), ALC 79% (79% alcohol by volume), and HP (High Proof). Plenty strong to be King. Other barrels that I have seen showed an alcohol content of 80% and 80.5%. As barrels of high-proof rum are aged, the amount of alcohol lost to evaporation varies, and the barrels contain different amounts of alcohol. Whatever the proof, ice sinks in Jack Iron.

Now I'm going to tell you what really happened. Jack Iron is actually made by Trinidad Distillers Limited for blending on the other islands. Since

> *The Carriacou Regatta takes place the first Monday of August, but the party begins before the previous Friday. In the early years, a bottle of Jack Iron was offered as a consolation prize for every boat. Now, thousands of dollars in cash prizes are offered in each class.*
>
> *The Regatta participants are all working freight and fishing craft built without engines. For the races, long battens and sprits are employed to increase sail area. If the wind is up, a few ballast stones are added, or if the wind dies, a few stones are thrown overboard.*

most blended rums are a base rum to which other light and heavy-aged rums are added, there is a demand for overproof rum as a base. To minimize shipping and handling costs, the high alcohol content is desired. Due to the economy of scale, T.D.L., one of the largest distilleries in the Eastern Caribbean, can make this light, high-proof liquor cheaper than a smaller distillery. Although Jack Iron is made in Trinidad, it isn't available there except by the barrel for export.

There are differences in the Jack Iron you will find in the various rum shops in Carriacou. Some add nuts, seeds, or spices to the large bottles, decanted from the barrel in the back room. A couple of enterprising shopkeepers have made labels and bottled Jack Iron; others will only fill your bottle.

No matter how you buy it, this is some plenty strong rum. When you order rum in Carriacou, you will be served Jack Iron—straight. So, order something else to chase it. Water is the most common chaser, but Coke is also popular.

Don't be surprised when you are served a small bottle of rum. Each of these sample-size bottles has been scientifically calibrated to deliver exactly *one-eighth* of Jack Iron. These small bottles are equal to one-eighth of a regular rum bottle and are usually shared among a few friends. Most tourists don't need more than an eighth to get started. The first time I ordered rum here, I couldn't finish the small bottle. No one seemed too surprised, and everyone willingly helped me out.

If there was any doubt that Jack Iron is King in Carriacou, it was dispelled when I tried to find a couple of bottles to take with me after the regatta. All of the fifty or so barrels unloaded at Tyrrel Bay before the regatta were gone. Next year, I won't wait so long to take the King with me.

RUMS OF THE WORLD

Jack Iron
Bottled Strength: 80% alcohol by volume
Age: Three years
Notes: Notice the color of this three-year-old rum straight from the barrel.

*N*ot everyone who has met Jack Iron has had such a memorable evening as the author of this letter, but then again this is strong rum.

Dear Mary and George Willy,
We have known each other for some time now, but I want to apologize for yesterday and last Thursday. As you know when I am sober, I am a polite, kind, generous person. But when I am drunk, I turn into a horrible animal. For the sake of my family as well as yourselves, please do not serve me Jack Iron or any other strong rum. I am witnessing this letter with the police to show my sincerity.

*T*o *make your next fruit pie memorable, marinate the sliced fruit in some good French wine, also available in Carriacou, and a shot of Jack Iron overnight in the refrigerator. Then, proceed as usual with your favorite recipe. Thanks to Mum at the Golden Eagle Bar (just south of the pier in Hillsborough). Jack Iron is also used in many locally prepared stews, fish water, goat water, and well, just about everything else.*

Grenada

You can't be in Grenada long before the "Spice Island" earns its name. Ninety-five percent of the world's nutmeg is grown here; it is even the focal point of the national flag. But nutmeg is only one of the spices on the "Isle of Spice."

If it is grown in the Eastern Caribbean, it probably grows better in Grenada than anywhere else as a result of the rich, volcanic soil and the diversity of the climate. The problem of relying on one or two crops has not plagued this small island nation. Family farms patchwork the hillsides, and sugar cane is often visible as you travel the island. A broad agricultural base and the lack of a consumption tax on alcohol have contributed to the survival of several distilleries that document the history of rum making over the last two hundred years.

Production techniques vary from pot stills capable of producing only a few gallons to a modern two-column still that yields several thousand gallons a day. Spirits are made from sugar cane juice, cane syrup, or molasses. Rum is also imported from other islands to be blended and bottled here.

During my travels, I encountered several illegal local stills. On some islands, I heard stories of stills that no longer existed; on others, I read about them in the daily newspaper. You probably won't see these stills on a casual island tour, but in the small, rural rum shops, if you ask—as an interested connoisseur—you may find "mountain dew, forest reserve, hogo, babash, or local rum." These spirits are usually fresh white rum, sometimes spiced, and as you might imagine, always quite strong. Without taxes or licenses, these illicit stills also have no regulations for the contents or processing of their rums.

If you are in the mood to party, plan on being in Grenada for Carnival. During the second weekend in August, you can see St. George's come alive with *color—lots of loud music, and, of course, plenty of rum. Rest up for this one. The party continues all night and doesn't slow down until Tuesday afternoon. St. George's is one of the most picturesque Caribbean cities; it really outdoes itself during Carnival. If you are on a boat, the lagoon is the best place to be. It is only a short dinghy ride from the party, so you won't feel left out even if you don't go ashore.*

While you are in Grenada, have a look around. There is a lot to see and an opportunity to witness rum being made as it was on the sugar estates centuries ago.

River Antoine Estate

When trying to identify the location of the distilleries on an island, I would go to a rum shop, talk to the shopkeeper, and look at the rum labels. I first heard of the River Antoine distillery at the Fat Rice Bar in Carriacou.

A few days later, I was in Grenada on a bus heading north from Grenville to the distillery. The road along the northeast coast was closed due to construction, so I had to walk about a mile in the hot afternoon sun. Signs on the open doors of neighborhood rum shops proclaiming, "Rivers Sold Here" raised my hopes that I would soon be at the distillery. When cane fields appeared on both sides of the road and a new bridge came into sight, I sensed I was close. Workmen on the bridge confirmed my expectations and pointed to a path through the cane to the west.

As the roofs of the distillery buildings became visible over the top of the cane, I felt transported back in time. The cornerstone on the boiling house proudly states the year 1785. Only the clothes of the seventy or so friendly people working here remind you that you are not in the eighteenth century. Some of the equipment at this estate has obviously been replaced, but there is no doubt that the people who worked here more than two hundred years ago, the ancestors of the present employees, would feel right at home here today.

The River Antoine Estate produces a variety of agricultural products, but is best known for its rum. Sugar cane, grown on the estate, is hauled on ox-drawn carts to the water-powered cane mill. All of the cane is then fed by hand, twice, into the three-roller press to extract as much juice as possible. The fresh-squeezed juice flows down a wooden sluice to the boiling house, where it is cooked in cast-iron pots over an open fire of dried cane stalks and wood. As the juice is ladled from pot to pot to thicken the sweet liquid, tempering lime is added to precipitate the unwanted impurities and to aid fermentation.

After the juice has boiled a few hours, the thickened liquid is ladled into another sluice that directs it to the fermentation tanks on the second floor of the still house. Fermentation relies on the natural yeast in the juice, taking about eight days. Once all of the sugar has been converted to alcohol, the wash is drained from the concrete tanks to the pot still and two retorts below.

Some of the products of a previous distillation are added to the fermented wash, then heated by a fire built directly under the copper pot. Vapor from the second retort is condensed in the heat exchanger and then piped to the sight glass on the ground floor of the still house.

The hydrometer in the sight glass indicates the alcohol content of the condensed liquid. The distiller then directs the product stream to one of the three concrete cisterns in the floor, depending on its alcohol content. Even though some of the clear liquid isn't fit to drink, it can be used to fill the retorts for the next distillation, as it contains some alcohol which can be recovered. Not much is wasted in this operation.

On a large chalkboard, in front of the sight glass, the depth of liquid in each cistern is recorded, then calculated into gallons, and entered in another column. From the chalkboard, you can see the daily production is only about thirty-five gallons. The distiller, Godfrey Williams, works year round to make enough rum to meet the demand.

This is one of the few distilleries where you can see all of the stages of rum making without any fanfare. After touring the operation, you can sample the clear rum that was probably distilled just yesterday, if not that morning. What you see is what you get. Don't be put off by the plastic cups or the warm water. Most of the work is done here in the morning, so get here early if you want to see the operation in motion. Around here, "Don't say rum, say Rivers."

RIVER ANTOINE ESTATE
ST. ANDREWS, GRENADA
Founded in 1785
Fermentation: Freshly squeezed sugar cane juice fermented for eight days
Distillation Equipment: Copper pot still with two retorts

Royale Grenadian Rum
(More commonly known as Rivers)

Bottled Strength: Up to 87% alcohol by volume, the strongest commercial rum in the Eastern Caribbean

Age: Unaged

Notes: Hot, raw rum straight from the still. Low production and high demand yields this less than a week old rum. My taste tends to favor an aged rum, but if you want to take home a bottle of white rum—right from the still—this is a rare opportunity.

Dunfermline

Only a few miles south of the River Antoine Estate lies the Dunfermline Estate. Established in 1797, this 300-acre estate produces rum, cocoa, and a variety of other agricultural products that includes virtually anything you can name.

If you take a morning bus from St. George's over the middle of the island, by the time you reach Grenville, you will be ready for lunch. From the bus stop, walk through the pool hall, north of the police station, and up the stairs on the outside of the building. Or ask for Bains on Albert Street. The view of the Atlantic Ocean, the cool breeze, and the delicious lunch are well worth climbing the three flights of stairs.

From Grenville, it's only a short bus ride north to the Dunfermline Estate. Pass Sam's Inn on your left, then turn left off the paved road, just before the single lane bridge and sharp right curve. Once off the paved road, take the left fork of the dirt road to the distillery and estate buildings.

In the shade of the old mahogany trees that line this well-traveled, rural road, I imagined the people that had traveled here before me, driving wagons loaded with barrels of rum and produce. Not far down this road a small, water-powered cane mill to your left signals your arrival to this distillery.

A pipe from the cane press delivers the fresh juice to the stone boiling house. Inside the boiling house, a 400-gallon copper measure is used to keep track of how much cane juice has been pressed.

The first job assigned to a new employee at Dunfermline is to build and maintain the fire under the sugar pots. When the steam is rising from the heavy iron sugar pots, temperatures inside this high-ceiling building can easily reach 100°F. A few hours of this work and I am sure the romance of working in a two hundred-year-old distillery would soon evaporate into a cloud of sweat. A single-cylinder diesel engine looks out of place in the boiling house, but greatly simplifies the job of pumping the boiled juice to the wooden and concrete fermentation vats on the second floor of the still house next door.

Depending on the sugar content of the cane juice, fermentation takes ten to twelve days. If there is not enough cane juice available, molasses is added to the fermentation wash. Trevor, the distiller, monitors the process with a hydrometer to determine when the wash is ready to be distilled. Then, the wash is drained into the copper pot still below, adjacent to the aging warehouse. Dunfermline's still is quite similar to the one in use at the River Antoine Estate.

After gathering and cutting the wood, the second job for a new employee is to maintain the fire for the still. The fire is lit before sunrise in order for the distillation to be completed by early afternoon. After the raw rum is condensed by the river water that passes through the estate, it fills the old copper sight glass on the floor of the still house. The sight glass contains three beads that float or sink depending on the alcohol content of the rum. This raw alcohol is then diverted to three cisterns that contain the rum to be bottled, the high wines, and the thirds. The high wines are used to fill the retorts. The thirds are mixed with the wash and redistilled the next time the still pot is fired.

This privately owned estate distills rum from the end of February to the end of September. Although not many tourists visit this distillery, Trevor, the distiller, and his assistant, Roland, were happy to show me around the distillery buildings and to help me understand what makes Dunfermline rum unique.

RUMS OF THE WORLD

DUNFERMLINE ESTATE
GRENADA
Founded 1797
Fermentation: Sugar cane juice fermented for ten to twelve days
Distillation Equipment: Copper pot still

Dunfermline Rum
Bottled Strength: 70% alcohol by volume
Age: Unaged
Notes: A white rum distilled, blended, and bottled by the estate. Slightly smoother than Rivers which is distilled a few miles north of Dunfermline.

Spicy Jack
Bottled Strength: 70% alcohol by volume
Age: Three years
Notes: A little darker than the other three-year-old rums bottled in Grenada. Similar to Jack Iron from Carriacou but with slightly less alcohol. Small spices are also added.

Westerhall Estate Ltd.

The Westerhall Estate dates from 1800 and is the third oldest distillery in Grenada. Easily reached by minibus, west of St. David's on the south coast road, this 70-acre estate produces sugar cane, cocoa, citrus, bananas, and rum. Privately owned by the Williams family, work was under way to restore this distillery to its original working order when I visited here.

This small distillery was designed to take advantage of water diverted from the St. Louis River that runs through the estate. The water was used to power a water wheel to crush the cane and then to condense the fresh rum from the still.

The copper pot still, visible from the road as you approach the estate, resembles the stills at the other old distilleries in Grenada. But its updated design incorporates a steam boiler to provide better temperature control than is possible with an open fire. From the still, the fresh rum is piped back to the first floor of the still house, to be aged, blended, and bottled.

In the cool, moist darkness on the second floor of this stone still house, bats sleep during the day, hanging from the ceiling. At night, they help control insects. Bats can be found in many of the aging warehouses, but their presence can be a little disturbing to unsuspecting tourists.

Although no rum was being produced here at the time I visited, Westerhall bottles five rum products. The blender, in addition to blending the rum, is responsible for keeping the secrets of the blend—a very important job. Rum is a very competitive business, and it is not uncommon for even the general manager of a distillery not to know all of the recipes of the blends used. In some cases, if the blender dies, everything goes out the window. All of the labels here are different blends, even though they may have similar character.

In addition to rum, Westerhall Estate Ltd. blends and bottles gin and vodka. These products are sold locally and exported to England.

WESTERHALL ESTATE LIMITED
GRENADA
Founded 1800

No longer producing rum, still blends and bottles a number of Trinidad rums.

Rum Sipper
Bottled Strength: Not less than 70% alcohol by volume

Age: Unaged

Notes: Imported in barrels which gives this white rum a smoother taste. Best enjoyed, as its name suggests, by sipping it.

Westerhall Strong Rum
Bottled Strength: 79% alcohol by volume

Age: Unaged

Notes: Like the Rum Sipper, this is imported in barrels, but bottled at a higher proof.

Superb Light Grenada Rum
Bottled Strength: 43% alcohol by volume

Age: Unaged white rum

Notes: A blend of several imported rums. Similar to Plantation Rum. This rum is not exported.

GRENADA

Jack Iron
Bottled Strength: 70% alcohol by volume
Age: Three years
Notes: This is similar to the Jack Iron in Carriacou, but bottled at a lower proof.

Westerhall Plantation Rum
Bottled Strength: 43% alcohol by volume
Age: Blend of rums aged up to three years

Notes: The premium rum of Westerhall. Plantation is the most popular Westerhall product among tourists and enjoys a good reputation as a blended, aged rum. Small quantities of this rum are exported.

Clarke's Court

The largest of the distilleries in Grenada, Clarke's Court is part of the Grenada Sugar Factory Ltd. The government is its principal shareholder. Built in 1937 in the southeastern part of the island, the Woodlands factory produces sugar, fancy molasses, rum, and methylated spirits.

Five hundred local farmers grow and harvest the cane processed at the factory. Since the sugar refinery and distillery are integrated, they can efficiently use the cane that costs EC $120 per ton. Depending on the production schedule of the sugar refinery, a combination of fresh cane juice, concentrated cane syrup, and molasses are fermented to make rum. During the cane-cutting season, from

February to June, fresh cane juice is used as it is available. In the fall, sugar cane syrup is used since it can be stored for a longer period of time than the fresh juice, which is not available in the fall.

According to the ingredients used in the wash, the time required for fermentation varies from eight days for fresh cane juice to only three to four days for concentrated cane syrup. The resulting wine, or dunder, is then distilled in a two-column continuous still. About 100,000 imperial gallons of rum at 96% alcohol by volume are produced annually. Distilling the rum to such a high purity helps reduce the variations in the final product normally associated with fermenting different raw materials.

The primary energy source for the sugar-processing operation is the bagasse from the crushing operation. To fire the boiler for the distillation process, fuel oil is burned since the bagasse is not available year round.

Distillery personnel are working hard to reclaim the solids from the *leeze*, or spent wash, collected from the distillation column after the alcohol has been distilled. By filtering the leeze and collecting the filter cake, usable products for paper production can be made. Utilizing these by-products as raw materials for other manufacturing processes reduces the amount of pollution generated, and produces additional revenue for the distillery.

The principal product of this distillery is Clarke's Court Pure White Rum. Available everywhere, this rum is the mainstay of Grenada and is drunk straight or with a dash of Angostura bitters, giving the drink a pleasing color. Water, or some other chaser, is usually served on the side. At about EC $14 a bottle, Clarke's Court is clearly the best-selling rum in Grenada.

GRENADA

After watching several men and women enjoying themselves at lunch, I tried a glass of this concoction and was pleasantly surprised. A splash of bitters really adds a lot to a shot of overproof rum. But make sure you have a glass of water in your other hand to chase this cocktail. It's hard to ask for water when you can't catch your breath! If nothing else, you will amuse all who are eagerly watching your reaction to their favorite drink.

Clarke's Court also bottles Kalypso White Rum. This is blended with "different water." But don't try to tell that to anyone who drinks this rum—they will undoubtedly tell you the virtues of this rum don't include just a little more water. In all of the islands, one's preference for rum is a very personal matter.

All of the distilleries in Grenada use some of the same 750 ml bottles. Paying EC 50 cents for recycled bottles contributes to a lower cost and helps ensure their supply. You won't see a lot of bottles on the roads in Grenada.

Relaxing and researching on Grand Anse Beach, just south of St. George's, I was introduced to a Grenadian Shandy. A shot or so of Clarke's Court is poured into a bottle of Carib beer. It's difficult to mix this Shandy in the beer bottle, but the vendors don't seem to worry about such details. After tipping the bottle to take a sip or two, it seems to be well mixed. This makes those small beers go a lot further on the beach during a hot afternoon.

GRENADA SUGAR FACTORY LTD.
WOODLANDS, GRENADA

Founded 1937

Fermentation: Wash varies from sugar cane syrup to molasses depending on the time of the year; molasses ferments for eight days and sugar cane syrup ferments for three to four days

Distillation Equipment: Copper and stainless steel two-column continuous still

Clarke's Court Pure White Rum

Bottled Strength: 69% alcohol by volume

Age: Unaged

Notes: The most popular white rum in Grenada. This rum is also used to make a plethora of spiced rums on the island. A strong rum usually served with a chaser on the side.

Clarke's Court Kalypso White Rum

Bottled Strength: 67.5% alcohol by volume

Age: Unaged

Notes: A little lighter than Clarke's Court because of its "different water" blend.

GRENADA

Clarke's Court Superior Light Rum

Bottled Strength: 43% alcohol by volume

Age: Six months in used oak barrels from Jamaica or Trinidad

Notes: Color is filtered to make this a clear rum.

Clarke's Court Dark Rum

Bottled Strength: 43% alcohol by volume

Age: Six months in used barrels

Notes: Colored with caramel to give this rum a dark brown color.

Clarke's Court Old Grog

Bottled Strength: 43% alcohol by volume

Age: Blend of rums up to ten years old

Notes: Introduced in 1996, this aged rum is the premium product from Clarke's Court.

Rhum Runner

Entering St. George's from the sea, the old city, with its red tile roofs, church bell towers, narrow streets, and colorful buildings, is the perfect island postcard. To enjoy the spirits of Grenada, you don't even have to go ashore. Floating bars on the waterfront serve refreshing drinks to beat the heat, or you can explore the waterfront from the deck of one of the tour boats. The harbor is always calm, so come prepared to enjoy yourself.

On board the tour boat *Rhum Runner*, their own Rhum Punch is served along with other drinks. This traditional blend of strong rum, fresh lime juice, natural spring water, raw cane sugar, Grenadian nutmeg, and bitters is served over ice. Compare this drink to the French ti punch. The addition of nutmeg and bitters make this a truly Grenadian drink with a very different character. This bottled punch is available on board or across the street at "The Best Little Liquor Store in Town."

I have not included most of the rum punches bottled in the islands because they would almost fill another book. This one, however, is made from Clarke's Court Pure White Rum, and is much stronger than most of the other punches, which are about the strength of a normal cocktail.

GRENADA

Rhum Runner
Rhum Punch

Bottled Strength: About 40% alcohol by volume

Age: Unaged

Notes: One of the strongest bottled rhum punches. This is made with Clarke's Court Pure White Rum. Bottled on board the *Rhum Runner* sightseeing boat in St. George's.

Just down the waterfront past the Rhum Runner *mooring, Young Street goes up a steep hill to the other half of this capital city. On the right, across from Tikal, is the Grenada National Marketing Board. An assortment of locally grown fruits and vegetables is available here, as well as numerous other products made in Grenada.*

Tamarind sauce, made from the fruit of the tamarind tree, adds a nice taste to stir-fried dishes. Tamarind is also an ingredient in Worcestershire sauce, but this locally prepared tamarind sauce is quite different. Another Grenadian delight is nutmeg jelly. You will find a lot of products made from nutmeg in Grenada. This is one of my favorites. I never have enough of this jelly on board Tafia.

I also found swizzle sticks at the Grenada Marketing Board. Called lele *in the French islands, this is my preferred tool to stir a drink. You will probably have to trim the forked branch to fit in your favorite glass, or get a bigger glass. This naturally grown, forked branch grows quite large and can be used to stir big pots of stew.*

Tradition

The label on Gerald Bowen's Tradition Specially Spiced Rum first caught my eye while I was shopping at the Food Fair in St. George's. Formulated according to an old recipe, Tradition is bottled with either an orange or a yellow label.

The bottles with orange labels have a filter to contain the spices when you dispense this rum. To extend the flavor, this bottle can be refilled with more rum when it is about half full. The contents of bottles with the yellow label have been filtered prior to bottling for convenience. Tradition can be mixed with milk, fruit juice, or soda. Mr. Bowen has extensively researched the uses of many of the spices and plants grown on his island. His company, Superior Foods Limited, also produces a 100% nutmeg oil, which is used in his unique nutmeg soap.

SUPERIOR FOODS LIMITED
GRENADA

Tradition Yellow and Orange Label

Bottled Strength: About 50% alcohol by volume

Age: Two months

Notes: Blend of Clarke's Court Pure White Rum, spices, barks, nuts, herbs, roots, and sea extracts. This rum is bottled with a yellow or orange label depending on whether the bottle has a filter built into the cap. Traditional Grenadian spiced rum.

GRENADA

*I*n Grenada, the numerous spices grown on the island, along with the many ingredients born in the sea, are combined to make the greatest variety of spiced rums that I have discovered. I do not claim to have been in every rum shop on every island, but I did see something new or unusual at almost every turn in Grenada.

In a small rum shop in St. George's, I met a friendly proprietor, who was eager to help me learn more about the unique rum he served. After examining a gallon wine jug stuffed with bits of bark, nutmeg, peanuts, tonic beans, cinnamon, assorted spice seeds, sprigs of fresh rosemary, sea moss, sea eggs, slices of star apple, strips of lamb, pieces of red meat, and several other objects that defied identification, I was told the bottle, which had captivated my attention, contained everything. But after I had examined the bottle a few more minutes, hoping to identify at least one more ingredient, it was conceded that the bottle in my hand did not contain everything.

From the top shelf behind the bar, the short man pulled down another bottle. As he turned it upside down, he handed this second bottle to me. "This contains everything," he grinned. Struggling to see the contents through the tinted glass in the dim bar, I could barely make out a centipede as it slowly descended into the mass of roots, herbs, and other still unidentified ingredients.

Barbados

In his log, Captain Thomas Walduck wrote, "upon all the new settlements, the Spanish do make, the first thing they do is build a church, the first thing the Dutch do upon a new colony is to build them a fort, but the first thing the English do, be it in the most remote parts of the world or amongst the most barbarous, is to set up a tavern or drinking house."

In 1627, the English established the first colony in Barbados. Twenty years later there were 120 drinking houses in Bridgetown. Lying to windward of the Caribbean island chain, Barbados had one of the best natural defenses for a naval attack. Bridgetown soon became a favorite place for soldiers and sailors to recuperate from the rigors of military life.

One of the more popular places of pleasure was a rum shop owned by Rachel Pringle. One night she nearly saw her shop destroyed by a group of naval officers that included Prince William Henry, the Prince of Wales. Not wanting to ruin their fun, she continued to serve the thirsty sailors until they were ready to go back to their ship in Carlisle Bay.

Early the next morning, Rachel hired a boat and presented the hungover prince with a bill for the damages. Being a gentleman, the prince promptly settled his account. By the time the sailors came ashore that night, Rachel was negotiating for a building that was to become the first hotel on the island.

An unnamed visitor to the island about that time called the local spirit, known as kill devil, "a hot and horrible liquor." This white, unaged rum was certainly the product of a copper pot still.

The technology of rum making has advanced significantly since the seventeenth century, but aged, pot still rum continues to be used in many of the blends bottled in Barbados today. Many of these blends are heavier and more flavorful than those found on the other islands in this book. Bajan rum *is unique, and the mélange of rum here makes it easy to find something that you haven't tried before. It is hard to pick a favorite. I found that the best rum in Barbados is the one in your glass.*

For the last five years, Caribbean Week *magazine has held a rum testing for the best Caribbean island rums. This event gives the distilleries an opportunity to show their products. (It is also a lot of fun for the editors of the magazine.) Even though not all of the distilleries participate, it is interesting to compare the results to your taste for rum. As new rums come to market, maybe you will pick a winner.*

Mount Gay Distilleries Limited

Refined Eclipse Barbados Rum is the most recognized label from this distillery. But the other products of this historic distillery should not be missed, especially while you are in Barbados. Mount Gay Distilleries Ltd. proudly traces its heritage to Ensign Abel Gay and Lt. William Gay. In 1663, William Gay bought the St. Lucy estate, including its small pot still. The details are a little sketchy, but the distillery has maintained production since that time. Although much has changed, the pride of the people I met at Mount Gay is deeply rooted in the history of the distillery.

The Mount Gay visitors center on Spring Garden Highway is a nice walk from the cruise ship docks, north along the waterfront. Built like a typical Bajan house, the visitors center is in front of the rum warehouse and bottling facility in St. Michael. It is the starting point for the informative tour.

After touring the aging and bottling operations, you will be invited to try the different Mount Gay rums at their elegant mahogany bar. If you want to see the coopers at work, come in the morning. But the afternoon is a little nicer time to sample the inviting spirits. The tours cost B $10, or US $5, and are a delightful way to spend an hour.

In Barbados, rum is made from molasses, which until recently was produced on the island. At the Mount Gay distillery in St. Lucy, the molasses is mixed with water and boiled to sterilize it prior to fermentation. The proprietary yeast culture used here is part of what makes Mount Gay rum unique. This special culture has been maintained for years at the closely guarded distillery laboratory in St. Lucy.

Once the yeast is introduced to the sterilized molasses wash, it is closely monitored for seventy-two hours. When the fermentation is complete, the wine contains six to seven percent alcohol by volume and is distilled by one of two processes.

Mount Gay employs both a pot still, similar to the one replaced in 1760, and a two-column, continuous distillation still, similar to the Aeneas Coffey still of 1832. The pot still produces heavy rum that contains flavors that are removed in the larger capacity Coffey still. This lighter rum, from the two-column still, is condensed at about 95% alcohol by volume and becomes the bulk of the final blend.

After distillation, the raw rum is loaded in tank trucks and transported to the St. Michael facility, where it is diluted to 68% for aging in oak barrels. According to a 1904 Barbados law, a distillery cannot bottle its products at the same location where they are produced. The aging warehouse at Mount Gay is one of the few that I have seen that was specifically designed for that purpose.

Small openings in the walls of the warehouse allow ventilation in a climate where it is important for air to circulate. To allow air to move freely around the barrels, they are stored on their sides in steel racks that nearly reach the ceiling.

Two-hundred-liter barrels are used for aging to maximize the contact between the barrel and the rum. The small barrels are used only three times to help minimize losses due to leaks and to maximize the effects of the aging process. Over 4,000 barrels of rum are sleeping within the moss-covered walls of the warehouse, undisturbed except by an inspection every three months to insure that the aging process is continuing properly. As you walk through the cool warehouse, the aroma of the sleeping rum is very agreeable, certainly better than reading about it.

Once the rum has aged from two to ten years, the barrels are emptied into large tanks where the rum is blended with other aged rum. As you might expect, the exact proportions of the blends are secret. After the flavors of the different aged rums in the blend have married, the mixture is filtered and chilled to a temperature of minus 10°C or just above 0°F. Chilling causes unwanted impurities in the rum to precipitate so they can be removed by filtering. This process of cold filtering insures that Mount Gay Rum will be consistent worldwide and will not contain any sediment in the bottle, regardless of the temperature it has been subjected to during shipping. Although not unique to Mount Gay, cold filtering is not widely used by other distilleries because few have such global distribution.

After the blended rum passes the final inspection, it is sent to the modern, 1,500 case-per-day bottling plant. Mount Gay bottles five different rums. In addition to the popular, two-year-old Refined Eclipse, Mount Gay also bottles Premium White Rum, Barbados Sugar Cane Brandy, and Extra Old Barbados Rum.

Most Mount Gay products are bottled in one liter and 750 ml bottles. When you sample the various rums of this popular distillery, look for the smoky wood, sweet vanilla, and bitter almond flavors that are the mark of Mount Gay.

You will see the A. Y. Ward signature trademark on every Mount Gay product. Audrey Ward was the distiller and blender at Mount Gay for many years. As the story goes, Mr. Ward had nearly one hundred children. At his funeral, his heirs ranged from senior citizens to youngsters still in their mothers' arms. Some of his children didn't even arrive in time for the funeral. One look in the local phone book will dispel any doubts about Mr. Ward's reputation.

You have probably noticed an increase in advertising by Mount Gay in recent years. The Ward family now owns forty percent of the company and the balance is held by Remy Martin. For the international seller of fine liquors, Mount Gay has been a good investment with its continued market expansion around the world.

MOUNT GAY DISTILLERIES LIMITED
ST. MICHAEL, BARBADOS
Founded 1663
Fermentation: Three days
Distillation Equipment: Pot still and copper two-column continuous still

BARBADOS

Mount Gay Refined Eclipse Barbados Rum

Bottled Strength: 43 and 77% alcohol by volume

Age: Two years

Notes: The most popular product of Mount Gay. This product's blend of pot still and continuous still rum made Mount Gay famous.

Mount Gay Premium White Rum

Bottled Strength: 43% alcohol by volume

Age: Two years

Notes: Light-bodied white rum, filtered to remove color.

Mount Gay Barbados Sugar Cane Brandy

Bottled Strength: 43% alcohol by volume

Age: Blend of rums up to five years old

Notes: Not available everywhere, certainly worth trying. Also bottled as Sugar Cane Rum for some markets.

Mount Gay Barbados Extra Old Rum

Bottled Strength: 43% alcohol by volume

Age: Blend of rums up to ten years old

Notes: The premium rum from Mount Gay. Don't miss this exceptional blend of mature pot still and continuous still rums. A good example of what aging does for a quality rum.

At one time, the coopers made rum barrels at the distilleries. Although today it is much cheaper to import used barrels, the cooper is still indispensable to fine rum.

When the barrels arrive, they are in pieces and have to be reassembled. The capacity of these barrels varies from about 165 to 250 liters, but their construction is very similar. Typically, the barrels consist of about twenty-seven oak staves, six hoops or bands, and two heads. Each head consists of pieces of flat wood that have been cut and fitted to form the ends of the barrel. Wooden pegs help keep these pieces of wood in place and keep them from warping.

The staves are not all the same width and come tied in a bundle to make assembly easier. If you look closely at an assembled barrel, you will see that the staves are alternated according to width.

The hoops are interchangeable between barrels of the same size and are called the head, quarter, and bilge hoop. During assembly, the cooper may use a piece of cane leaf to fill gaps between the staves. This is one of the few distilleries where you can actually see barrels being assembled—a process that I urge you to see.

Once the barrels are assembled they are filled with water. Water makes the dry wood swell so the barrel becomes watertight before it is filled with precious rum.

West Indies Rum Refinery Limited

On the waterfront, just north of Bridgetown, the West Indies Rum Refinery Ltd. has been a pioneer in scientific rum making since 1893. All of the alcohol distilled in Barbados, except that made by Mount Gay Distillers Ltd., is made here. The West Indies Rum Refinery makes alcohol for bottlers on this island and others around the world, but does not bottle any of its own products.

Beginning with the five-day fermentation, every step of the process is performed under the strict control of the distiller. A small quantity of molasses is used to grow the special yeast culture for twenty-four hours in the laboratory. This is transferred to a larger container and then outside to the large, steel vats where the fermentation is completed.

After fermentation, most of the fermented wine is distilled in a four-column, continuous still to a strength of 95% alcohol by volume. The remainder is distilled in a steam-fired pot still to about 75% alcohol by volume. The products of these two stills are light and heavy rums, respectively.

Since rum is made here from molasses and there is no bagasse to burn, the West Indies Rum Refinery burns fuel oil to make the steam necessary for the still pot and four-column distillation equipment. Conveniently, one of the major fuel depots in Barbados is located next to the distillery.

After distillation, the rum is shipped to customers or stored for aging in the warehouse adjacent to the distillery. On the head of each barrel, markings indicate the alcohol content, the owner's name, the date the barrel was filled, and a lot number for identification. The barrels are also marked with yellow and black bands. If the rum came from the continuous still, the barrel will have a black band. Yellow bands designate rum from the pot still.

In addition to distilling alcohol for the rum bottlers, high-strength alcohol produced here is also bottled as vodka or flavored with juniper berries and bottled as gin. Other products made from the alcohol produced here are Malibu Coconut Rum, Gilbey's Gin, and Chelsea Gin.

To make a high quality product, you have to start with quality ingredients. One of these ingredients is water. In Barbados, the island itself contributes to the high quality of the water. The coral formations that support most of this island are credited with filtering the well water used to make the rum here.

Hanschell Inniss Limited

In 1884, Valdemar Hanschell founded the company that has evolved to be known as Hanschell Inniss Ltd. Like all of the rum bottlers in Barbados, except Mount Gay, this company buys rum from the West Indies Rum Refinery. The different blends of the Cockspur label are born at the Hanschell Innis blending and bottling operation in Fontabelle, north of Bridgetown. From here, rum is shipped all over the world in either bulk containers or in bottles, depending on the market destination.

All the rum blended by Hanschell Inniss Ltd. is bottled under the Cockspur label. Like most distilleries, the West Indies Rum Refinery buys once-used barrels from the States. The day I visited the distillery, barrels from Kentucky were being assembled to be filled the next day. Unlike the barrels used to age rum for other blenders, the charred wood on the inside of the staves is removed before assembly.

In 1989, on the 350th anniversary of the first parliament in the new world, Hanschell Innis Ltd. introduced a special blend called 1639. I was told this rum would be discontinued in the near future when the current stock of blending rum was exhausted. However, judging from the popularity of this blend, in Barbados and aboard *Tafia*, I have no doubt that, even if the label is changed, a new blend of two-year-old rums will replace the void left in the market when 1639 finally leaves the shelves.

In the United Kingdom, United States, Canada, Germany, Japan, and Sweden, Cockspur is bottled locally. You may not be able to find all of the blends listed here, but look for new products as the company increases distribution through its joint venture agreement with International Distillers and Vintners, which was completed in July of 1993. Although rum from the West Indies Rum Refinery is sold to several bottlers, the differences in the aging barrels and the variations in the blends is dramatic.

I had seen the Cockspur label in bars and on the shelves of the Caribbean liquor stores before I arrived in Barbados. Here, however, I was introduced to more Cockspur rum than expected. Researching this book was a lot of work; I sailed over 3,000 miles and traveled hundreds of miles ashore. Discovering new rums made all the work worthwhile, confirming the fact that the only way to really know the islands and its rum is to go there yourself. You, too, will be rewarded.

Unfortunately for the tourist on a schedule,

Hanschell Inniss Ltd. does not have a visitors center where you can get to know these fine rums. They do, however, sponsor the *Where De Rum Come From* luncheon tours. Every Wednesday, this production, which includes transportation from your hotel, is staged for visitors who would like to know more about rum, and those who just want to get out for a good meal and some lively, steel-band music.

On my second trip to Barbados, I went on the $27.50 lunch tour that begins across the street from the West Indies Rum Refinery in Brighton. If possible, arrive a little early and sign up for one of the first tour groups. After you have seen the distillery and are back in the shade of the tents, you will enjoy the delicious Bajan buffet and rum punch even more.

Everyone enjoys this outing, but bring a hat. The sun, at noon in Barbados, is "plenty hot." You will also have an opportunity to sample all of the Cockspur products and take home a small bottle of Cockspur Five Star Rum.

Even if you are not an experienced rum drinker, with some practice you should be able to identify at least one of the fine Bajan rums available on this friendly island.

HANSCHELL INNISS LIMITED
FONTABELLE, BARBADOS
Founded 1884

Hanschell Innis Ltd. buys rum from the West Indies Rum Refinery Ltd. to be blended in the products under the Cockspur label.

Cockspur Five Star Fine Rum

Bottled Strength: 40% alcohol by volume

Age: Blend of rums up to two years old

Notes: This rum is bottled as both a golden and a white rum. The white rum is filtered to remove the slight color gained during aging.

Cockspur Old Gold Reserve

Bottled Strength: 43% alcohol by volume

Age: Blend of rums up to five years old

Notes: A fine rum almost too good to mix.

Cockspur Very Special Old Rum (V.S.O.R.)

Bottled Strength: 43% alcohol by volume

Age: Blend of rums up to ten years old

Notes: The premium rum from Hanschell Innis. A serial number on the back of every label authenticates each bottle of this premium rum.

R. L. Seale & Company, Limited

When I reached the entrance to this seventeenth century estate, I knew this was going to be a very interesting visit. An air of tradition and pride in workmanship was apparent everywhere.

As I walked through the cane fields in the southern parish of Christ Church, horses were being worked out. The stables, next to the estate house at Hopefield Sugar Plantation, are state of the art. (These horses have won the prestigious Cockspur Gold Cup more times than any others.)

R. L. Seale & Co. Ltd. is certainly one of the Bajan success stories of the century. The wholly Bajan-owned rum company R. L. Seale & Co. Ltd.

From time to time in the islands, you may consume more rum than you realize, especially when the rum is very good. Sleep is the best cure. A glass of water and an aspirin before you go to bed can be helpful. But sometimes this is not enough. When you get up in the morning and your knees are a little wobbly and your head is a little dizzy, Doctor Frankie will diagnose your condition as kneemoania.

Don't worry, this affliction is temporary and rarely fatal in itself. Doctor Frankie's prescription is easily filled. Two rum and Cokes. One for the patient and one for the doctor. Then take a taxi home. In extreme cases, you may need a second dose of medicine, but this should be taken after some sleep.

Kneemoania is not usually fatal, unless you insist on driving.

is the third largest bottler in Barbados. The owner, Mr. Seale, is the celebrity you would expect him to be. David Seale's empire is smaller than that of Cockspur or Mount Gay, but his company is known for the distinct Bajan products that have become symbols of the island by selling more rum in Barbados than either of the giants.

In 1996, a new distillery was commissioned but it will be a few years before the new rum will be aged sufficiently to bear the label of the old rums. Until then rum will continue to be bought from the West Indies Rum Refinery and then blended at the modern Hopefield blending and bottling facility. All the rum sold by the Seale company is bottled at this facility in order to maintain the highest standards of quality control.

The first rum in Barbados was made not far from here in St. Philips by the Stade brothers, who had immigrated from Germany. In 1909, Erstin Sanford and Friends established E. S. A. Field, one of the labels now bottled at Hopefield. Commonly referred to as "see through," E. S. A. Field or Stade's is the best-selling white rum in Barbados by a large margin.

The West Indies Rum Refinery also ages rum for its customers. After seven years, the customers must take possession of the aging barrels. In July of 1993, when the assets of Alleyne Arthur & Hunte Ltd. were acquired by the R. L. Seale & Co. Ltd., more than a thousand barrels of ten-year-old and older rum were part of the deal. These aged reserves were for sale when I visited Hopefield. Who wouldn't like to have a few barrels of aged Bajan rum?

Still bottled under the Alleyne Arthur name are Old Brigand and Special Barbados Rum. Doorly's, another label owned by R. L. Seale & Co. Ltd., is recognized as an essential part of any connoisseur's bar in Barbados. All of the Doorly's rums are exported as Martin Doorly & Co., Ltd., Bridgetown.

Doorly's Harbor Policeman is very popular and is bottled in a regular bottle with the label on the next page or in a hand-painted glass figure from Italy that looks like the harbor policeman from the past. Before I left Barbados, I heard this uniform is coming back. If you would like one of these bottles for your collection, check at Big B's grocery and you might save a few dollars.

Before the new port was built, arriving vessels anchored in Carlisle Bay and all of the goods were brought to the carenage by lighters, or small sailing boats. The lighter crews were paid on the quantity of goods brought ashore or delivered to the ships at anchor. Since the ship captains engaged the fastest crews in order to spend as little time in port as possible, competition was high.

As it was not uncommon for many ships to be at anchor, the entrance to the river was the busiest place in Barbados. Traffic here was so busy that it was directed by a Royal Barbados Harbor Policeman, standing in a boat at the entrance to the carenage.

Falernum, a unique sugar cane liqueur born and bred in Barbados, is also bottled by R. L. Seale & Co. Ltd. As the story goes, if you want to learn to make Falernum "you haf a learn um." John D. Taylor's Famous White Falernum is another staple of the Bajan bar. The 8% alcohol liqueur is mixed with an equal part of rum to make the Bajan corn 'n' oil. For Christmas, a special 14% alcohol Velvet Falernum is bottled.

R. L. SEALE & CO. LIMITED
CHRIST CHURCH, BARBADOS

Blends and bottles rum under a variety of labels

Stade's White Rum
Bottled Strength: 43% alcohol by volume

Age: Filtered aged rum

Notes: The best-selling white rum in Barbados by a large margin. Available everywhere, in almost any size bottle you want. Bajans drink Stade's with water on the side or with a little bitters and ice, and then eat, sleep, and forget.

Barbados Gold Fine Rum
Bottled Strength: 43% alcohol by volume

Age: Blend of rums up to five years old

Notes: First place winner in the 1993 Caribbean Week Rum Testing Competition.

Special Barbados Rum
Bottled Strength: 40% alcohol by volume

Age: Blend of rums less than five years old

Notes: Bottled under the Alleyne Arthur label, this rum is primarily exported to Europe.

RUMS OF THE WORLD

Old Brigand White and Black

Bottled Strength: 40% alcohol by volume

Age: Blend of rums less than five years old

Notes: Old Brigand White is filtered and Old Brigand Black is colored. These rums are also bottled at different proofs for export markets.

Old Brigand Black Superior

Bottled Strength: 40% alcohol by volume

Age: Blend of rums up to thirteen years old

Notes: Although made primarily for export, it is available in Barbados. Black Superior is hard to find, but worth the effort.

Doorly's Fine Old Barbados

Bottled Strength: 40% alcohol by volume

Age: Blend of five-year-old rums

Notes: Also known as Doorly's Five Year Old.

Doorly's Macaw

Bottled Strength: 40 and 75.5% alcohol by volume

Age: Unaged

Notes: Macaw is bottled as White and Dark. Macaw Dark is a colored rum commonly used in rum punches.

BARBADOS

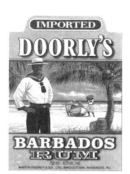

Doorly's Harbour Policeman

Bottled Strength: 40% alcohol by volume

Age: Not available

Notes: Bottled in a sculptured, hand-painted glass bottle, this is a popular souvenir from Barbados.

M. E. R. Bourne & Company, Limited

The smallest bottler in Barbados, M. E. R. Bourne & Co. Ltd. is primarily a food wholesale company but also bottles XXXX Superior White Rum. This clear rum is bottled at 47% alcohol by volume, a little stronger than the other white rums in Barbados. According to the advertisements, "It's the best shot of the day."

M. E. R. BOURNE & COMPANY, LIMITED
CHRIST CHURCH, BARBADOS
The smallest bottler in Barbados

XXXX Superior White Rum

Bottled Strength: 47% alcohol by volume

Age: Not available

Notes: A light white rum that is commonly drunk with water on the side.

Trinidad and Tobago

On his later voyages of discovery, Columbus sailed farther south to explore more of the New World. As he approached the South American continent, the equatorial current and the Amazon River helped move his ships northward in the light breezes. When he saw the opening at the Serpent's Mouth, Columbus knew he was entering a large bay. The three mountain peaks to his starboard could only be an island to the north.

In the calm waters of the Gulf, the sailors sounded drums in hopes of bringing the native inhabitants to the shore in a festive mood. Instead, the Indians interpreted the noise as a sign of war and forced the intruders to move on. It wasn't until 1532 that the first Spanish conquistador, Don Antonio Sedeno, came ashore at the Amerindian fishing village of Cumucarapo, now Mucarapo.

In the following century, the fertile land attracted planters. French corsairs were drawn to the nearly helpless, heavily laden, cargo ships as they made their way north in the light air around the islands and narrow passes, or Bocas, which lead to the Caribbean Sea. The difficulty of navigating under sail in characteristically light winds contributed to the slow development of Trinidad. Finally, in May of 1796, the H.M.S. Lebra came to Trinidad to rid the small islands near the Bocas of the troublesome corsairs. Under the protection of the British Crown, trade began to increase.

A few miles northeast of Trinidad, on neighboring Tobago, cocoa, tobacco, cotton, and sugar cane were cultivated by Dutch, French, English, and Courlander planters. Pirates, privateers, and the navies of the European powers all sought to control Tobago's wealth. In Europe, "rich as a Tobago planter" was the badge of success. By the end of the eighteenth century, sugar cane dominated this *small island that produced a half million gallons of rum in 1793.*

After an overnight sail from Grenada, I arrived at Chaguaramas to clear customs and immigration. During the formalities, I stated the purpose for my visit: to research the rum made in Trinidad and Tobago. The efficient immigration officer looked me straight in the eye and firmly directed me, "Beware the Puncheon."

"Beware the Puncheon." She repeated the admonishment. Without a clue as to what she was talking about, I vowed that I would, "Beware the Puncheon." Whatever she was talking about, this was a warning to heed.

Angostura Bitters Limited

The distinctive slender bottle of bitters, wrapped in a label that fits like an older brother's coat, is as identifiable as the name itself. The colorful story of Angostura aromatic bitters began in Venezuela.

In 1820, Dr. J. G. B. Siegert, a decorated, twenty-four-year-old surgeon from the Napoleonic Wars, followed his heart for adventure and enlisted in the cause of South American independence under the great liberator, General Simon Bolivar. Four years later, as Surgeon General of the military hospital in Venezuela, Dr. Siegert perfected his mixture of tropical herbs, spices, and alcohol to be used as a tonic for the debilitating tropical disorders that faced the European armies in the South American jungles.

Originally known as Dr. Siegert's Aromatic Bitters, the secret blend later took the name of the town on the banks of the Orinoco River where Bolivar headquartered his liberation army. Soldiers and ship crews returning home from

South America spread the versatile bitters around the world. Inevitably, the demand for the prescription grew and became sought after as a stomachic, pick-me-up, and an important ingredient in mixed drinks. By 1850, Dr. Siegert had left the military to concentrate his efforts on the manufacture of the flavorful liquid.

The revolutionary atmosphere of Venezuela in 1875 persuaded Dr. Siegert's sons to move the family business to the British West Indies island of Trinidad. The formula for Angostura aromatic bitters is one of the most jealously guarded Caribbean secrets I have encountered. I can, however, tell you that no Angostura bark is used in the preparation of this world-renowned product.

In 1936, Robert W. Siegert, the great grandson of the founder, established a scientific approach for the company to successfully expand its manufacturing and quality control. Angostura soon began making its own rum and alcohol to be used in the famous bitters.

The Angostura compound on the East Main Road, east of the coconut-processing plant, is hard to miss. The color-coded, five-column still looks more like a petroleum processing plant than a rum factory. Actually, the processes of distilling petroleum and alcohol are quite similar.

Angostura buys molasses produced in Trinidad, a major sugar-producing country in the region. After the raw material has passed a laboratory inspection, it is pumped to the fermentation vats located behind the still. Utilizing their own proprietary yeast, fermentation is accomplished in twenty-four hours. Only distillate from the first and last of the five columns, varying from 75 to 95% alcohol by volume, is collected to be blended and bottled as rum. The combination of light and heavy distillate allows Angostura to blend a variety of different rums.

From the still, rum is stored in stainless steel vessels before being aged, bottled, or shipped in bulk containers. The contents of the thousands of rum-filled, oak barrels are inspected annually. Some of this aged rum is sold to other distillers and bottlers to be blended on other islands.

Although there is not a public tour here, I was introduced to the plant engineer, John Georges, who showed me what makes this the most advanced distillery in the Eastern Caribbean. Almost every aspect of the process is monitored by sensors connected to computers that record the measurements. The temperature profile, for example, of the twenty-four-hour fermentation process can warn the distiller of potential problems. An unusual temperature rise may be the result of a lack of cooling water or an indication of a more serious problem with the wash.

In addition to extensive testing of the rum and the ingredients that go into it, the water for blending is also scrutinized in the laboratory. Filtering and demineralization are essential steps in the quality control process at Angostura. After blending, all of the rums are filtered and random samples of the bottled products are again tested before shipment.

Rum is produced here by Trinidad Distillers Limited, a wholly owned company of Angostura Holdings that manufactures rum for Angostura Bitters Ltd. and Fernandes Distillers (1973) Ltd. In 1973, Angostura Holdings acquired the assets and name of the distillery that had been located across the street.

While surveying the local taste for rum, I was surprised how many people told me they only drank either Angostura or Fernandes Rum. Even though all of the rum sold by these two companies comes from the same still, each is a different blend of the various light and heavy rums distilled here.

The Fernandes label is one of the most diverse in the islands. The alcohol content of some of the blends described below is adjusted slightly depending on the export destination.

All of these rums are bottled in Trinidad, but only account for a small part of the total production. Angostura also sells bulk rum to be bottled around the world. If you arrive by yacht, on the northwest side of the anchorage, you can see several large tanks with a horizontal black stripe painted around the circumference. These bulk alcohol tanks are part of the bulk terminal storage at Chaguaramas.

ANGOSTURA BITTERS LIMITED
TRINIDAD
Founded 1875
Fermentation: Molasses fermented for twenty-four hours
Distillation Equipment: Stainless steel and copper five-column continuous still

Old Oak (Angostura label)
Bottled Strength: 43% alcohol by volume
Age: Not available
Notes: The leading rum brand in Trinidad and Tobago. A light, flavored blend of rums made as a Gold and a White. Old Oak Gold is colored with caramel for color uniformity; Old Oak White is a clear rum. They are available in one liter, 750 ml, and 375 ml bottles.

TRINIDAD AND TOBAGO

Royal Oak (Angostura label)
Bottled Strength: 43% alcohol by volume

Age: Not available

Notes: The premium blend of the finest rums made by the House of Angostura. Slightly colored with caramel for uniformity, this smooth, aged spirit is only bottled in 750 ml bottles.

Forres Park Puncheon Rum (Fernandes label)
Bottled Strength: Not less than 75% alcohol by volume

Age: Not available

Notes: A clear, light rum popular as a high-proof mixer in punch and cocktails. Remember: "Beware the Puncheon."

Vat 19 (Fernandes label)
Bottled Strength: 43% alcohol by volume

Age: Not available

Notes: Blend of matured rums. One of the most widely recognized labels in the Eastern Caribbean, with much market appeal. Natural color from aging is adjusted with caramel.

Black Label (Fernandes label)
Bottled Strength: 43% alcohol by volume

Age: Not available

Notes: Slightly more expensive than Vat 19. Has a distinctive light character and is widely used in cocktails. Available at most retail outlets in the sister island republic.

RUMS OF THE WORLD

White Star (Fernandes label)
Bottled Strength: 43% alcohol by volume
Age: Not available
Notes: Smooth, light-bodied rum, a blend of mature light and heavy rums colored with caramel.

Ferdi's (Fernandes label)
Bottled Strength: 43% alcohol by volume
Age: Not available
Notes: Premium blend of very mature, light and heavy rums. Called a medium-type rum. Has a dark, rich color due to the long aging time of its blended components.

Crystal White Rum (Fernandes label)
Bottled Strength: 43% alcohol by volume
Age: Not available
Notes: A very light rum, clear as water.

Caroni (1975) Limited

It wasn't difficult to identify Caroni as one of the distilleries in Trinidad, but finding it took a little longer. I quickly located the Caroni Sugar Factory on a map of Trinidad and assumed the distillery would be close by. After I got off the bus, on the way to the government-owned factory, I found I was only half right. The distillery was built next to the sugar factory, but the factory was moved years ago. Now they are separated by more than twenty miles.

The Caroni Sugar Factory began distilling rum in a cast iron still in 1918. Twenty-five years later, a wooden Coffey still was installed. Then, in 1957, Caroni Limited took over the Esperanza Estate and the single-column still from that estate was moved to Caroni. When the market for Caroni rums grew, a new four-column still was commissioned in 1980. The new still increased production capabilities and enabled the distillery to improve the quality of its lighter rums. The different stills that have been employed over the last century reflect the changes in consumer tastes and the markets where these rums are sold.

After the sugar-processing season is over (the first six months of the year), rum making begins. In the process of removing most of the sugar from the fresh cane juice, other minerals and nonsugar organic compounds are concentrated in the molasses. The molasses can be fermented after it is diluted with water, but in order to increase the amount of alcohol produced, ammonium sulfate is also added to the wash. It isn't uncommon for the distillers to add chemicals to the wash; yet many of the people that I interviewed for this book flatly refused to admit that anything was added to the wash to accelerate fermentation.

After the wash is fermented for three days, it is distilled in a modern four-column still. Although the operation of the still is quite complex, I hope you can follow this simplification. In the first column, the analyzing column, alcohol is concentrated to about 50 to 60% by volume. A small amount of this effluent is condensed and aged two years for blending as heavy rum.

The rest of the effluent is condensed and fed to the second column, the hydroselection column. Water is added to the condensate from the first column so that esters and aldehydes can be more efficiently removed from taps in this column. The remainder of the product from this column is condensed and then distilled a third time in the rectification column. The bulk of the production from the still, a high-purity alcohol called neutral spirits, is condensed from this column. Fusel oils and isobutyl alcohol are also removed from other taps in this column. The remainder of the effluent is fed to the last and smallest column, the recovery column.

From the recovery column, the final product stream is condensed and aged to be used as a rum blend flavoring; other condensate from this column is condensed and reintroduced to the hydroselection column to increase the overall efficiency of the still.

A variety of rums are blended and bottled from the different product streams collected. The lightest rums bottled are the puncheons.

The rest of the bottled products are blended with aged ingredients. During aging, rum is lost to evaporation and, to a lesser extent, leaking barrels.

In Trinidad, alcohol is a bonded product that must be accounted for by the distilleries. To compensate for losses incurred during aging, the government Customs and Excise Division allows the distilleries to deduct 19.5% for rum aged five years. Considering that the losses are generally in the range of 8 to 12% annually, this is a small allowance. To help minimize the actual losses, the rum is diluted to about 80% alcohol by volume before aging. The barrels are also regularly inspected and refilled annually to help keep the losses to a minimum. The recasking operation is the same as *houillage* in the French islands, but in the English islands, the angels aren't given credit for the losses.

Most of the 500,000 proof imperial gallons of rum produced annually is exported to European, Canadian, and Caribbean markets as unaged bulk shipments of neutral spirits. Aged rum, blended for private labels, is also exported—a growing market as tourism in the Caribbean continues to expand.

CARONI (1975) LIMITED
TRINIDAD
Founded 1918
Fermentation: Fresh cane juice fermented for three days
Distillation Equipment: Modern four-column still

Caroni Puncheon Rum
Bottled Strength: 75% alcohol by volume
Age: Unaged
Notes: A clear, light rum.

Stallion Puncheon Rum
Bottled Strength: 78% alcohol by volume
Age: Unaged
Notes: Stallion is the strongest rum bottled for local consumption.

Felicite Gold
Bottled Strength: 43% alcohol by volume
Age: Blended with three-year-old rum
Notes: Felicite Gold is colored with caramel.

RUMS OF THE WORLD

White Magic Light
Bottled Strength: 43% alcohol by volume

Age: Blended with three-year-old rum

Notes: White Magic's color is removed with activated carbon filtering.

Caroni Special Old Cask Rum
Bottled Strength: 43% alcohol by volume

Age: Blended with rum up to ten years old

Notes: Called red rum for its coloring. The premium rum blended at Caroni.

While compiling the information for this book, not only was I introduced to some of the finest spirits anywhere, I had an opportunity to work with some of the finest people in the world. I hope you will take advantage of the opportunity to meet some of them yourself. Like the spirits in this book, if you visit the islands with an open mind you will certainly be surprised at what you will find.

It is often said that this part of the world lives on island time. Considered too slow or uncaring by many, island time is really an attitude and a way of life. If you allow yourself to be concerned with only what is really important, you will begin to appreciate your island time.

A taxi driver, asleep in his car under a palm tree, was woken by a man who had recently arrived in paradise. As he yawned, the driver was told how if he would drive his taxi instead of sleeping he would be able to make enough money to buy another taxi. By hiring someone else to drive the second taxi, he would be able to make more money and ...

"And then I could take a little rest," the driver yawned as he pulled his hat back down over his eyes.

Puerto Rico

In 1509, Governor Ponce de Leon established the first European settlement as part of the Spanish conquest. The Spanish hoped to exploit the gold rumored to flow from every stream in the Caribbean. By the time it was confirmed that San Juan island was not full of the precious metal, the all-weather harbor had become an important port for exporting gold from the western Caribbean to Spain. Meanwhile, sugar, which had been introduced on Columbus's second voyage, was showing an affinity for the soil and climate of this tropical island. For the next three hundred years, sugar, not gold, was the basis of the island economy.

The Puerto Rican economy has had more than a few false starts since the island became an American possession in 1899. Ponce, on the southern coast, was the site of the first sugar cane plant and the center of the industry on the island for many years. After World War II, the emphasis on development has moved towards industrial exports and tourism.

Although the sugar business has been losing ground each year, a traveler leaving the urban center of San Juan can still see narrow green leaves of sugar cane all over the island. In spite of declining sugar cane production, the production of rum, or ron, as it is known to the Spanish-speaking people of the island, is growing. Distilleries have been forced to buy molasses from other sugar-producing countries, principally in the Caribbean basin, to meet rising rum demands.

Today only two distilleries are operating on the island, Bacardi in San Juan and Serrallès in Ponce. Over the last two decades, several other distilleries have closed; their labels having been bought by other distillers. One distillery that used to produce their own rum now buys alcohol from Bacardi to be blended and bottled under the Barrilito label.

Unlike many of the other islands, rum must be aged at least one year in oak barrels before it is bottled in Puerto Rico. To meet U.S. bottling requirements, an age statement on a bottle of alcohol must represent the youngest rum in a blend. Although many of the rums from Puerto Rico are much older than the one year minimum, none of the labels state an age on them. After consulting with those who appear to be driving the marketing of rum in the United States and the Caribbean, I expect to see age statements on rum labels from all the islands in the near future.

All of the alcohol distilled in Puerto Rico is made from fermented molasses. Puerto Rican rum is also characteristically lighter than that bottled on the other islands. Although caramel is added to many of the blends to enhance the natural color attained during aging, it is typically used sparingly to allow the distilled alcohol flavor to dominate the spirit's taste.

Bacardí Corporation

The San Juan headquarters of the Bacardi Corporation is known as the largest distiller in the world. The picturesque trip across the harbor gives an interesting perspective on historic Old San Juan and the sprawling development that defines the largest metropolis in the Eastern Caribbean. Once you board the ferry to Catano, you are only a few relaxing minutes from the Bacardi distillery and tourist center.

In the second half of the nineteenth century, founder Facundo Bacardi Masó was a wine and blending merchant in Cuba. Searching for a lighter rum than was being made in pot stills, Bacardi installed the first Coffey still in Cuba and began to make a name for himself with his new lighter product. After growing to a sizable company in 1958, Don Secuto Bacardi moved his operations to its present site in response to the political instability of his homeland. It was a decision that helped propel the Bacardi Corporation to a position of international importance.

Today the Bacardi distillery in San Juan is a show place of technology and efficiency. The four-column still is capable of distilling nearly two million proof gallons of alcohol per day. To generate the tremendous amount of steam required for such a sizable distilling operation, an innovative system has been incorporated to reduce the quantity of polluting effluent while providing the majority of the plant's energy needs.

After the alcohol has been stripped from the fermented wash, the resulting leeze is piped to a covered tank where anaerobic bacteria convert most of the organic waste into methane gas. This gas is stored in large tanks before being burned in high efficiency boilers. Since the distillery operates continuously, only shutting down for periodic scheduled maintenance, the methane storage tanks are actually quite small compared to the amount of gas generated.

The small amount of waste that isn't converted to gas is periodically removed from the bottom of the tank by a conveyor and used as fertilizer. Although this process was an expensive investment for Bacardi, it contributed significantly to the preservation of the water quality in the bay adjoining the distillery and is part of a continuing program of ecological responsibility.

Bacardi presently distills and bottles six different rums and a couple of rum-based liquors. Bacardi Superior White is a blend of one-year-old rums which has been filtered to remove the color attained from the oak aging barrels. Bacardi Superior Gold is a blend of two-year-old rums bottled as Light, with the color removed, and Dark, which has some added color.

Bacardi Black is a blend of rums up to four years old with added color. Bacardi Añejo is a smoother blend of rums that have been aged up to six years with a taste that reflects well on the additional aging. The premium rum, Bacardi Reserve, is also a blend of rums up to six years old with an emphasis on finer rums. Bacardi 1873, introduced a few years ago, is blended with three-year-old rums and reminds the drinker of fine scotch. All of the above rums are blended at 40% alcohol by volume.

Bacardi Limon is a new blend of one-year-old rum with grapefruit, lemon, and lime flavoring for a mixable liquor bottled at 35% alcohol by volume. The clear glass bottle has received significant product recognition in the markets where it is being sold. More recently, Bacardi Spice made its debut on the market. This is a unique blend of golden rums, cinnamon, nutmeg, and other Caribbean spices that results in an extremely smooth and great tasting spiced rum—whether you mix it in your favorite cocktail or drink it on the rocks. Although Bacardi was not the first to introduce a bottled spiced rum, Bacardi Spice has been very well received and will certainly take its place in the market.

When you enter the 127-acre Bacardi complex, you will put the busy metropolis of San Juan in the distance and immediately feel pampered in the spacious landscape of the park. Tour trains depart regularly from the large visitors center for guided tours of the distillery area.

It is impossible to see all of this large facility, so tours concentrate on areas of historical value and the distilling processes. You will also learn the significance of the Bat logo which appears on many of the Bacardi products. From here, you move on to the fermentation tanks and then to the tasteful product displays. Back at the visitors center, you are invited to try the Bacardi products and to visit the Bacardi rum and gift shop. The tour requires only a little walking and is certainly a relaxing break from the fast pace of the largest city in the islands.

BACARDI CORPORATION
SAN JUAN, PUERTO RICO
Founded 1873
Fermentation: Molasses fermented for twenty-four hours
Distillation Equipment: Stainless steel, four-column continuous still

Bacardi Superior White
Bottled Strength: 40% alcohol by volume
Age: One year
Notes: Blend of one-year-old light rums which have been filtered to remove the color.

Bacardi Superior Gold: Light and Dark
Bottled Strength: 40% alcohol by volume
Age: Two years
Notes: Light has been filtered to remove the color, while Dark has some added color.

Bacardi Black
Bottled Strength: 40% alcohol by volume
Age: Blend containing rum up to four years old
Notes: This rum is being reintroduced in some markets as Bacardi Select.

Bacardi Spice
Bottled Strength: 40% alcohol by volume
Age: Blend of golden aged rum
Notes: Unique blend of golden rum and spices.

Bacardi 1873
Bottled Strength: 40% alcohol by volume
Age: Blended with three-year-old rums
Notes: Blended to remind the drinker of scotch, resulting in an unusual blend of smooth rums.

Bacardi Añejo
Bottled Strength: 40% alcohol by volume
Age: Blend of rums up to six years old
Notes: Smooth, colored blend of mature rums.

Bacardi Reserve
Bottled Strength: 40% alcohol by volume
Age: Blend of rums up to six years old
Notes: Emphasis in this blend is on the older rums. The premium rum from Bacardi.

Edmundo B. Fernández, Inc.

One of the treasures of Puerto Rico is certainly Ron del Barrilito. By no means the largest brand on the island, Barrilito is known to all who take their rum seriously. No tour of Puerto Rico's rum would be complete without at least tasting this spirit.

After graduating from engineering school in France in 1871, Pedro B. Fernández returned to the Haciendo Santa Ana in Bayamón, Puerto Rico to live with his family who had emigrated from Spain in the late 1700s. Sugar cane was grown on the family estate and, like most plantations of the day, a small still was part of the sugar works on the property.

Rum was made by many people at that time, but Señor Fernández' secret blend ingredients and aging made his rum special. His friends named his rum "ron del barril," or rum of the barrel. In 1880, Pedro Fernández began selling his rum commercially. His unique blend has held a special place in the hearts of Puerto Rican rum drinkers ever since. Today you are encouraged to visit the hacienda where only a few of the original buildings still stand.

It is refreshing to see this oasis of history in the fast developing metropolis just outside the capitol city of San Juan. The foundation of the windmill, built in 1827, now serves as an office next to the aging warehouse which was built right after World War II. Since all of the surrounding land has been developed and there is no longer a source of sugar cane to make rum on the property, bulk alcohol is bought from Bacardi and blended with the special formula to make Ron del Barrilito.

This is the only blender I know of that blends the rum before it is aged. Barrilito is also unique in that the barrels are larger than those found at other rum warehouses, about 132 gallons, and they aren't moved around to be filled or emptied. When one of the 3,000 barrels is almost empty, it is refilled from the blending room adjacent to the aging storeroom at very nearly the strength that it will be bottled at years later.

The secrets of the blend are a closely guarded family secret but it is interesting to note that unlike the whisky barrels used elsewhere in the Caribbean to age rum, oak wine barrels from Europe are employed to work their magic on the blend.

Only two products are bottled here at Edmundo B. Fernández, Inc. The blue label, or Two

Star, which was introduced after the end of prohibition and the dark blue, Three Star. The stars are found on the neck band above the label that has been recognized for years as a truly unique Puerto Rican rum. Both labels show the French influence of the founder and depict a cherub offering the highest quality liquor to the mythological gods of Olympus. The initials "P" and "F" are for the founder Pedro Fernández. Silver and gold medals won in expositions also have been incorporated into the label.

Only 11,000 cases of these spirits are sold annually with distribution almost exclusively on this island. But much of this fine rum goes back home with Puerto Ricans who have moved to the United States and Canada. This is an especially popular gift for the holidays. The distillery is also the best place to buy their rum by the bottle or the case.

I was given the rare opportunity to sample rum that had been in the barrel since the warehouse was built in 1946. This was my first taste of rum that was older than me and I can only say that it exceeded my expectations. But I shouldn't have been surprised, I have enjoyed Ron del Barrilito Three Star for years. It can be a little hard to find, so stock up while you are here. Gracias, Que Rico.

To visit this friendly facility take Hwy #5 from Bayamón toward Cataño and get off at Kilo 1.6. On the west side of the highway look for the signs and the trees that are part of the hacienda. The public is welcome from 8:00 A.M. to 11:45 A.M. and from 1:00 P.M. to 4:45 P.M., Monday through Friday. Manuel B. Fernández, the president, and his brother Edmundo will welcome you to their family operation. (Tel 809-785-3490)

RUMS OF THE WORLD

EDMUNDO B. FERNÁNDEZ, INCORPORATED
BAYAMÓN, PUERTO RICO
Founded 1880

Blends and bottles rum under the Barrilito label

Barrilito Two Star
Bottled Strength: 43% alcohol by volume

Age: Blend of rums at least three years old

Notes: Two Star is best enjoyed with ice and a little water.

Barrilito Three Star
Bottled Strength: 43% alcohol by volume

Age: Blend of rums at least six years old

Notes: More mature taste than Two Star, this is one of the treasures of Puerto Rico.

Serrallès

Not every sixteenth century Spanish conquistador was in search of the fabled golden city of El Dorado—Ponce de Leon was obsessed with the fountain of youth. After serving as the first governor of Hispaniola and cultivating large tracts of sugar cane, he left the Caribbean to continue his search for immortality. The fountain of youth evaded him but his name lives on as one of the most beautiful cities in Puerto Rico. Today Ponce is the second largest city in Puerto Rico and one that should not be missed. Quieter and less hectic than San Juan, this south coast city deserves more than just a passing look from a fast moving car or bus.

Just east of Ponce's Mercedita airport, the faded name Don Q can be seen on the brick smokestacks of the Serrallès distillery. In the second half of the nineteenth century, Sebastian Serrallès came from Catalona, Spain and bought a small plot of land known as the Hacienda Teresa. As was common at that time, crude rum was made from fermenting the scrapings from the sugar boiling pots in a copper pot still. Only a small quantity was produced to be shared with the estate workers and friends.

In 1865, a five-tray continuous distillation column was imported from France to increase production. Ponce was becoming a commercial center and the demand for spirits increased. Rum from the hacienda gained local acceptance, becoming well known in Ponce. In 1890, Sebastian Serrallès moved from Puerto Rico for Barcelona, leaving the growing estate in the hands of his Puerto Rican born son Don Juan Serrallès Colón. The tradition of Serrallès has continued to be handed down from generation to generation. Many of today's 375 employees are descendants of the people who built the company more than one hundred years ago.

When Prohibition closed the distillery operations, the Serrallès family concentrated on sugar production until the end of the spirits controversy. With a burgeoning market to fill and an established reputation among rum drinkers, the Serrallès distillery was built on its present site and the Don Q label was inaugurated. Today Don Q, named after the famous horseman of Spanish literature, means rum in Puerto Rico.

The flat land between the Caribbean Sea and the mountains that rise from east to west in the center of the island provided the right combination of soil, rain, and climate to become the center of the Puerto Rican sugar business. Although the sugar business has been declining in the last two decades, the production of rum is actually increasing.

Until recently, the molasses used to make Serrallès rum came from the local sugar factory located next to the distillery. Today molasses is bought on the world market and arrives via tanker at the port in Ponce. Proprietary yeast is carefully cultivated and introduced to the clarified molasses wash where it is allowed to ferment for thirty-six hours. Since the distillery was built in 1935, it has been upgraded to include six continuous distillation columns. Temperature, pressure, and flow are carefully controlled during the fermentation and distillation process to produce several distillates which are later blended into a variety of rums under the Serrallès name.

Since the days of Sebastian Serrallès, the rum making operation has grown to a capacity of

55,000 proof gallons per day. Aging warehouses that contain nearly 500,000 barrels of rum are maintained in Mercedita and the old Puerto Rico Distillers warehouse in Camuy. To complement the rum production, neutral spirits are also produced to be bottled as vodka, gin, anisette, and other cordials.

With the 1985 acquisition of Puerto Rico Distillers Inc. from the Canadian giant Seagrams, Serrallès gained manufacturing facilities in Camuy and Arecibo on the north coast of the island and more than doubled its sales. Although the distilling operations at these facilities have been shut down, the Camuy aging warehouses are still in use as well as the bottling operation.

In addition to White and Gold Don Q and premium El Dorado rum bottled in Mercedita, Serrallès ages and bottles Palo Viejo, Ron Llave, Ron Granado, Ronrico, and Captain Morgan in Camuy. (The latter under a manufacturing agreement with Seagrams.)

Serrallès maintains two retail outlets called La Cava—one at the Mercedita facility and another in Miramar on the north coast. Both offer the consumer a variety of products which are made or distributed by Serrallès. Since the expansion of the marketing side of the business, Serrallès has become the distribution representative for wines, scotch, whiskey, wine, brandy, and other specialties.

SERRALLÈS
PONCE, PUERTO RICO
Founded circa 1865
Fermentation: Molasses fermented for thirty-six hours
Distillation Equipment: Stainless steel, six-column continuous still

Don Q: White and Gold
Bottled Strength: 40% alcohol by volume
Age: Blended aged rums
Notes: Don Q White is the largest selling rum in Puerto Rico. Like many of the other rums, White has been filtered and Gold has been slightly colored before bottling.

El Dorado
Bottled Strength: 40% alcohol by volume
Age: Blend of light rums up to five years old
Notes: The premium rum from Seralles. A mature light rum.

Dominican Republic

Not to be confused with Dominica, the Dominican Republic occupies the eastern two-thirds of Hispaniola, less than 100 miles west of Puerto Rico. Santo Domingo, on the south coast of the island, is the oldest port in the Western Hemisphere. It quickly became the center for exploration in the New World—a status never regained after Francis Drake sacked the city in 1586. (Drake was an English explorer well versed in exploring wealthy cities under foreign flags.) French buccaneers took the western third of this fertile island in the late seventeenth century and began importing slaves to work the sugar plantations. By the beginning of the eighteenth century, the French had wrestled control of the whole island and renamed it Saint Dominigue.

In 1804, the first black republic in the world was established in Haiti following a slave revolt that left most of the plantations in shambles. Five years later, the island was divided when the Spanish regained control of the Dominican Republic, which became independent in 1844. Though not as famous for its rum as neighboring island Haiti, the distilleries in the Dominican Republic offer an opportunity to discover several of the little-known treasures of the Caribbean. Several distilleries make rum for the local market and three of the distilleries have established an export market, though it is not well developed.

Like many things in the islands, the rum sold today reflects the past. When a distillery produces more rum than it can sell as in times of economic hardship, the surplus is stored in oak barrels and continues to age. If hard times persist it is not uncommon for a distiller to accumulate stocks of aged rum. The result is often a supply of rum, ten or more years old, offered at very attractive prices.

Exports of rum will probably increase in the future as international trade increases in the Caribbean region, reducing the stocks of old rum.

When you visit the Dominican Republic, you will undoubtedly find some unusually fine rums. I have found something new almost every time I visit the island and always look forward to returning. Small cruise ships have visited the north coast city of Puerto Plata for some time, but in the late 1980s, the waterfront got a facelift in anticipation of increased tourist arrivals that haven't materialized—yet.

In Puerto Plata, you can visit the Brugal bottling facility which is within walking distance of the port. Or, if you have more time, a trip to the mountain city of Santiago and the Bermúdez distillery is worth the effort. Tourism has remained relatively undeveloped on the island as a result of political strife on both sides of the island but the Dominican Republic certainly shouldn't be overlooked for fine spirits.

J Armando Bermúdez & Company, C. X. A.

When J Armando Bermúdez founded the Bermúdez distillery in 1852 with a small pot still, sugar was the major export of this Caribbean nation. In spite of the economic hardships in the Dominican Republic due to dwindling sugar exports, the Bermúdez family has continued their tradition of distilling fine rum in the city of Santiago for nearly one and a half centuries.

Molasses from the sugar mill in the Dominican Republic is fermented over three days before it is distilled in a four-column continuous still that replaced the original pot still in 1927. Constructed of copper and stainless steel, this is one of the oldest four-column stills in the islands.

Once distilled, the fresh rum is aged in used

oak barrels from England at only 55% alcohol by volume. The combination of a low cask strength and small barrels contribute to the character of Bermúdez fine rums.

After aging, six Bermúdez rums are bottled. Like many distilleries, Bermúdez bottles an overproof rum, but this 151 proof rum is aged nine months, making it a much smoother liquor for mixing in punches. Bermúdez Blanco and Dorado, (white and gold) are aged three years and readily available in the Dominican Republic. Añejo Selecto is a smoother blend of fine six-year-old Bermúdez rums. The eight-year-old Don Armando and the premium, twelve-year-old Aniversario are harder to find because they are produced in smaller quantities but your efforts to find these rums will be rewarded. In the older rums, you can taste the vanilla flavor imparted by the complex sugars in the barrels' oak wood.

Like many of the small distilleries in the islands, distribution of Bermúdez rums is limited to the Dominican Republic, St. Martin, Spain, Italy, Honduras, Ecuador, and Peru. Not all of the Bermúdez family of rums are available in these markets, so the best way to appreciate the finest products of this distillery is to visit the distillery in Santiago.

Tours to the distillery can be arranged through local tour operators or by calling (809) 581-1852.

J ARMANDO BERMÚDEZ & COMPANY, C. X. A.
SANTIAGO, DOMINICAN REPUBLIC

Founded 1852
Fermentation: Molasses fermented for three days
Distillation Equipment: Copper, four-column still

151 Proof
Bottled Strength: 75.5% alcohol by volume
Age: Nine months
Notes: Strong rum for punches and cooking. This rum is not exported.

Bermúdez Blanco
Bottled Strength: 43% alcohol by volume
Age: Three years
Notes: Aged at 55% alcohol by volume, this rum is filtered before bottling.

Bermúdez Dorado Rum
Bottled Strength: 43% alcohol by volume
Age: Three years
Notes: Golden rum whose color is the product of its low alcohol content during aging.

Añejo Selecto
Bottled Strength: 43% alcohol by volume
Age: Six years
Notes: Smoother than Dorado or Blanco, look for this rum in the Dominican Republic.

Aniversario
Bottled Strength: 43% alcohol by volume
Age: Twelve years
Notes: Premium rum sometimes referred to as 1852. A rum to be drunk neat.

Brugal

Visitors to Puerto Plata will find the Brugal bottling facility near the waterfront. When I sailed *Tafia* here in the late '80s, the tour was conducted for a few hours whenever a ship came into the harbor. After the tour, a heavy metal door was opened at the exit of the building and tourists from the ships would appear to taste the rums mixed in a variety of fruit cocktails.

Invariably sailors from the yachts moored at the dock would appear at the back door and be invited to sample the rum. We soon came to know our hosts by their first names. No one seemed to mind that we hadn't gone on the tour that day and were just there for the delicious fresh fruit punches that flowed from the bar just inside the back door.

I became familiar with three of the Brugal rums, but there are more. Since that time, I have been pleased to find Brugal products in the United States. I have been unable to confirm much of what I have heard about the distillery, but I hope you will try these rums when you find them.

Brugal operates a distillery outside Santo Domingo where molasses is fermented and then distilled in a continuous column still. The alcohol is then aged and bottled in Puerto Plata. To tour the bottling facility, check at the warehouse reception desk or ask the guard.

BRUGAL DISTILLERY
SANTO DOMINGO, DOMINICAN REPUBLIC
Fermentation: Molasses
Distillation Equipment: Continuous column still

Brugal White Label
Bottled Strength: 43% alcohol by volume
Age: Three years
Notes: Light flavorful white rum. Mixes well with lime and a little cane syrup.

Brugal Gold Label
Bottled Strength: 43% alcohol by volume
Age: Three year
Notes: Slightly colored, but popular wherever this rum is available.

Brugal Añejo
Bottled Strength: 43% alcohol by volume
Age: More than three years
Notes: Packaged with gold netting around the bottle, this rum is not as popular as the rums above, but has a very attractive presentation.

Barceló

In addition to the Bermúdez and Brugal distilleries, Barceló also distills and bottles aged rums on the island. Unfortunately I was unable to confirm reliable information about the distillery, but I can tell you with certainty that some of the Barceló rums are worth looking for.

Bottled in shorter bottles than other rums, Barceló's products are exported to St. Maarten and only a few other countries. Like most other rums from the Dominican Republic, exports of these rums are scarce.

Two other distilleries should also be mentioned: Macronix and Carta Viejo. I have not seen rum from either of them outside the Dominican Republic. Macronix and Carta Viejo distill rum for local consumption. I have no doubt that both of these distilleries have fine rum stocks and I look forward to discovering them on my next trip to this beautiful country.

BARCELÓ & COMPANY, C. POR A.
SANTO DOMINGO, DOMINICAN REPUBLIC

Fermentation: Molasses
Distillation Equipment: Continuous column still

Ron Barceló Añejo
Bottled Strength: 40% alcohol by volume
Age: Aged in oak barrels for one to three years
Notes: This is the most widely available rum from the Dominican Republic in the Caribbean. A good rum that is representative of the quality of the rums from this side of Hispaniola.

Ron Barceló Imperial
Bottled Strength: 38% alcohol by volume
Age: Aged in oak barrels up to six years
Notes: Introduced in 1980, this is the premium rum from Barceló. Production is limited to only about 8,000 bottles per year.

Ron Barceló Gran Añejo
Bottled Strength: 40% alcohol by volume
Age: Aged one to four years
Notes: A more aged version of Ron Barceló Añejo.

Jamaica

Like the other English islands, the first exports of Jamaican rum were sold to the Royal Navy pursers and given to the sailors who served on the Royal Navy ships. In addition to the daily ration, extra rations were distributed to the crews before battle to bolster bravery and after battles to reward acts of heroism.

This crude white rum was also claimed to have medicinal powers far greater than any other medicine of the time and used liberally by the ships' doctors. Until the late nineteenth century, all manner of surgery was done without the aid of pain killers other than that provided by the patient drinking a large portion of alcohol before the surgeon began his work.

For the plantation owner, the distillation of rum meant more profit from the cultivation of sugar cane. But more importantly, selling rum to the ships at discount prices encouraged the navy ships to stay nearby and helped deter the pirates that infested the islands.

Everywhere you travel in the Caribbean the Jamaican influence is present. The reggae music that began in Jamaica is practiced by every band in the Caribbean. You can't miss the music of Bob Marley being played on every radio station, taxi, and bus. Jamaica is also credited with making the first dark-colored rums, which have become popular around the world.

There is much to see in Jamaica. Cool mountain waterfalls are irresistible in the tropics and everywhere you go you will be met with a smile. Rum is as much a part of life in Jamaica as reggae and beautiful beaches. Jamaican distillers sell a variety of rums. While you are in Jamaica, taste for yourself why Jamaican rum is famous all over the world.

JAMAICA

Since the seventeenth century, rum has been made all over the island in small pot stills. After World War II, many of the Caribbean islands suffered economically while their resources were being used to rebuild England and Europe. The Caribbean island sugar cane industry was particularly hard hit by competition from sugar beets and the development of vast sugar cane fields in southern Florida where more modern sugar production plants were being built. Many Jamaicans worked at the Florida plants because there was little or no work at home.

In the early 1960s, the Jamaican government nationalized their island sugar industry, as did many of the other islands. Today there are only two distilleries that distill the bulk of the rum in Jamaica, Wray & Nephew and National Rums of Jamaica.

I have read several stories that Jamaican dark rums are made from cane juice that was cooked too long or even burned, accounting for the dark color of the rum. It should be understood that alcohol is always clear when it leaves the still. Color is only the effect of aging in barrels or the addition of caramel, or burnt sugar, after the distillation process. It has nothing to do with the color of the raw ingredients.

Jamaican law recognizes that many popular rums are colored with caramel made from cane sugar and allows the addition of caramel as the only additive in rum bottled on the island. You will, however, find every combination of overproof white rum, herbs, spices, and such used for both medicinal purposes and consumption on the street.

A few years ago, barrels of rum from a wrecked ship moored in Port Royal. An earthquake had sunk the ship, then buried it beneath the ocean floor in 1692. Sunk for nearly two hundred years, the spirits were auctioned off to a number of curious observers. I did not taste any of this rum myself, but I have heard from several sources that it was not the velvet smooth spirit you might imagine.

The fact that the barrels were exposed to salt water influenced the aging and prevented the rum from evaporating but exposing alcohol to wood for that long brings a very heavy wood taste to the rum. I would speculate that even if this special rum didn't live up to some people's expectations it was probably more to my liking than it would have been in 1692.

Wray & Nephew

Wray & Nephew is not only the largest distiller and blender of fine rums in Jamaica, but also an integral part of the culture and lore of the island. Mr. Wray began blending rums from several estates in 1825. Today the company he founded owns and operates three estates that make world famous rum.

Starting with molasses from Jamaican sugar cane, the wash is allowed to ferment for forty-eight hours before being distilled in traditional pot stills or modern continuous three-column stills. The equipment has been upgraded over the last century and a half—without losing the dedication to quality. After distillation, the raw alcohol is carefully analyzed in a modern laboratory.

Before the raw rum is aged in once-used American oak barrels, it is diluted with water to help minimize evaporation losses and to maximize the effects of the wood and alcohol interacting. Depending on the final product, rum from the pot still is blended in closely guarded proportions with rum from the continuous stills. It is this blending that gives Wray & Nephew rums their character.

Wray & Nephew bottles and blends a variety

of rums under the Wray and Appleton labels. The world's best selling overproof rum, White Overproof, is drunk in Jamaica with water. Commonly "overproof" is served with water on the side. Mix one finger of rum with four fingers of water. With a little experimentation, you can taste when you have the right proportions.

You will also notice that it doesn't take much of this overproof rum to render you unable to carry on the experiment if you aren't used to drinking overproof rum. This 126 proof white rum is credited with warding off evil spirits, or duppies, as they are known in Jamaica. Wray & Nephew Overproof accounts for 90% of the rum consumed in Jamaica; everywhere you go you will be served this white Jamaican "wine."

C. J. Wray Dry Rum is a light clear rum that has been carefully aged and then charcoal filtered. This light rum can be drunk on the rocks but also mixes well with tonic or fruit juices. Named for its founder, this is the lightest rum bottled by Wray & Nephew.

Jamaica is famous for its dark full-bodied rums. Coruba is Wray & Nephew's dark rum. The full flavor of this rum mixes well in punch and is popular in the tropical cocktails that make Jamaica such a pleasure to visit.

Wray & Nephew operates the Appleton estate where rum has been made for 250 years. Under the Appleton label, Appleton Special White and Gold are medium-bodied aged rums, blended from pot still and continuous still distillates.

Appleton Estate V/X (Very eXceptional) is a rare blend of rums that have been aged in small barrels then blended in large vats where the delicate flavors marry. This full flavor rum owes its character to the aged pot still component in the blend and the natural spring water on the estate.

Connoisseurs will know Appleton Estate 12-Year-Old, a very smooth blend of rums that have aged at least twelve years and are comparable to fine cognacs. In spite of the longer aging time, this extra old rum doesn't have the heavy wood tones that can detract from the flavor of an aged spirit.

The newest addition to the list of fine rums from Wray & Nephew is Appleton Estate 21-Year-Old. Following the traditions of distillation and blending that has made Appleton the largest producer of fine aged rums in Jamaica, this rum has to be tasted to really be appreciated.

Wray & Nephew rums are exported to sixty countries around the world. In addition to rum bottled in Jamaica, bulk shipments are also made to bottlers who maintain the specifications and standards of the distillery.

Tourism is more than an emerging industry in Jamaica. You are invited to visit the Appleton Estate daily from 9:00 A.M. until 4:00 P.M., Monday through Saturday. Tours include demonstrations of crushing sugar cane and blending rums. You can sample the rums that have made Jamaica famous and see how these great rums are crafted. To arrange transportation, contact your hotel tourist desk or call (809) 963-9215 for more information.

JAMAICA

WRAY & NEPHEW
KINGSTON, JAMAICA
Founded 1825
Fermentation: Molasses and cane juice fermented for forty-eight hours
Distillation Equipment: Copper pot stills, two and three-column continuous stills.

White Overproof
Bottled Strength: 63% alcohol by volume
Age: Unaged
Notes: Commonly referred to as Jamaican wine. The best-selling overproof in Jamaica.

C. J. Wray Dry Rum
Bottled Strength: 40% alcohol by volume
Age: Aged in small barrels
Notes: The lightest white rum from Wray & Nephew.

Coruba
Bottled Strength: 40% alcohol by volume
Age: Aged in small barrels
Notes: Dark rum with a full flavor due to the pot still rum used in this blend.

Appleton Special: White and Gold Rum
Bottled Strength: 43% alcohol by volume
Age: Aged in small barrels
Notes: White rum is filtered to remove color of aging. Blended from pot still and continuous still rum.

Appleton Estate V/X
Bottled Strength: 43% alcohol by volume
Age: Aged in small barrels
Notes: Aged blend of pot still and continuous still rum. Aged less than the twelve-year-old, this rum is surprisingly smooth and a very mixable rum which can be drunk on the rocks.

Appleton Estate 12-Year-Old
Bottled Strength: 43% alcohol by volume
Aged: Blend of rums aged at least twelve years, up to twenty
Notes: This blend of aged rums shouldn't be overlooked. It is rare for a large production distillery to bottle rum of these dimensions.

Appleton Estate 21-Year-Old
Bottled Strength: 40% alcohol by volume
Age: Blend of rums aged a minimum of twenty-one years
Notes: Recently introduced, the premium rum from Wray & Nephew.

National Rums of Jamaica also operates a distillery as part of the National Sugar Company Ltd. Alcohol from this multicolumn still is sold to several bottlers around the island who bottle such rums as Denrose Overproof, Gilbert Overproof, Conquering Lion Overproof, and others. Most of these rums are not aged for many years but have very loyal followings in Jamaica and in those places where they are imported.

Unfortunately I was unable to get any reliable information on Myer's Rum. I can tell you that this famous rum, available nearly everywhere in the world, is heavily colored with caramel. In order for rum to have attained such a dark color from aging in barrels, it would have had to sleep for fifty years or more—by then the rum would have evaporated.

Haiti

Perhaps the least understood of the islands, Haiti is one of the smaller rum producers in the Caribbean basin. The art has been practiced here since Columbus brought sugar cane from Madeira to Hispaniola, or Little Spain, on his second voyage of discovery. When the French took control of the island, Haiti became known as Saint-Dominique. Rum distilled here began to gain a reputation in France where it compared favorably to the finest French brandies. Even after Haiti gained independence on January 1, 1804, Haitian rum maintained its place among the most sought-after liquors in the world.

Plagued by internal conflicts for the last two hundred years, Haiti continues to attract interest in its culture, art, and spirits. Stories of voodoo and black magic seem to be suspended in the humid tropical air. As in most of the Caribbean, the saying that "things are not as they appear" is certainly true here. In many respects, Haiti is in contrast not only to its neighbors and the rest of the world, but to itself.

To appreciate Haiti, you have to visit this microcosm of humanity where in spite of oppression—from both inside and outside its borders—there is a human spirit that cannot be conquered. Even though the future is sometimes uncertain here, there is no doubt that Haitian rhum will continue to take its place as one of the country's great achievements for years to come.

Barbancourt

About ten miles from the capital city of Port-au-Prince, is the rural town of Damiens—home to the Barbancourt distillery since 1862. From the fertile fields surrounding the distillery, sugar cane is grown to maturity and then harvested by hand. Once cut, the cane is hauled to the distillery by ox-drawn carts or small trucks. Planting and harvesting cane by hand is very labor intensive, combined with the distillery operations, Barbancourt provides employment for about two hundred people in a country where unemployment and political turmoil have been part of the landscape for generations.

Following centuries of tradition, rum making takes place from December through May during the dry season when the cane contains the most sugar. A steam-powered cane mill crushes the cane as soon as it arrives at the distillery. From the mill the freshly squeezed juice is fermented for three days in stainless steel vats before it is distilled by a method called *charentaise*.

From the fermentation vats the wash is distilled in a single-column continuous still called the "rectification column" after which the condensate is collected to be redistilled in a traditional copper pot still. Double distillation in this manner is time-consuming and requires the skills of an experienced distiller but the results cannot be denied. The raw alcohol from the pot still is condensed at about 90% alcohol by volume and then diluted with filtered rain water to only 50% alcohol by volume before it is allowed to age in the old warehouse.

The magic of aging Rhum Barbancourt takes

place in a variety of oak aging vats imported from Limousin, France ranging in size up to 70 hectolitres. Since the losses due to evaporation are directly related to the ratio of the volume of a vessel to its surface area, the larger vessels employed here help reduce the percentage of alcohol lost to the atmosphere. Aging at a low alcohol content also maximizes the benefits of the time spent in the oak vats.

There are a number of small pot stills in Haiti that produce white rum for local consumption, but all Rhum Barbancourt is aged before it is bottled in the distinctive brown bottle.

All of the Barbancourt products are bottled at the distillery and then shipped to markets in the United States, Italy, Panama, Germany, Ecuador, Canada, Belgium, and St. Maarten. There is a good chance that all of these fine rums won't be available in your area because production is fairly low but throughout the world Barbancourt is revered as a standard of quality and excellence.

There is not presently a tour at Barbancourt, but visitors are welcome to come and see the distillery and experience why Rhum Barbancourt is known as one of the finest rums in the world. Tourists are encouraged to visit the Barbancourt distillery Monday to Friday from 10:00 A.M. until 1:00 P.M.

RHUM BARBANCOURT
PORT-AU-PRINCE, HAITI

Founded 1862

Fermentation: Freshly squeezed sugar cane juice fermented for three days

Distillation equipment: Copper and stainless steel single-column continuous still and copper pot still.

Barbancourt Three Star Rhum

Bottled Strength: 43% alcohol by volume

Age: Four years in large oak vats

Notes: Lends itself to being mixed with tropical fruit juices served with ice, or it can be enjoyed with just a little lime juice, cane syrup, and ice. The higher degree of distillation makes this rum a very different drink than the rhum agricole found in the French islands.

Barbancourt Reserve Speciale-Five Star

Bottled Strength: 43% alcohol by volume

Age: Eight years in large vats

Notes: More mature than Three Star, I drink this rhum with ice. The flavor changes as the ice melts. This rhum is the reason Barbancourt is one of the great rums of the world.

Barbancourt Reserve du Domain

Bottled Strength: 43% alcohol by volume

Age: Fifteen years in large vats

Notes: Despite the 40,000 gallons of spirit distilled annually, Barbancourt can only produce this premium rum in limited quantities. To really appreciate the full flavor of the distiller's efforts, this fine spirit should be drunk straight or with a little ice.

United States

The first North American distilleries fermented and distilled Caribbean molasses in New England. Some of this rum was then shipped to England and sold or traded for supplies needed in the fledgling colonies. Another quantity of New England rum was shipped to Africa and traded for slaves who were transported to the Caribbean for sugar plantation labor, completing the triangle of trade.

To control the economy of their colonies, England and France prohibited their island colonies from exporting distilled spirits. This led to smuggling, but supported the rum industry in New England. Over the next century, whiskey distilled in Tennessee and Kentucky began to find its way to New England as transportation routes in the Mississippi Valley were developed. In the nineteenth century, slavery was abolished and the chain of trade was broken. Over the next century, the aging New England distilleries closed in the face of competition and the rising costs of raw materials.

During World War II, a distillery was built in the small rural town of Lake Alfred, Florida to make beverage alcohol from fruit. All the alcohol made from grain was utilized for munitions and/or rationed as part of the war effort. After the war, the distillery made rum from the by-products of the sugar industry developed in the south central part of the state and continues to make a brandy from citrus fruits. Today, there are only two distilleries in the continental United States producing rum. About ten miles from the Lake Alfred distillery, Florida Distillers Company also operates a distillery in Auburndale.

Molasses from the U.S. sugar mills in Clewiston is delivered by truck and rail car to the Lake Alfred and Auburndale distilleries where it is fermented in a three-day process. From the stainless steel fer-

mentation vats the fermented beer, as it is called here, is distilled in the beer column and then stored in a cistern before it is further distilled in a four-column still. Since the distillery is not presently operating at its full capacity of 20,000 proof gallons per day it is more efficient to schedule the distillation process in two operations.

After distillation, the raw alcohol is stored in tall stainless steel tanks before it is put into aging barrels or shipped in bulk containers to other bottlers around the world. In the early 1990s, the raw rum storage at the Lake Alfred distillery caught fire when a welder's spark ignited the flammable vapor on top of an adjacent tank. Over a million gallons of alcohol burned during the next three days.

Fire is an ever-present danger in the distillery business. When the aged rum stocks are lost, it takes years before the distillery can produce the products that have earned it a loyal customer base. It is not uncommon for distilleries to suffer the effects of fire for a decade or more; others never fully recover.

Florida Distillers Company distills and bottles rum under a variety of labels. Conch Republic Rum Company and Old Florida Rum Company, for example, are owned by Florida Distillers Company. Others are contract bottled for various companies, and some are private labels for chain accounts. Fruit-based liqueurs and cordials are also distilled and bottled here as well as rum from the Virgin Islands and Puerto Rico.

There are no facilities for tourists to visit Florida Distillers Company at the present time but when you see Lake Alfred or Auburndale on the label you will know that the rum came from the only rum distilleries in the continental states.

South of Miami there are a string of islands known as the Conch Republic, also referred to as the Florida Keys. The label on Conch Republic Rums best describes the distillery's origins.

UNITED STATES

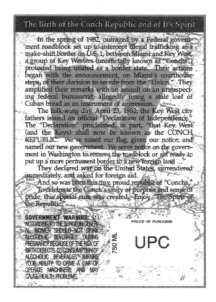

Down in the Conch Republic, the most important part of the day is sunset. And the best way to enjoy it is with a rum drink in your hand, but not just any rum will do. Durdy White Rum is cask aged for two years and then bottled without filtering to remove the color it has gained from the barrels. The label is reminiscent of a parrothead fantasy but this is one of the few rum labels that tells you right up front, Cask Aged 2 Years. Before you add your favorite mixer, take the time to smell this rum and then taste what two years in the barrel will do for distilled spirits. Life just got a little better in the Conch Republic.

The Old Florida Rum Co. also bottles Islamorada Light Rum, Matecumbe Dark Rum, and the 151 proof Knockemdown Key Rum. All of these rums are named for islands in the Conch Republic and are available in finer patriotic bars in Key West. Or look for it in selected Conch Republic liquor stores.

FLORIDA DISTILLERS COMPANY
WEST PALM BEACH, FLORIDA

Molasses-based rums from continuous still

Durdy White Rum

Bottled Strength: 40% alcohol by volume

Age: Blend of two to six-year-old rums aged in oak barrels

Notes: This rum is not filtered before bottling to maintain all of the color, taste, and aroma of the aged rum. The premium rum from the Conch Republic.

Islamorada Light Rum

Bottled Strength: 40% alcohol by volume

Age: Blend of two-year-old rums

Notes: Filtered prior to bottling.

UNITED STATES

Matecumbe Dark Rum
Bottled Strength: 40% alcohol by volume

Age: Blend of two-year-old rums

Notes: Colored with caramel for those who prefer a colored dark rum.

Knockemdown Key Rum
Bottled Strength: 75.5% alcohol by volume, 151 proof

Age: Two years

Notes: Strong rum for punches and those Conch Republic parties.

Cuba

Only ninety miles south of Florida, Havana was the playground for the rich after World War II until the end of the 1950s when Fidel Castro took power. Ernest Hemingway spent much of his later years in Cuba writing about what he loved most—fishing and drinking rum.

Bacardi was founded in Cuba and then moved to Puerto Rico in 1958, just before Castro nationalized the sugar industry and many others. Another rum label, Ron Matusalem, was founded in Cuba in 1852 but is now bottled in the Bahamas and Florida. Havana Club continues to produce rum from molasses made in Cuba. Until recently, Havana Club maintained a distribution network that included most of the Soviet empire. With the breakup of the Soviet Union, the distribution of these light flavorful rums has deteriorated but they continue to be considered among the world's best.

Made in continuous distillation stills, the Havana Club rums are aged in oak barrels and then bottled as white, gold, and aged rums. The distillers have suffered as foreign trade in rum and almost every other export from this island has diminished. In spite of the problems of the last ten years, the industry's future looks very bright.

In the early 1990s, Haiti's rum export market suffered because of the country's political troubles, including the U.S. blockade. Once the crisis subsided, the demand for rum actually increased, due in part to the temporary shortage of supply. While exports were suspended, the distillery aged more of their product. Despite difficulties for everyone involved, all was not lost because supplies of aged rum actually improved.

Sugar cane is still a large part of the lush mountainous landscape in Cuba. A number of distilleries continue to produce rum in old copper stills. Most *of the production of these small distilleries is sold in the local market, but as changes in the power structure inevitably take place, look for an introduction of a wide variety of Cuban rums to the market. Havana Club, in particular, is anticipating increased tourism to the island and is in the process of opening a new visitors center and rum museum.*

Australia

No discussion of rum would be complete without mentioning Bundaberg, or "Bundy" as it known down under. On the northern coast of Queensland, the Bundaberg Distilling Company has been making spirits since 1889.

Unlike the northern hemisphere, down under cane harvest is done between July and November. Traditionally the cane fields are burned to remove the dry leaves from the stalk and rid the fields of snakes making the work of cane cutting a little easier. For more than a century the sweet cane was cut by hand, one stalk at a time, but more recently machines are employed to cut the cane.

Shortly after sugar cane was introduced to Australia in 1872, dozens of sugar mills were built to process the cane from the rich volcanic Queensland soil. The Millaquin sugar mill, one of the surviving mills, supplies the molasses for Bundy rum. At the Bundaberg distillery, the molasses is fermented for thirty-six hours using specially prepared yeast before the wash is distilled in the two-stage distillation process.

The first stage of distillation takes place in the single-column continuous still called the wash column. From the wash column a low alcohol content distillate is condensed then redistilled in the second stage, a pot still. Although some pot stills are used to distill rum, very few use a pot still to redistill alcohol from a continuous column still. The raw *rum condensate from the pot still then matures for two to three years in 60,000 liter American white oak vats before it is bottled in the distinctive square-based bottle.*

Until the 1950s, Bundaberg Rum was only sold in casks to agents who bottled the rum with their own labels throughout Australia. Today Bundaberg distills and bottles all of its rum at the distillery in Queensland. It is also bottled in Australia Stubbs White Rum. Stroh Australia is the only rum is I have seen that actually says it contains coloring additives.

Most of the five million liters of rum produced annually is bottled as the original Bundaberg Rum. But in 1985 a vat was selected to become the pride of Bundaberg. In 1995, the first vat of this especially smooth, mellow rum was bottled as Bundaberg Black. Each numbered bottle of this special rum is a collector's item and since no two vats of rum age in exactly the same way, each batch of Bundaberg Black will be unique.

In addition to its rum, The Bundaberg Distilling Co. also bottles two ready-to-drink cocktails. Dark & Stormy is a Bundaberg combination of ginger beer and rum. The other product, Bundy & Cola, needs no explanation.

The Bundy polar bear is the mascot of the distillery. To find out why, you'll have to visit the distillery in north Queensland. There you can tour the distillery and learn for yourself what makes Bundaberg Australia's favorite rum.

England and Scotland

Even before rum was adopted as part of the Royal Navy's daily rations in 1687, rum was gaining popularity in Europe. Drought conditions had caused shortages of grain and in 1675, the production of gin, fermented and distilled from grain, was limited in order to provide more food for the population. Imports of the Caribbean spirit soared and rum punch became a staple of European drinking houses.

In the eighteenth century Lemon Hart, based in British Guyana, began importing rum from Guyana and became an official rum supplier to the Royal Navy. Today Lemon Hart is based in England and buys rum from distilleries in Guyana and Jamaica to be aged in the cooler northern latitudes. Lemon Hart blends and bottles a number of rums including a 151 proof, colored rum as well as rums aged five years and more.

Cadenhead from Cambelton, Scotland also buys Jamaican rum and ages it in warehouses in Scotland. Rums aged as much as thirty years are bottled at cask aging strengths of up to 146 proof. In the Caribbean, rum is rarely aged more than twenty years due in part to the higher evaporation losses in warmer climates. At a conservative evaporation rate of 8% per year, a barrel of rum is depleted by almost 50% in only eight years in the Caribbean. After seventeen years, evaporation will claim over 75% of the contents of the aging barrel. As the volume in a barrel is depleted, the chances of the barrel leaking increases and further complicates the task of aging spirits.

Some of the rums aged more than fifteen years in the Caribbean take on a very distinct woody, sometimes burnt, taste. I have not found this to be as dominant in the taste of the Cadenhead aged rums, even in their thirty-year-old cask strength rum.

Some distillers claim older barrels age rum better than newer barrels. All of the rum distilleries use barrels several times before they are discarded. Some distilleries remove the head of the barrel after each use, which may be many years, and burn the inside of the barrel again to increase the desired effects of the aging process. This is an expensive process and is not widely practiced since it requires the expertise of a skilled cooper.

In spite of the controversy regarding what are the best conditions of temperature and humidity for aging, it is agreed that oak is the best wood for aging alcohol. In the United States, most of the oak used for barrel making comes from the central states of Kentucky, Missouri, and Arkansas. In Europe, France is the biggest supplier of oak aging barrels and vats. Oak is preferred for the strength, flexibility, and low porosity of the heartwood.

Although some woods are toxic, the natural sugars in the form of cellulose and lignin in the oak fibers account for the vanilla taste of spirits aged in oak barrels. The vanilla tones of aging are evident in fine scotch, whiskey, and rum. It should also be noted that oak contains other natural sugars such as glucose, fructose, and xylose that combine with the aging alcohol to impart other flavors and effects.

Venezuela

In addition to the islands, all of the countries that border the Caribbean also make rum. Venezuela has the biggest variety of rums made from molasses. Cacique, Pampero, and Santa Teresa are a few of the labels. Each company has its own range of rums which vary in age from a year or less to more than ten years. Aniversario from Pampero is probably the most famous aged rum from Venezuela. Packaged in a leather pouch and spherical bottle, this premium rum is a special find—but don't overlook some of the other rums from Venezuela. The value of the Venezuelan Bolivar has fluctuated considerably in the last few years, making some of these fine rums very affordable.

Guyana

Southeast of Trinidad, Guyana has been exporting rum for hundreds of years. Demarra Rums are famous among rum drinkers. Some of the Demarra rums are aged fifteen years and more. Distilled from fermented molasses, these rums are also exported to the United Kingdom for aging or to other islands for blending. During the wars in the early part of this century, the coasts off of Trinidad and Guyana were very active, making the threat of invasion quite real. I have heard stories of rum being warehoused in caves that were closed off to hide the precious liquor and then either forgotten or lost until many years later.

RUMS OF THE WORLD

Surinam

Like its neighbor to the north, Surinam produces aged and unaged rums. Sailors from South Africa that stop in this tropical country are in for a treat. Like so many places where rum is distilled, production exceeds demand from time to time and the result is stocks of aged rum waiting to be discovered.

Africa

Off the east coast of Africa, a variety of rums can be found on the island of Madagascar. Some are blends of several rums made on the island, others are blends of imported spirits. The people of Madagascar have historically relied heavily on trading and the sea for their livelihoods—as a result their taste for rum has been influenced by many places around the world. The spirits bottled here today are representative of the diverse background of the people, where clear overproof spirits and colored, if not aged, rums are readily available.

When the sugar cane plant was transplanted from Africa westward to Spain, Portugal, and the Canary Islands, spirits were also made in these places from the fermented juice. In South Africa, alcohol was manufactured for fuel during World War II. Since alcohol for human consumption was difficult to find during the war, the cane spirits were drunk. After the war, the economy was in shambles but the alcohol production was bottled for consumption in the local market. Today cane spirits are bottled in South Africa under the Mainstay and Red Heart labels.

Guatemala

Anyone who has been to Guatemala has drunk Ron Botran, made from distilled molasses. These medium-bodied rums are well worth getting to know. In addition to their white and dark rums, Botran also bottles Ron Botran Añejo and a special Ron Botran Solero. I have not had the pleasure of visiting the distillery but while I was continuing the research for this book I was invited to have a drink on board the ketch, Sunshine II. As the evening progressed, and more friends arrived with some of their favorite rums, the research became less than scientific but I can tell you that just when you think rum can't get much better you will be surprised. Without paying a king's ransom you can drink some very good rums—Ron Botran is one of them. Botran is one of the special rums that has begun to gain a following in the United States where it is imported in small quantities.

The Pacific

Sugar cane is grown in the Pacific in many places but seldom was as pivotal to the economies of these islands as in the Caribbean. Today, the French islands of Reunion and Mauritius make rhum agricole for local consumption and export mostly to France.

The Hawaiian islands also make rum from molasses as well as a number of fruit-based liquors, such as pineapple cordials and liqueurs. Whaler's is a popular label but there are others that can only be found in the local market. In the Philippines, Negrita and Tanduay are aged and then colored with caramel. Small quantities of very old rum can also be found, but you must be persistent in your search.

In the islands, I heard of many stills or boilers that were inoperative because of leaks or had never been completed due to a lack of materials. It was late in the year and final preparations were under way for this book. Soon, I would have to go back to the States for publication, without actually seeing one of these stills in operation. Even though I had walked many miles, chasing leads about local stills without success, I was excited when I heard that one might be nearby. The directions were not very clear, but I was going to look for it anyway.

All I had to go on was part of a conversation I had overheard: "As the road began to rise, a young man came down a small path from the hill up to the right and asked us for a cigarette. He invited us to the shack for a taste of local rum, but we were in a hurry to get to town so we didn't stop. The shack didn't look big enough for a still. But, if you want some local rum, you might find some there." The directions were not very clear, but I was going to look for it anyway.

On my next trip to town with two friends, I was careful to notice the grade of the road. As it began to rise, my heartbeat quickened, partly from the exertion of walking uphill in the hot afternoon sun and partly from the excitement of meeting someone who might be willing to let me see a still in operation. It was Thursday afternoon, and if I was right, the rum would be distilled sometime soon, probably before the weekend.

A few hundred yards after the road began to rise, a small footpath led to a shack up the hill to the right. As we approached and tried to make ourselves known, it became obvious that no one was there. We looked between the pieces of rusted sheet metal that formed the door, and only saw a cup and some clothes inside. There was no still. But it was early in the afternoon, so we walked back to the dirt road and continued toward town.

The next field shack was also to the right. As we approached, we heard people talking and a woman laughing. A black dog announced our arrival, and a smiling young man with a piece of cloth tied around his forehead appeared. Before I could tell him we were looking for some local rum, he invited us into the shade. Just before the last step into the low-roofed shed, the young man stopped us and pulled a piece of wood with nails pointing up through it out of the grass. "We've had some thieving around here. This is a trap for the thief to step on." He held the primitive, but effective trap up for us to see, then tossed it under a bluggoe tree at the corner of the shack.

I first thought this was a banana tree, but the fruit were much shorter and fatter than bananas, like swollen fingers sticking out of the single, fruit-bearing branch.

Inside the shed, a woman, who appeared to be old enough to be the young man's mother, was sitting on a few boards across the right side of the shed. When I told her that we were looking for some local rum, her broad smile lit up in the dark shadows of the shed. "Come in, come in out of the sun. Get another cup of water," she instructed the young man who was outside playing with the dog.

She pulled a bag from the shelf behind her and poured a little clear liquid from a nearly empty bottle into an already wet cup. As she handed it to me, the young man appeared with another cup, larger than the first, half full of water. I was reluctant to taste this liquor. But I was surprised that it did not have a harsh smell. It had a pleasant fragrance, more like a sweet flower than the petroleum-like smell that I have come to associate with the rum from the other small stills in the Caribbean.

As I carefully let the liquid touch my mouth, the coolness of the alcohol evaporating on my lips convinced me that this was strong. I forced my mouth open to taste the liquid that I knew was going to burn not only my mouth, but also my throat, eyes, and probably my heart and lungs by the time it hit my stomach.

I handed the cup to my friend who eagerly took it from me as he watched my reaction. My mouth was not burning, my throat was not scorched, and my eyes were not full of tears. Even the aftertaste was not unpleasant. The young man handed me a cup of water, I sipped it, and handed the cup to my friend. Unsure of my experience, he waited for the water before he committed himself to the small cup.

Without saying a word, he sipped from the cup, then the water, and handed both to his wife. Her eyes became bigger as she held the two cups, a small plastic tea cup with a broken handle and a much larger porcelain-covered metal cup, rusted where the thin ceramic coating had been worn away by years of use. She hesitated until she was aware that we were looking at her, then sipped from the cups in turn.

Without noticing the man or his mother, we looked at each other as if we alone had just witnessed some extraordinary event that none of us was capable of relating to anyone else. As I formed my mouth to speak to my friend's wife, I became aware again of the young man standing behind me and the woman sitting on the bench, silently watching our reactions.

Behind the woman, a partition of rusted metal,

which did not reach the ceiling, divided the shed. I looked over the partition and saw an old metal drum and some sticks on the floor, but hardly enough to convince me that this was what I had been looking for. Without any disappointment, I asked where the rum was made and tried to explain that my interest was solely—"Come see over here," the young man interrupted with an approving nod from the woman.

As we moved to a larger open space facing the hill behind the shack, I saw another barrel on its side, slightly inclined, perched on a few rocks. A rectangular hole had been chiseled into the top side of this barrel and it was nearly full of water. A piece of pipe protruded from its ends. We were in the right place! But the still had been dismantled.

We moved to the first barrel I had seen. My host removed a piece of wood from on top of the barrel and exposed a cleanly cut, round hole, too small to put my head into. He told me to smell the contents. I could just make out some brown bubbles coming from the dark liquid that filled more than half the barrel. Judging from the bubbles, the fire would be lit in the next day or so. If I was lucky, I would be allowed to witness the magic in this small shack.

While my companions examined the barrel, the young man pulled a long copper pipe from the roof of the shed and placed it between the two barrels. He began to explain the operation of the still when the woman appeared with another sip of rum.

Once it was disclosed that the fire would be lit Sunday afternoon, I asked if it would be all right to come see the boiling. Without hesitation, the woman assured me that we were welcome. Since the boiling would take the better part of the night,

I asked what we should bring. "No, come just then and join us. After, if you want to buy some rum, you can then."

As we walked back down the hill to the main road, we quickly agreed that, in spite of the fact that it was unmistakably strong, this was some of the best rum we had ever tasted. But in our euphoria, we had forgotten to ask to buy some of the fragrant spirit to take with us. But never mind, there would be plenty of rum on Sunday. Just a couple of sips of this powerful spirit had shaken our senses.

My friends had to leave before Sunday, so I assured them that I would let them know all of the details that I could remember. This is the account I promised them, as best as I can recall.

After a couple of sips of rum and the excitement of the previous visit, I was unsure of the time that the boiling would take place, so I rowed ashore and headed for the shed about five o'clock Sunday afternoon. Not far from the footpath that led up the hill to the camp, I stopped to catch my breath under the shade of a tamarind tree.

As I turned to pull one of the figlike fruit from the tree, I saw two figures coming up the road from the well. They were carrying some bags and a white plastic jug, which even at this distance appeared to be empty. The woman waved to me like a young girl. They were the people I had met a few days earlier.

The conversation was light as we made our way up the hill to the camp. The young man went ahead with his bags and the black dog barked as he approached. He filled a can with water for the animal and met us at the entrance to the camp. As the woman and I took the last steps up the incline we looked for the trap. "It's over there," the young man grinned, pointing to the piece of wood with sharpened nails shining in the sun. We entered the shade of the rusted structure and the jovial mood of the gathering changed to one of purpose.

The young man removed the cover of the barrel where the dark liquid had been bubbling. Now, no bubbles were visible. To fill the round hole in the top of this barrel, he pushed a large, dry-milk powder can, without a lid, upside down into the barrel a couple of inches. The metal drum looked like it was wearing a party hat. A hole in the dry-milk can was cut toward the uphill end of the inclined barrel with water in it.

Next, he took another four-gallon, metal container with rounded ends and placed it on three rocks near the high end of the inclined barrel. In the side of this container there was a hole large enough to slide over the pipe that extended through the water-filled barrel. When this was done, another hole, near the top of the rounded container, lined up with the hole in the milk-powder can. Then, the copper pipe was put in place between the hole in the milk-powder can and the hole near the top of the rounded container.

While the boiler was being assembled, the woman had been making a paste of white flour and water. Then, she pulled some stringy material from a coffee can where it had been soaking in water. This was the dried stalk of a bluggoe plant, and would give the crude stucco the strength to seal the joints so that none of the precious vapor would escape. With sure, sculptor-like hands, she coated the fibers with the white paste and forced it into the cracks between the boiler and the dry-milk can. Next, she put some of the paste around the copper pipe where it fit into the can. The young man took some and applied it to the two holes in the round-topped container where the pipes fit into it.

Standing straight, she surveyed their work, then told the young man to cut a plug for the drain hole in the bottom of the rounded container. Until now, not one word had been spoken since we had entered the camp. When he had finished fitting the plug, she offered the last of the sticky mixture from between the callused fingers of her large hands. Without noticing me, she began to sing as she dipped water from another drum that collected rainwater from the roof. When her hands were clean, she sat down on another round-topped container, no longer used because the holes in it had rusted until they were too big to be sealed with the flour and bluggoe stucco.

Below the lower end of the inclined barrel, a hole had been scooped out of the dirt floor of the shed. On a rusty piece of metal in the hole, she placed the small tea cup on top of the coffee can. The cup sat a couple of inches below the pipe that passed through the water-filled barrel. In a few minutes, the still was in position, though not quite ready for operation.

To complete the still, she reached toward the metal wall of the shed and, as if by magic, produced a piece of forked branch. The smooth branch was inserted into the pipe above the small cup.

Finished with her preparations, she crossed her ankles and pulled a crumpled bag of tobacco and a delicate clay pipe from the folds of her skirt. Satisfaction covered her broad features as she arranged her skirt to hold the plastic bag. Through an opening in the shed behind her, the last of the day's sun formed a collage of pastel colors that framed her radiant silhouette. She took a deep breath, held her unlit pipe in her mouth, and looked at her son who was busy getting the fire ready to light.

The metal boiling drum sat on several rocks to get it off the ground. The young man was arranging small kindling under the front of the barrel, then lit it with a single match. Soon, the flickering flames of the kindling chased shadows around the shed. The pastels were fading from the sky, replaced by a sliver of the new moon and Venus, on their first trip that month into the tropical sky.

Without being asked, he handed her a lit branch for her pipe. While he waited, she lit her pipe, then asked him to put some more wood on the fire. We all watched the fire begin to lick the front of the barrel. "If the fire is not under the barrel, the flames be rushing up the top and the rum will be slow to come," the smoke from her pipe mixed with her words.

The old woman looked at me and smiled. I asked how long she had been making rum. "I been boiling since nineteen hundred and seventy-six," she said hesitantly. Almost every week since then, with the help of her adopted son, she had willed the fire to turn the fermented cane juice into rum.

I knew this was illegal, but asked anyway. "Does anyone care you make rum?"

"Well, in before times, when the other government was here, they was bad for it. But now, they don't be so bad for it. The last time I really heard of someone to get in trouble for it, the man had three barrels of rum when they come to his camp. That was, like I say, before."

Once the fire under the boiler was hot, a second fire was built between some rocks near the inclined barrel. The young man had pulled his fish traps this morning and taken a few small fish. Fish stew was put on this fire in a dented pot with a lid that barely covered it. Then, the woman again directed the young man's attention to the fire under the boiler. "Shake the fire! Shake the fire!"

The larger pieces of wood in the fire were removed and all of the coals were brought out to the side of the boiler with a forked stick. He put the largest pieces of smoking wood back on the fire and reached to his left for more dry branches. She sprinkled water on the coals, and the rusty shed coughed smoke and steam in all directions. This charcoal would be used for cooking at home during the coming week.

"Are you from here?" I asked when the smoke cleared.

"No," she said. "I'm really not from here, since I was small I live here, but I'm really not from here. Before, I used to sell charcoal in the market with those other women in town, you know. One time, a woman gave me some charcoal to sell that looked good, it was black and shiny, but it couldn't boil a pot. Then, a woman that I sell the charcoal come to my house and ask me why I sell charcoal that don't have any heat. The Lord knows, I didn't know that it was no good until I, myself, try to boil a pot on it. And you know, after one-and-a-half hours, the pot, it wouldn't boil. I don't like that business. For what? You work all day and maybe you get a few dollars, but I give it up now. Now, I just work here in me garden."

Her dark skin glowed as she looked out the opening of the shack into the dark garden. There were spices, watermelon, cantaloupe, bodi, squash, corn, and sugar cane. It had been too dry this year for tomatoes, cucumbers, cabbage, and sugar apples.

The black dog barked once, but didn't alarm

the woman or her son. A man, older than the woman, entered the shed through the small area. As he put his folded cardigan sweater over the metal divider, he greeted the young man, hugged the woman, and called her by her first name. Then, he turned to me as the woman introduced me.

He was a strong, fit man with a quick, sincere smile and short, gray hair under his hat. His pullover shirt was neat and his just-washed, polyester slacks fit him well. He looked like he was on his way to the prayer house except for his rubber shoes, which he soon took off to reveal his wide feet.

He had been here many times before and, after looking in the cup and seeing it empty, took a step toward the long copper pipe that separated us. He put his hand on the dark pipe, looked to the heavens through the metal roof, and silently asked the Lord's will to bring the rum to the cup as he moved his hand closer to the boiler. It was too soon, the pipe was not hot yet.

The old man stood reverently in the middle of the dirt floor. The woman said almost laughing, "If you have any questions about boiling, this is the man to ask." She didn't want to reveal that he had taught her how to boil nearly twenty years ago.

The old man looked at me. "You want to know about boiling?" And he began to tell me about the apparatus that stood between us in the shed.

"First, you have to set up. You have to take four pails of water and four gallons of cane syrup. Then, you add one pail of leavener from the last boiling, and some yeast. You mix that up and let it set. You let it set about five days, according to the syrup. After five days, if it is ready to boil, you will know because the bubbles will fall."

"If it fall before it's time, you can know that it won't be so good," the woman offered.

"How much yeast do you use?" I asked.

"One ounce of yeast. But," the woman warned as she smiled, "if you use too much yeast, when you drink the rum, you will be certain to get loose bowels." The men laughed with her as she pulled the folds of her shirt around her stomach to keep her tobacco from spilling on the floor.

"Then, you assemble the boiler and light the fire, like so," he continued as he turned to the fire. The woman and her son held their laughter until the old man turned back to me. "The set will heat up, but not too hot or the rum will taste burnt. After, when the set turn to steam, the pipe will get hot like so. And, as the heat moves down the pipe, then the steam in the boiler pushes the heat into the extractor." He held his hand over the rounded can in front of me.

"The extractor extracts the water from the rum. The water comes same as the rum and is separated in the bottom. When you get one jar of rum, you might get one of water, so you must condemn and remove it from here." He pointed to the drain on the extractor, then waited for my eyes to meet his before he continued. "Only the rum vapor will pass the extractor. Unless," he paused to make me understand the gravity of what he was saying, "the waste forgets to drain and runs down this pipe in the cooler and into the jar."

"Can you use the water for anything?" I inquired of my tutor.

"No!" The old man was forceful. "Some people collect it, then put it back in the boiler through the bung in the head, but it makes the rum taste as bad as that water smells."

"If you drink that in your rum, you won't want

to talk to your wife in the morning," the woman added, "that's what give you bad breath when you drink the other rum." The two men nodded in agreement. She obviously knew what she was talking about. "Some people use it for rheumatism; you rub it all over your body before you go to bed at night. But," she grinned, "if you use it, they will know that you be coming from a camp." The three of them laughed out loud, looking first at me, then each other.

With his hand in the water of the inclined barrel, the old man continued. "Only the rum vapor will pass the extractor, then it makes drops in the pipe in the cooler and comes out there." Pointing to the nipple above the cup, he looked over the barrel to see if the rum had come yet. "If you stroke the pipe in the barrel to cool it, the rum will come better. You understand?" I nodded and everyone began to laugh at the old man leaning over the cooler with his hand in the water up to his elbow, caressing the pipe that passed through it, willing the rum to come.

The young man got up and put his hand on the pipe to check the heat. The heat had moved down the pipe and was nearly in front of me, only a foot or so from the rounded extractor.

It was dark now. A piece of rag had been shoved into the top of a bottle, two-thirds full of kerosene. Lit from the fire under the boiler, the flame provided just enough light to see the branch where the rum would appear.

Silence filled the shed. The flame got smaller as it was batted about the top of the bottle by the draft in the three-walled area. The young man moved from his place, a board between two cans, and tipped the bottle to soak the rag wick, which didn't reach the flammable liquid. Tipping the bottle caused the flame to become very orange and give off thick, black smoke for a few seconds.

I looked toward the fish, and noticed that the small fire had gone almost completely out. "No problem," the young man said. As he moved the lid, the smell of fish stew was a pleasant relief from the charcoal cooling next to the boiler and the soot from the kerosene flame.

The old man was the first to smell the smoke from the still. He leaned closer to the cup and the woman peered into it. There was no rum yet. I reached to feel the extractor in front of me. Even before I touched it, I could feel the warmth of the rounded metal can. Then, I caught the sweet smell of the smoke. "The rum is behind the smoke," the woman said. "Since you are smelling it, the rum will come just now."

I moved closer to the cup and saw a little bit of smoke come from the pipe above the cup. The old man reached behind me and again stroked the pipe in the cooler. As we laughed, the young man began. "Put some more oil in the lamp." And the others joined him.

"Keep it burning, keep it burning till breakaway."

"If it's a quarter, it's better than water."

"Bring it with your willing mind."

"Bring it, Mr. Chairman, bring it with your willing mind."

The rum had not yet come, but the sweet smell of the cane liquor was filling the air. I knew the first liquor would be the harshest to come out of this still. I also knew that I didn't want to be the first to taste it. I asked the woman, "Who will be the first to taste the rum?"

"You will be the first," she smiled, "strangers are always first." The young man laughed as he willed the rum to come with his nose close to the empty cup.

"I'll be the first to taste the rum," the old man proclaimed, as if taking the responsibility for the stranger, but without any indication that he ever expected anything in return. The woman laughed and again focused her dark eyes on the cup. A wisp of smoke emerged, then one drop of clear liquid, then another, followed quickly by another, and another, until an almost steady stream of liquid flowed from the whittled stick to the cup. As soon as the rum appeared, the young man moved to the fire. After he had pulled the fire from under the kettle, he quickly rebuilt it with smaller wood. And the rum continued to come.

When the cup was about one-quarter full, the woman removed it. The old man removed the coffee can and replaced it with a one-gallon, wide-mouth jar. The liquid was steadily dripping into the bottom of the jar, but everyone's attention was on the small cup she held in the palms of her large hands.

She sniffed at it, then poured a little of the first liquor into the palm of her left hand. She handed the cup to the old man, then rubbed the liquid on the back of her right hand. The coolness of the alcohol on her hands made her smile. The rum was strong. After the rest of us had tasted this first rum, the cup was returned to her with just a few drops left in it. She threw what was left into the fire causing blue flames to reach the smoke-blackened metal roof over the boiler. We laughed as she replaced the gallon jar with the cup and the coffee can.

"The first rum is called high wines," the old man began. The woman sat down in front of the cup and pulled her bag of tobacco from her skirt.

"After the high wines is the seconds, and then come the low wines. The low wines are not so high temperature as the high wines, and so, we mix the first and the seconds with the low wines to lower the temperature of the rum." Finally, it occurred to me that the temperature was not a measure of heat, but an indication of the rum's strength.

The stream of rum into the jar was growing. "Remove the fire, remove the fire!" she ordered the young man. "Remove the fire, don't burn the rum!" When he didn't respond, she carefully stepped around him and tended the fire herself. In a minute, the rum was back to a steady, smaller stream and the jar was again replaced by the cup and its rusty pedestal.

The young man brought four deep bowls in from the smaller area. His mother, of the last thirty years, looked into the cup, then turned and smiled at him. Dark, round eyes gleamed back at her. Then he turned his attention to the cup in the dim, yellow light of the flame.

The old man took the bowls and began to serve dinner. When he had finished, the woman removed the cup as her son replaced the gallon jar. "Now, no more until the jar is full," she said. The cup of rum and another of water were passed around twice. The first time we each took a drink; the second time we spilled a little of the fresh rum into our bowls. The old man held the cup up to get the last drop before he placed it on the cooler where it would be handy. The first jar of rum was filling up.

The fish stew had been seasoned with spices grown in the garden and was simply good. The rum made a much better condiment than the usual hot sauce used in the islands. Soon, everyone had cleaned their bowls. Being the closest to the pot, I served seconds.

After dinner, the woman held the cup to collect some more rum. The clear stream pleased her as it flowed into the cup. She took a sip, then moved from her seat in front of the jar to the bench behind the partition. The old man stood up and stretched his arms, then looked for the cup. It had a little left in it and he handed it to me. "Have a drink, my friend."

I took the cup and said, "She sure is a nice woman."

"She sure is." He repeated. "I love her," he whispered.

"You are high, you've been drinking too much, you are getting high," the voice came from the other side of the partition.

"I am not," he said. "I am not, I won't have another drink till morning."

"OK," came the reply.

"She really is wonderful," he continued, this time in a lower voice. "She has been my friend for a long time now. Yes, she is a wonderful woman. You won't find a better woman than her, and none with a camp." The young man had been pulling more coals from the fire and started laughing at his friend. Feeling a little ashamed, the old man stood up and began again. "I've been a fisherman, boat builder, I can do macheting." As he spoke, he imitated the actions of each of the trades he had done in his life. "Plumbing, masonry with bricks, carpentering."

"Carpenter," she was beside him now, and corrected him like she would a young school boy.

"Carpenter," he repeated, as if he were her pupil. She smiled at him as their eyes met.

The jar was just about full. The woman replaced

it with the cup and the small can. "Tippy, tippy, tippy," the old man whispered. The woman looked at him, her white teeth shining as she smiled. She was happy, the rum was coming, and it was still strong. Her happiness was contagious. She passed the full jar to the young man. While I held the funnel, he poured the fragrant rum into the plastic jug that would carry it home at the end of the night.

When we had finished, the young man removed the plug from the extractor. A foul smell filled the shed as the condemned water spilled from the container. The old man said, "Don't forget to plug back the extractor," as he handed first the cup of rum, and then the water, to his younger friend.

"Thank you, I hold it in me hand." He held the wooden plug between his knuckles so the older man could see it as he tipped the cup of rum toward his mouth. The politeness of the moment surprised me. The old man chuckled approvingly. He envied the young man, living with the woman he loved, but he did not resent him in the least. They had been friends most of the younger man's life.

"How do you know when the seconds come?" I asked, peering into the jar.

"See the beads in the bottom?" she asked, as she leaned over me with her warm hand on my shoulder. The bottom of the jar was just covered with liquid, and the beads formed by the rum splashing into it were floating to the outside of the jar. "When the seconds come, the beads won't stay like that."

It was hard to see, but in the next few minutes, I am sure I saw a difference in the behavior of the little bubbles of clear rum in the jar. Or at least I think I did. The old man was trying to focus on the jar in the dim light. "When the moon be new, the rum will be plenty. When the moon be filling, the rum be getting stronger. After, when the moon falling, the rum be getting weaker."

There was plenty of rum, and I thought it was very strong. I tried to think of where I planned to be when this moon would be full. Never mind, I thought, plans made for sailing boats are foolish. Enjoy where you are and don't worry about the full moon, just be free to see it.

The simplicity of the experience mixed with the rum had a warm, numbing effect on me. Like the old man, I, too, loved the woman. She was as fair as a human could be. What a delight to spend time with these people, who, by their own assessment were poor, honest people, thankful for whatever the Master gave them. But they were richer than anyone I could think of, and I hoped to learn the secret of their wealth.

As the second jar filled, the conversation became more animated and several more songs were sung, but to be honest, I can hardly remember a word of any of them. When the one song I knew was sung, I joined in. It reminded me of singing in church when I was a young boy; all of the songs had a gospel rhythm and feeling to them. As I looked at each of the three people with me, we all smiled and admitted our unabashed friendship.

There was no doubt that I would visit the camp again. My thoughts condensed into words. "Would you mind if I came again, to see how you make the rum?"

"Of course not," they said in unison. Then, the woman spoke out. "As long as I am the boss of this camp, you are welcome!"

"How do you know when the low wines are

coming?" I asked.

"The beads will not form and the jar will get cloudy in the top," the woman said. As I leaned toward the jar, I could still see the beads. The top of the jar was clear, but I wasn't sure exactly what she meant. In time, I was sure that I would understand.

"Tippy, tippy, tippy," the old man began to sing. "Tippy, tippy, tippy," echoed his young friend. The woman couldn't help but smile.

"Okay," as she spoke, the old man took the cup and put it under the peeing twig to catch the rum right out of the cooler. She leaned forward and removed the jar. Soon, the cup had enough rum in it to pass around. "Stand up, and tell me do you like me rum." The young man began singing.

"I want to know, oh yeah. I want to know if you like me rum."

Then, very softly. "A little more oil in the lamp." This time, I was pleased to join them.

"Keep it burning, keep it burning till breakaway."

"If it's a quarter, it's better than water."

"Bring it with your willing mind."

"Bring it, Mr. Chairman, bring it with your willing mind."

This was a happy night and everyone laughed between singing the lines of the old boiler's song. My new friends had been very patient with me. But then, they were polite and patient with each other. Only kindness had been spoken or felt here in the garden and I was surprised how quickly they had accepted me into their old circle of friendship. I felt like I was at an evening church social rather than in a rusty shack, watching illicit rum being made.

The second jar of rum was nearly full and the

cut was the topic of discussion. The cut was the point when the seconds turned to the low wines. It didn't seem to me that it really mattered, since all of the rum was mixed in the end anyway, but it was important. Finally, the second jar of rum was full. The cup once again replaced the jar, while the gallon of raw rum was emptied into the plastic jug.

When we had finished, the drip of rum into the cup almost stopped. "Shake the fire, shake the fire," the woman said. The old man leaned over the fire, and I put my hand in the cooler. It surprised me that the water in the top of the cooler was so hot. When I stepped back, I could see steam coming from the hole in the top of the inclined barrel. "Is this too hot?" I asked.

The young man put his hand in the cooler and agreed. We took about ten gallons of water out of the cooler and replaced it with water from the barrel behind the woman. The stinking water was again removed from the extractor.

Soon, the fire was hot again, the rum was coming, and the woman took her seat in front of the jar. As the old man stepped back from the fire, he came close to the flame and the woman scolded him, "Don't kick the flame, don't kick the flame!"

"Yes, yes," he comforted her, as he sat down next to her. He looked at me and cautioned. "You have to be careful about the flame to get too close to the rum." The woman smiled and the young man laughed. I nodded in agreement.

"Have you ever had a fire?" I wondered out loud.

"One time, the flame get too close and the fire go in here," the old man was pointing to the nipple, "and around there, and back to the boiler and all blow up! But that was not here. You have to be careful."

"Have you had a fire?" I asked the woman.

"No," she looked up to thank the Master. "No, not as of yet," she said, with her chin still pointing toward the heavens.

The jar was beginning to collect moisture around the inside of its wide mouth, as if it had just been pulled from a tub of hot water. "Is this the low wines?" I asked.

"This is kill prick," the woman laughed. The old man laughed, but he did not think it quite as funny as the woman.

"You know what is kill prick?" the young man asked. I shrugged my shoulders, and asked him with my eyes to tell me.

The woman laughed again. "If you drink this one, you won't be any good for any woman!"

As we passed the cup of rum and another of water, we all laughed. "Some rum, it make you strong. Some rum, it make you weak," the old man said.

"Some rum make you stand," the woman was looking directly into my tired eyes, "and some rum make you sleep." We all laughed again. Even though it was dark in the camp, and the woman's face was black from tending the smoky fire and the kerosene flame, I could see her blush. She really was beautiful.

By now, the cup wasn't getting much lighter as it was passed around. All of us had drunk plenty of rum and were now tired. The young man stood up and walked outside to shake off the long night. It was well after midnight when the drip of rum from the nipple quit again. The woman started to get up, but I offered to shake the fire. When the fire was a little hotter, the rum began to drip again. She put the empty cup under the nipple and collected a few drops, then smelled it, and threw it into the fire. A blue flash lit up the shed, and the young man appeared.

After a few more minutes, the rum again refused to come. This time, the woman removed the jar and asked me to shake the fire. When a few drops had come, she held them into the cup, then raised it to her nose. Knowing that all of the rum had come, she threw it into the fire. The liquid hissed as it hit the hot coals.

"That's breakaway," she smiled at me and turned to the old man, asleep against her shoulder.

(The land where this story took place is now being considered for a golf course location. I guess that is progress.)

Rum Line

1492 Columbus discovers many of the Eastern Caribbean islands.

1502 Sugar cane is brought to Puerto Rico.

Portuguese colonists bring sugar cane to Brazil.

1526 Brazil exports first sugar to Europe.

1623 Sir Thomas Warner establishes the first English colony in the West Indies on the island of St. Kitts.

1630s Sugar cane brought to Barbados from Brazil.

1637 Sugar cane from St. Kitts is successful in Martinique.

1647 Richard Ligon arrives in Barbados as a Royalist refugee from the English Civil War.

1650 Ligon writes his *History of the Island of Barbados*, which gives a detailed account of sugar and rum making in Barbados in 1650.

1651 Navigation Act, the first of a series of British attempts to monopolize trade with the American colonies, is passed.

1654 Connecticut Court prohibits the importation of any Barbados liquors.

1675 Grain crop failure in England leads to a shortage, limiting gin production and giving rum a foothold in the English market.

RUM LINE

1687 Rum adopted as the daily ration in the Royal Navy.

1690 Golden age of piracy begins.

1692 Port Royal, Jamaica is destroyed by an earthquake.

1694 Père Labat arrives in St. Pierre, Martinique.

1709 Barbados with 409 windmills and 76 animal-powered cane mills produces more sugar than any other island.

1718 November 22, Blackbeard is killed off the coast of North Carolina by Lieutenant Robert Maynard.

1720 Golden age of piracy ends.

1733 Molasses Act forces American colonists to buy more expensive British West Indian sugar which leads to increased smuggling and ultimately the American Revolution.

1740 Admiral Vernon dilutes the Royal Navy rum ration, earning it the name *grog*.

1763 French islands allowed to import rhum to France.

Denmark buys the Virgin Islands leaving the duty-free status that prevails today.

1780 Hurricane destroys much of the English fleet in Carlisle Bay.

1782 Admiral George Rodney defeats Admiral de Grasse off Dominica and secures his place as a Royal Navy hero.

RUM LINE

1787 Sugar is produced from the sugar beet and competition with sugar cane begins.

1790 Captain William Bligh arrives from Tahiti with breadfruit sprouts in St. Vincent.

1789 French Revolution begins.

1804 Haiti is established as the first black republic.

1807 Slave trade outlawed by Britain.

1824 Angostura Bitters first blended by Dr. J. Siegbert.

1825 Wray & Nephew founded in Jamaica.

1832 Coffey still perfected which leads to higher production and greater distillation purity.

1833 Abolition of slavery in the British islands.

1844 Dominican Republic declares independence.

1852 The Bermúdez distillery is founded by J Armando Bermúdez.

1856 Cessation of letters of marque at the Convention of Paris is the first step to the abolition of privateering.

1862 Barbancourt distillery begins production.

1872 Commercial production of sugar cane commences in Queensland.

1879 Tobago exports 500,000 gallons of rum.

1883 Sugar production from sugar beets equals that of sugar cane.

RUM LINE

1888 The Bundaberg Distilling Company is incorporated.

1902 Mount Pelè erupts in St. Pierre leaving only one survivor.

1917 Virgin Islands purchased by the United States from Denmark.

1920 Prohibition starts in the United States.

1933 Prohibition ends in the United States.

1950 The Bundaberg Distilling Company is still selling all its rum in barrels, overproof, to agents who bottled the rum with their own labels, just as it had at the turn of the century.

1957 Hurricane Janet destroys Grenada.

1958 Bacardi moves from Cuba to Puerto Rico.

1963 Sugar is nationalized by many Caribbean governments.

1966 Barbados gains independence.

1970 Rum ration abolished in the Royal Navy.

1974 Grenada becomes an independent nation.

1976 Trinidad and Tobago gain Republican status after attaining independence in 1962.

1978 November 3, Dominica becomes independent, 465 years, to the day, after its discovery by Columbus.

1979 Charles Tobias begins blending and bottling Pusser's Old Navy Rum in Tortola.

St. Lucia, St. Vincent, and the Grenadines gain independence from Britain.

1981 Antigua and Barbuda gain independence.

1983 St. Kitts-Nevis becomes an independent nation.

1989 Hurricane Hugo destroys many of the islands, including St. Croix.

1994 Competition from Central and South American banana growers forces the Caribbean Islands to look for new sources of trade.

1996 Hurricanes Luis and Marilyn leave St. Bart's, St. Martin/St. Maarten, the U.S. Virgin Islands, and the Leeward Islands of Antigua devastated.

Recipes

If you have never tried anything but a rum and Coke, I am sorry. Here are a few ideas to enhance your enjoyment of the Caribbean spirit. Although I have tasted nearly every spirit in this book, I have not tried every one of these concoctions, so I accept no responsibility for any circumstances arising out of their consumption. I swear that I didn't make any of these up and have tried to give credit to those who gave them to me.

In the islands, it is possible to find pure cane syrup. This sweet syrup mixes well in cocktails, especially if you are mixing cold drinks without a blender. The taste is also superior to granulated sugar.

Punch

There are many rum punch recipes that claim to be the original. These vary from the simplest—rum, sugar and lime—to the complicated concoctions of ingredients that I would hardly ever have all at the same time, much less remember.

It is agreed, as much as anything in the islands is agreed upon, that the word *punch* comes from the Hindustani word for five—*panch*. The term *punch* sailed with the English traders to the Caribbean colonies from India.

The rhyming recipe from Barbados is for a traditional punch. Try the different recipes. On other islands, sometimes only three or four ingredients are recognized. The addition of bitters and fresh ground nutmeg gives punch a unique island flavor.

Barbados Punch

One of sour,
Two of sweet,
Three of strong,
Four of weak.
Five drops of bitters and nutmeg spice.
Serve well chilled with lots of ice.

This recipe calls for one part lime juice, two parts sugar or cane syrup, three parts rum, and four parts water, juice, or nectars.

Planters punch includes fruit and fruit juices. The options are all yours—usually orange, pineapple, guava, or passion fruit are used. The best fruit punch I drank was made by Charles Briggs in Barbados, but he isn't telling me the recipe until I give him a book.

Mango Rum Punch

Mix 1 cup mango juice, 1 cup pineapple juice, the juice of 1 fresh lime or lemon, and sugar to taste. Add 2 cups dark rum and ice. Pour over pieces of cut pineapple in chilled glasses.

Pusser's Traditional Rum Punch

Mix 2 ounces Pusser's Rum and equal parts of guava, orange, and pineapple juices, and the juice of ½ lime. Pour over ice and top with a touch of nutmeg and a fresh fruit garnish.

Party Punch

In a large punch bowl, mix 1 bottle of rum, ½ cup lemon juice, ¼ cup sugar, 1 cup cranberry juice, 1 cup orange juice, 1 cup strong tea, 1 dozen cloves, and ice. Garnish with thin lemon slices.

Island Planter

Mix the juice of 1 orange, 1 lime, 1 lemon, 3 dashes Grenadine, ½ cup pineapple juice, ½ cup fruit juice or fruit punch, 2 ounces dark rum, and 3 teaspoons cane syrup. Pour over crushed ice and garnish with an orange slice.

Haitian Planter's Punch

Nearly every island has its own planter's punch. Here is Haiti's.

Mix 3 ounces Barbancourt, 2 ounces orange juice, 1 ounce passion fruit juice, and ½ ounce lime juice. Pour over crushed ice.

Traditional Cavalier Rum Punch

Mix 1½ ounces Cavalier Dark Rum, 2 ounces orange juice, ½ ounce lime juice, 2 ounces pineapple juice, ½ ounce sugar cane syrup, and 2 dashes Angostura bitters. Pour over cracked ice. Add a dash of Grenadine for color and sprinkle freshly grated nutmeg on top.

Almost any fruit juice will make a good rum drink. Grapefruit juice, because it is tart, will mask the strength of even the strongest rum. This can yield a very potent drink and a spectacular hangover.

Daiquiris

Daiquiris come in all kinds. But to be a daiquiri, the drink must have lime and rum. Most often white rum is used for this drink. The simplest is a good measure of white rum, a splash of lime juice, and a little sugar. Shake well and strain into a glass. These are the same ingredients in a ti punch, but don't be fooled. A daiquiri is prepared quite differently than a ti punch.

Frozen Daiquiri

If you have a blender, you are ready. Instead of straining the drink above, blend it until the chunks of ice are small enough to suck through a straw—you have a frozen daiquiri.

Frozen Banana Daiquiri

In a blender, mix 2 ounces white rum, the juice of ½ lime, 1 teaspoon cane syrup, 1 ripe banana, and ice. Blend until smooth.

Banana Mango Daiquiri

In a blender, mix 6 ounces white rum, the juice of 1 lime, a peeled ripe mango or pineapple, 1 ripe banana, and 2 cups ice. Blend until smooth.

By now, you should have the idea. Substitute or add whatever you have in the galley—orange, pineapple, passion fruit, kiwi, grapefruit, etc. The hardest thing about daiquiris is naming them.

RECIPES

Rum 'n' Ginger

Rum and ginger ale. This is popular in Barbados with a dash of Angostura bitters.

Ginger Syrup

For a zesty cocktail, mix a spoonful of this syrup in a glass with some rum to taste, a little water, and a squeeze of lime. Or use a little ginger syrup in your favorite drink.

Grate ½ cup of fresh ginger into a small saucepan, cover with water, and add 2 cups of brown sugar. Bring this to a boil and stir to keep the mixture from boiling over. This is a mess if it boils over in the galley. Strain into a small jar for later use. This will keep for several weeks unrefrigerated. If you don't use enough sugar, the ginger will ferment, so don't skimp on the sugar.

Christina on board Sea Gypsy, *London*

Rum Swizzle

Strong, but not too sweet. For 2 drinks, mix 6 ounces white rum, the juice of 2 limes, 1 tablespoon caster sugar, 2 tablespoons orange liqueur, and 2 lime slices with ½ pint crushed ice.

St. Brendan's Grog

Sugar cane syrup is not always available, but you easily can make a good syrup by filling a quart bottle with sugar, then filling it with water. Shake well and keep in the refrigerator. Pour the syrup off the top and refill with water as you use the syrup.

To make St. Brendan's Grog, fill a 12-ounce glass, with diameter equal to height, with cracked ice. Add white rum to taste and juice from ½ of a lime and 2 teaspoons syrup. Top with a little Angostura bitters. Add syrup to taste because limes vary. Dark rum makes a nice variation but it's not a St. Brendan's Grog. Using Campari instead of Angostura bitters is another variation.

Paul and Linda on board St. Brendan

Ogoun Feray Grog

3 oz Barbancourt
2 tbsp honey
1 oz passion fruit juice
Garnish with a dash of cinnamon and nutmeg.

Magical Rum

1½ oz Barbancourt
½ oz lime juice
1 tbsp sugar cane syrup
1 oz pineapple juice
Stir over crushed ice and serve in a highball glass. Garnish with a slice of pineapple and a mint leaf.

Port-au-Prince Cocktail

1 oz Barbancourt
½ oz coconut cream
½ oz lime juice
Stir over ice and serve in a cocktail glass.

Bacardi Cocktail

1½ oz Bacardi Rum
juice of ½ lime
½ tsp Grenadine
Shake over ice and strain into a cocktail glass.

RECIPES

Bahama Mama

½ oz dark rum
½ oz coconut liqueur
¼ oz 151-proof rum
¼ coffee liqueur
juice of ½ lime
4 oz pineapple juice

Mix and pour over cracked ice into highball glass. Garnish with strawberry, cherry, or fresh fruit of your choice.

Banana Cow

1 oz light rum
1 oz Creme de Banana
1½ oz cream
dash of Grenadine syrup

Serve over crushed ice.

Beachcomber

1½ oz light rum
½ oz Triple Sec
½ oz Grenadine syrup
1 oz sour mix

Shake with ice and strain into a cocktail glass with sugared rim. Garnish with a lime wedge.

Coconut Water & Rum

With a machete, cut the top off a green coconut. (Shake it first and listen for the sound of the milk or you may be disappointed.) Mix this water with your favorite rum and you are a winner.

Cool Runnings, *Miami*

In the islands, coconuts are plentiful and the milk from the seed, or coconut water as it is called, makes a good mixer. A friend of mine keeps a plastic container of coconut water in his refrigerator. He buys fresh coconut water from coconut vendors on the street and avoids the risk of cutting his fingers off with a machete.

In the past, sailors were not allowed to go ashore except on leave. Local women came to the ships to sell fruits and vegetables and often brought coconuts that had been filled with rum. *Sucking the monkey* was the term used to describe drinking the contents from these spiked coconuts.

Lebenho

On board sailing vessels, from time to time—most of the time—things are born from what is available. This is one that deserves to be noted, even if there are other mixers available. Mix Tang orange drink powder (or orange juice) with instant tea, then add rum to taste.

From the yacht Lebenho

Cannonball

Pour 2 ounces of Pusser's Rum over ice, top with orange juice, and float 4-5 dashes of Angostura bitters on the top. Sip through the bitters to savor the flavor.

Blue Lagoon

Mix 2 ounces Bounty Crystal White Rum, 1 ounce Blue Curacao Liqueur, and a glass of lemonade with crushed ice.

RECIPES

Royal Navy Fog Cutter

Shake 2 ounces Pusser's Rum, ½ ounce brandy, ½ ounce gin, 1 ounce orange juice, 3 tablespoons lemon juice, and a splash of Orgeat syrup. Strain into a tall glass filled with ice. Top with a teaspoon of sweet sherry and garnish.

The Lady Hamilton

Into a tall glass, pour 1½ ounces Pusser's Rum, a teaspoon of fresh lime juice, and equal parts of passion fruit juice, orange juice, and ginger ale. Add ice and mix well.

Tortola Lullaby

Mix 1 ounce Pusser's Rum, 1 ounce coconut rum, ½ ounce cane syrup, ½ ounce lemon juice, and 2 ounces pineapple juice. Pour over ice and relax.

Nelson's Blood

After Admiral Nelson died of a wound received in the Battle of Trafalgar, his body was put in a cask of rum to preserve him until he could be buried with full honors at St. Paul's Cathedral. When the cask arrived, there was no rum in it and the crew was accused of drinking Nelson's blood.

Mix 3 ounces Pusser's Rum with equal parts of cranberry, orange, and pineapple juices. Top this off with fresh West Indian lime. Add fresh grated nutmeg and a cinnamon stick to stir.

Mai-Tai

Mix 2 ounces dark rum, 1 ounce Curacao, ½ teaspoon sugar, 1 tablespoon Orgeat or almond-flavored syrup, and 1 tablespoon Grenadine. Pour over ice and garnish with pineapple and a cherry on a toothpick. Sometimes a shot of overproof rum is added to top off this tropical drink.

Pusser's Reef Juice

Pour 1½ ounces Pusser's Rum, 1 ounce banana liqueur, ½ ounce gin, ½ ounce unsweetened lime juice, 1 teaspoon Grenadine, and 2 ounces pineapple juice into a tall glass and garnish with pineapple and cherry. Float the squeezed lime on top.

Modern Navy Grog

Blend 2 ounces Pusser's Rum, ½ ounce fresh lime juice, 1 ounce orange juice, 1 ounce pineapple juice, 1 ounce guava nectar, ¼ ounce Falernum, and ½ cup crushed ice at low speed for about 15 seconds. Pour into a glass and garnish to your taste. (This is one of the few recipes I came across that uses Falernum, a sugar cane liqueur made in Barbados.)

Blue Virgin

Blend 1 measure dark rum, ½ measure Blue Curacao, 2 measures pineapple juice, and 1 measure cream of coconut with crushed ice.

Bushwhacker

There are a few of these in the islands. This one is Carol's favorite. Blend equal parts of dark rum, vodka, Kahlua, Bailey's Irish Cream, Amaretto, Frangelica, and Creme de Cacao. Sip and good night.

Bossa Nova

Shake 4 parts golden rum, 1 part lime juice, 1 part lemon juice, 2 parts passion fruit juice, and ice. Pour into a glass and garnish with slices of orange and lime.

Rum 'n' Coffee

Into ½ cup freshly brewed coffee, pour 1 ounce Old Fort Reserve Rum, and 1½ ounces cream liqueur. Top with whipped cream and ground nutmeg for garnish.

Barbados Rum Cocktail

Shake a shot of golden rum, 2 dashes of Angostura bitters, a little sugar to taste, and ice. Strain into a glass and enjoy.

Caribbean Sky Cocktail

Mix ¾ ounce Bounty Crystal White Rum, ¾ ounce Blue Curacao, ¾ ounce fresh cream. Garnish with a slice of orange and a cherry.

Pineapple Delight

Mix 1 measure Cavalier Rum and 4 measures pineapple juice. Add ice, maraschino cherry, and a dash of bitters.

Antiguan Kiss

Pour 1½ ounces Cavalier White Rum, ½ ounce apricot brandy, and 2 ounces pineapple juice over cracked ice and stir. Garnish with cherry or pineapple.

Rum Sour

Shake 2 ounces of golden rum, ½ teaspoon sugar, the juice of ½ lemon, and ice. Strain and serve in a glass garnished with a lemon slice and a cherry. Try this drink with cane syrup instead of sugar. The syrup mixes easily—even in an iced drink.

Rum Julep

Lightly crush 3 sprigs of mint in 1 teaspoon sugar and a dash of water, add a shot of white rum and fill the glass with your favorite chunks of fruit. Garnish with mint leaves.

Rum Martini

Pour 3 parts Cockspur white rum and 1 part dry vermouth over ice and shake vigorously. Strain into a chilled martini glass. Twist a slice of fresh lemon rind over the glass and then use it as a garnish.

RECIPES

Rum Bloody Mary

Mix a shot of rum, 5 ounces tomato juice, and a dash of Tabasco and Worcestershire sauce. Salt to taste and add a squeeze of lemon. This is a good drink made with white rum.

Naked Lady

Shake a shot of rum, a shot of sweet vermouth, 4 dashes apricot brandy, 2 dashes Grenadine, 2 dashes lemon juice, and ice. Strain and serve in a cocktail glass.

Holiday Eggnog

Beat 12 egg yolks until light, add ½ pound sugar and continue beating until thick. Stir in one quart of milk and one bottle (750 ml) dark rum. Put this in the refrigerator for three hours. Pour into a punch bowl and fold in one quart of stiffly whipped heavy cream. Chill for another hour, then dust with nutmeg before serving. Serves 24.

Even in the Caribbean it can get cold. Well, cool. To warm up the crew, here are a few suggestions.

Hot Toddy

Mix a teaspoon of brown sugar and a shot of dark rum in a cup. Fill with boiling water to heat the mixture and garnish with a slice of lemon and cloves.

Hot Buttered Rum

Pour boiling water over 2 ounces rum, 1 teaspoon brown sugar, 4 cloves, a slice of butter, and a pinch of fresh nutmeg in a mug. Stir with a cinnamon stick.

Hot Punch

Blend 1 tablespoon powdered ginger and 1 teaspoon grated nutmeg with 2½ pints warmed beer and heat. Beat 3 eggs with ½ pint beer and 2 tablespoons of molasses. Slowly add the warm beer mixture to the egg mixture, beating all the time. Add ¼ pint golden rum and serve at once.

If you try enough of the spirits in this book, you will end up with a bottle of liquor that you just can't drink. If, after you have tried a few different things, the bottle is still not getting any lighter, put some of your special spirit in a squeeze bottle. The next time you hook a big fish, give it a shot of rum before you try to bring your trophy aboard. This will immediately take the fight out of any fish, and won't hurt the flavor of your prize catch.

I also discovered a number of good food recipes that, of course, include rum. Try a few of these and you will appreciate the spirit of the Caribbean even more. Some of these recipes call for white or dark rum. With a little experience, you will know what suits your taste best.

RECIPES

Rum 'n' Coffee

This is easy. A half shot of dark rum in your morning coffee. Too much rum and the coffee will be cold. This also makes going back to bed easier, if you are on island time.

Rum 'n' Honey

In Tobago, I bought a bottle of honey that was, of course, in a rum bottle. The honey had a slightly different but delightful flavor. There must have been a little rum left in the bottle before it was filled with honey. A little rum in pancake syrup is also a welcome treat. In both cases, it doesn't take much rum. Heating the honey or syrup makes it easier to mix with the rum. I prefer to use a colored, aged rum as opposed to a light, clear rum.

Rum Pancakes

Some of the colored rums make a great addition to pancake batter. Too much of a good thing, though, and the pancakes stick to the pan. I also add a cup or so of leftover, cooked rice to the batter. Believe it or not, some people who thought I was crazy before they tried this, now always leave a little rice for tomorrow's pancakes.

Rum French Toast

Mix 3 eggs, ¾ cup of milk, half-and-half or cream, 3 tablespoons dark rum, ¼ tablespoon nutmeg, 1 tablespoon sugar, and a pinch of salt. Dip slices of bread in batter and fry in 2 tablespoons oil on a hot griddle. Garnish with fresh fruit, butter, and maple syrup. Please don't forget to add a few drops of dark rum to the syrup.

Drunken Fruit

Slice pineapples, bananas, mangoes, or even canned peaches in a glass pan, sprinkle with brown sugar, lime juice, and some dark rum. Let this sit in the refrigerator for a few hours, then sprinkle with fresh nutmeg or cinnamon before serving. Serve your guests toothpicks and they can pick the fruit of their choice.

Rum Barbecue Ribs

Cut 6 pounds pork spareribs in pieces. Place them in a pan and cover with cold water. Bring to a boil and simmer, uncovered for 20 minutes. Drain. Combine two 8-ounce cans tomato sauce, 1 cup dark rum, 1 cup honey, ¼ cup red wine vinegar, ½ cup minced fresh onion, 2 minced garlic cloves, 1 teaspoon Worcestershire sauce, salt, and pepper to taste in small pan. Bring to a boil and simmer for 5 minutes. Preheat broiler or prepare barbecue grill. Grill the parboiled ribs slowly in oven broiler 5-6 inches from the heat. Baste often.

Express Ribs

The Food Center in Cole Bay, St. Maarten sells marinated ribs in large containers. At least one of the charter boats uses these prepared ribs for their beach barbecues. The ribs always get rave reviews. For a special taste, a splash of dark rum is added to the ribs before they are put in the refrigerator overnight.

RECIPES

Flaming Shrimp

In Martinique, I was served a great meal with a great presentation. Shrimp were sautéed in a little olive oil and a lot of garlic. Just before the pan was brought to the table half a cup of white rhum was poured over the seafood and quickly lit with a match. Once the flames died, the dinner was delicious.

Rum & Bananas

Mash 8 bananas in a mixer. Add 4 tablespoons brown sugar, 4 cups white rum, and 1 tablespoon lemon juice per serving. Add vanilla to taste, if you have some, and spoon mixture into glasses. Top off with soda water.

Yergin on board Malu, *Charlotte Amalie*

Limes

Limes are also an integral part of many rum drinks. To enjoy the most from this fruit, proper preparation is essential.

Before you cut a lime and squeeze the juice into your glass, roll it on a wooden cutting board to break up the juice-bearing pulp inside the skin. A wooden board will absorb some of the citric oils in the skin. A cloth towel will remove some of the residual oils released by rolling the lime. Using a sharp knife, cut the middle of the lime perpendicular to the stem with a sharp knife. Cutting the lime in this way will allow the juice to escape from the sections with a minimum of pressure on the skin, reducing the amount of oils that ends up in your glass.

Papayas & Bananas

Slice and remove seeds from a firm papaya, mash 3-4 bananas with 1 teaspoon of coconut cream, ½ teaspoon of fresh nutmeg and 1 teaspoon of rum. Fill papaya halves with the mixture, top with a dot of butter, and bake 10-15 minutes depending on the ripeness of the papaya.

Anne on board Sandpiper

Flamin' Fruit

Prepare like Drunken Fruit, but while you are eating dinner, add a little butter to the top of the fruit and put the pan in the oven on low heat. After dinner, heat a shallow pan of water. Turn off the stove! Pour a shot of rum per person into a heavy glass and place the glass in the hot water and cover for a few minutes to safely heat the rum. When you are ready to serve, pour the rum over the fruit. Carefully light with a match.

Mango Chutney

Mangoes came to the Caribbean from India with the traders in the sixteenth century. Today, many different varieties are grown in the islands. You will hardly ever be short of these delicious fruit during mango season, which roughly coincides with hurricane season.

Make a syrup of ½ cup brown sugar and 2 cups vinegar. When it comes to a boil, add 5 cups chopped mango (about 15 peach size mangoes), 1 seeded lemon, 1½ cup raisins, ¾ cup chopped ginger, ¼ teaspoon cayenne pepper, and a spice bag of ¾ tablespoon coriander seeds, 15-20 whole cloves, and 1 cinnamon stick. Simmer this for 15-

RECIPES

20 minutes, then remove the spice bag and let cool.

You may want to add garlic, hot peppers, chopped onion, or mustard seed. But don't forget to add some rum to the brown sugar and vinegar.

Peggy on board Elisabeth, *Miami*

Poncho de Crema

This drink is traditionally served at Christmas in Trinidad. Beat 1 egg and grate the rind of ½ lime, add 7 ounces condensed milk, 12 ounces golden rum, and 8 ounces crushed ice. Finish with a dash of Angostura bitters and grated nutmeg.

Banana Rum Mousse

1. Sprinkle 2 tablespoons powdered gelatin over 4 tablespoons rum and leave for five minutes. Then simmer over water for 2-3 minutes and set aside.

2. Put 3 mashed ripe bananas, 6 ounces rum, and 2 teaspoons vanilla essence in processor for one minute to form a smooth puree. Set this aside.

3. Whisk 5 egg whites and a pinch of salt, gradually add 1½ ounces sugar until stiff.

4. Whisk 1½ ounces sugar with 5 egg yolks until light and fluffy. Beat in 6 ounces double cream and continue beating for five minutes.

5. Add banana mixture to cream mixture, then fold in the eggs and gelatin.

6. Pour the mousse into a decorative glass bowl. Cover and refrigerate for 2-3 hours or until set.

7. Whisk another 6 ounces double cream in a bowl until firm. Remove the mousse from the refrigerator. Decorate the mousse with whipped cream, sprinkle with nutmeg, and serve.

Rita's Rum Cake

Mix 1 cup sugar, ½ teaspoon salt, 1 teaspoon soda, 2 cups flour, ½ cup butter, 2 eggs, ¼ cup buttermilk, 1 cup mashed bananas, 1 teaspoon vanilla, and 2 tablespoons rum to make a batter. Bake in a greased and floured pan at 350°F until done.

Let the cake cool on a rack, then drizzle with a sauce of ¼ cup melted butter, ⅛ cup confectioner sugar, and ¼ cup rum. (I prefer dark rum for frostings like this one.)

Anne on board Crosstown Traffic

John's Brownies

If you are in a hurry and want more than you usually get from brownie mixes, use one third less water and replace that amount with rum, preferably dark rum.

John on board Meeling, *Miami*

Apple Rum Float

Mix 2 cups applesauce, 1 cup brown sugar, a handful of pecan pieces, 1 cup raisins, ⅔ cup dark rum, 2 teaspoons cinnamon, 1 teaspoon nutmeg, and ⅛ teaspoon allspice in a saucepan. Bring to a boil. Pour into a glass casserole. Beat 4 egg whites, and add ½ cup white sugar to make meringue. Bake at 325°F until the meringue browns. Serve hot.

Jack's Favorite Chocolate Malt

Add a bottle of rum to a quart of milk and a quart of chocolate ice cream. Mix it all up and enjoy.

Jack on board Triton, *Charlotte Amalie*

Rum Raisin Brownies

Melt 4 ounces unsweetened chocolate and 1 cup butter in a saucepan. Remove from the stove and mix in 1 cup sugar and 2 eggs. Keep mixing, and add ⅓ cup dark rum and 1 tablespoon vanilla. When this is smooth, slowly add 1 cup flour and ½ cup raisins. Bake in a greased baking pan at 375°F for half an hour or until done. When this is cool, cut into pieces.

I hope you enjoy these recipes as much as I do and that you will look for more ways to use rum in your cooking. Just the addition of a rum glaze to a cake can turn the ordinary into something special.

Glossary

acre – unit of surface measurement equal to 43,560 square feet, or 0.4 hectare.

agricole – Fr., agricultural. Rhum agricole is rhum made from fresh cane juice, as opposed to rhum industriel, which is made from molasses.

aldehyde – colorless, volatile liquid obtained from alcohol by oxidation.

alembic – pot still.

analyzing column – first column of a multiple-column still.

babash – locally made rum, generally illicit.

bagasse – sugar cane stalk fiber after it has been crushed or pressed to remove the juice. Commonly burned to fire the boiler for distillation.

beer – fermented sugar cane juice.

beer still – first of the four distillation columns. Nomenclature specific to the Cruzan Distillery in St. Croix.

brix – describes the % of suspended solids. For example, 95 brix denotes a liquid which is 95% suspended solids by weight. Also a name used for fermented wash.

chairman – person who sits in front of a small pot still and directs the operation.

chêne – Fr., oak. Fut de chêne means oak barrels.

condenser – heat exchanger that condenses the alcohol vapor after distillation.

GLOSSARY

congeners – impurities in the alcohol after distillation. Congeners account for the difference in the taste of rum and other liquors.

culture – illicit rum, term widely used in Nevis and St. Kitts.

distillation – process of concentrating a component of a mixture by heating the mixture and then collecting and condensing the vapor.

distillerie – Fr., distillery.

dunder – fermented wash.

esters – formed by the reaction of alcohol and acids, esters are compounds formed during fermentation that are present in small quantities after distillation. Esters are also formed during aging.

fermentation – process of yeast, either naturally occurring or introduced from the outside, changing sugar into alcohol.

foudre de chêne – Fr., large cask, generally 35,000 to 65,000-liter capacity, used for storing rhum blanc or aging rhum paille.

fusel oil – light oils formed during fermentation that accumulate during distillation. Can be removed in multiple column stills or through successive distillations. Used to flavor other alcoholic beverages.

fût – Fr., barrel, generally accepted to be less than 650 liters.

fût de chêne – Fr., oak barrels used for aging rum.

gallon – liquid measure of four quarts, 231 cubic inches, or approximately 3.8 liters.

gooseneck – connects the pot or kettle of a pot still to the condenser or retorts.

grand arôme – Fr., rhum industriel made from fermented molasses and vinasse.

guildive – Fr., rhum.

hammond – illicit rum. This term is most prevalent in St. Kitts and Nevis. It is disputed whether Mr. Hammond was a customs officer or a renowned distiller.

heads – the first condensate that comes from the still. Also called high wines, or the flat ends of a barrel.

hectare – metric unit of surface measurement equal to 10,000 square meters, or 2.471 acres.

high wines – the first liquor that comes from the still, also called heads.

hogo – fusel oils that can be seen floating on top of crudely distilled rum. Also a name for locally distilled rum, generally illicit.

houillage – recasking, the annual ritual where rum from the same production year is used to fill other barrels of rum to replace the angels' share.

hydrometer – device that compares the density of a sample with the density of water to directly indicate the alcohol content of the spirit.

hydroselection column – third column of a four-column still.

imperial gallon – equal to 277.42 cubic inches.

industriel – Fr., industrial. Rhum industriel is rhum made from molasses, as opposed to fresh cane juice.

GLOSSARY

lele – Fr., naturally grown swizzle stick with generally five branches that grow perpendicular to the stem.

leeze – residue left after the alcohol has been distilled from the fermented wine, also called vinasse.

let off – leeze, term used at some of the older distilleries for what is let off after distillation.

liter – volume of one kilogram of water, or 61.05 cubic inches.

low wines – the last liquor that comes from the still. Low wines contain less alcohol than the seconds that precede them.

melasse – Fr., molasses.

millésimé – Fr., vintage.

molasses – the thick black liquid that remains after all of the commercially producible sugar has been recovered.

neutral spirit – distilled spirit which is 95.5% alcohol by volume and contains no congeners, the remaining 4.5 % by volume is water.

paille – Fr., rhum paille is straw-colored rhum that has aged less than the three years required to be called rhum vieux.

pot still – still consisting of a pot where the fermented wash is heated. With a gooseneck and condenser, a pot still may also incorporate one or more retorts.

rectifying column – second column of a multiple-column still.

retort – closed vessel used to double distill alcohol as an accessory to a pot still. Hot vapor enters the bottom of the retort and heats the liquid in the retort to vaporize the alcohol in the liquid.

rhum – Fr., rum, used in this book to differentiate between the products of the French West Indies and the products of the English-speaking islands.

rhum agricole – Fr., agricultural. Rhum made from fresh cane juice as opposed to molasses.

rhum industriel – Fr., rhum made from molasses, as opposed to fresh cane juice.

rhum paille – Fr., straw-colored rhum aged less than the three years required to be called rhum vieux.

rhum vieux – Fr., rhum that has been aging in a barrel for more than three years. The barrel must be less than 650 liters.

rum – spirit distilled from the fermented sugar of the sugar cane plant. This sugar may be in the form of fresh juice, cane syrup or molasses.

strong – referring to rum that is more than 50% alcohol by volume.

sucrerie – Fr., sugar factory.

tafia – Fr., rhum.

tails – the last condensate collected from the still, also called the low wines.

très vieux – Fr., very old rhum, generally aged more than ten years.

vieux – Fr., old. Rhum vieux is rhum that has been in a barrel of less than 650 liter capacity for more than three years. In the French islands, the first of July is the anniversary date for rhum. All rhum in the barrel by July first is one-year-old on this date.

vesou – Fr., sugar cane juice.

vin – Fr., wine, refers to fermented sugar cane juice.

vinasse – Fr., residue left after the alcohol has been distilled from the fermented wine.

wash – mixture of yeast, water, and molasses to be fermented.

wine – fermented sugar cane juice.

• • •

When I began writing and compiling this book, I knew it would be impossible to cover every rum from every distillery in the world. Having researched rum and most of the books in print on the subject, I also knew there was a huge void in reliable information for the connoisseur and that the project had to be attempted.

As the public awareness of rum grows in the twenty-first century, I have no doubt that there will be many more books written on the subject and I look forward to reading them. If I have not included your favorite rum please let me know; I would love to learn more about it and would like to include it in the next edition of this book.

In an effort to help the rum connoisseurs of the world find their favorite spirit, I have gone on-line at the Office of the Minister of Rum. **http://www.ministerofrum.com.**

Information about the islands and the availability of these spirits can be found at this address. If you would like to share more information about anything concerning the industry, you can do it on-line here.

Keep the wind behind you and your glass half full. Cheers. The research continues.

Index

151 proof, 244

A. H. Riise, 37-38
A. H. Riise 3-6 years old rum, 38
A. H. Riise 6-12 years old rum, 38
A. H. Riise Apothecary, 37
A.H. Riise Gifts and Liquor Store, 37
ABC liquor stores, 68
Admiralty Bay, 171, 173
Admiralty Board, 44
Afoos Supermarket, 56
Africa, 3, 4, 143, 156, 167, 259, 270
aging, 20-21
Ajoupa Bouillon, 129
Albert Street, 183
alcohol content, 23-24
Alleyne Arthur & Hunte Ltd., 211, 213
Alteza, 56
Amaretto, 310
Amazon River, 216
AMC et Cie Supermarket, 62
Ame-Nöel, Francois Joseph, 80
Ame-Nöel, Jean-Antoine, 80
American West India Company, 54
Añejo Selecto 243, 244
Angostura bitters, 302, 304, 305, 307, 310, 318
Angostura Bitters Limited, 217-222, 297
Angostura Holdings, 219
Aniversario, 243, 244
Aniversario (Pampero), 269
Antigua, 59, 65-75, 299
Antigua Distillery Limited, 60, 66-70, 71, 72
Antigua Sailing Week, 70
Antiguan Kiss, 311
Antwerp Exposition, 37
Appellation d'Origine, 119, 155
Apple Rum Float, 319
Appleton Estate 12-year-old, 252, 254
Appleton Estate 21-year-old, 252, 254
Appleton Estate V/X (Very eXceptional), 251, 253
Appleton label, 251-254
Appleton Special Gold Rum, 251, 253
Appleton Special White Rum, 251, 253
Archard, Franz Karl, 7
Arecibo, 239
Arkansas, 268
Arundel Dark Cane Rum, 42
Arundel Estate, 40-43
Arundel White Cane Rum, 42, **C1**
Astaphan, R. A. J., 116
Atlantic Ocean, 65, 68, 129, 137, 161, 183
Aubrey, M., 160
Auburndale, 259, 260

Australia, 265-266
Australia Stubbs White Rum, 266

Bacardi, 228, 229-233, 234, 264, 298, 305
Bacardi 1873, 231, 233
Bacardi Añejo 231, 233
Bacardi Black, 231, 232
Bacardi Cocktail, 305
Bacardi, Don Secuto, 230
Bacardi Limon, 231
Bacardi Reserve, 231, 233
Bacardi Spice, 231, 233
Bacardi Superior Gold Dark, 231, 232
Bacardi Superior Gold Light, 231, 232
Bacardi Superior White, 230, 232
Bahama Mama, 306
Bahamas, 264
Baie du Galion, 145
Bailey's Irish Cream, 310
Baillif, 81
Bains, 183
Bajan, 60, 208, 210, 211, 212
Bally Rhum, 53, 61, 124
Banana Cow, 306
Banana Daiquiri, 303
Banana Mango Daiquiri, 303
Banana Rum Mousse, 318
Barbados, 5, 6, 12, 31, 45, 53, 59, 60, 61, 72, 116, 198-215, 295, 296, 298, 300, 301, 304, 309
Barbados Gold Fine Rum, 213
Barbados Punch, 301
Barbados Rum Cocktail, 310
Barbancourt, 256-258, 297, 302, 305
Barbancourt Reserve du Domain, 258
Barbancourt Reserve Speciale-Five Star, 258
Barbancourt Three Star Rum, 258
Barbuda, 67, 299
Barceló & Company, C. Por A., 246-247
Barcelona, 237
Bark Fantome, 66
Barnard family, 166
Barnard, Laurie, 167
Barreto, John "Bushy" Angelo, 71, 72
Barrilito rums, 228, 233-236
Barrilito Three Star, 235, 236
Barrilito Two Star, 234, 236
Basse Pointe, 129
Basse-Terre, 81, 83, 90, 96
Battle of Trafalgar, 308
Bayamón, 233, 235, 236
Beachcomber, 306
Belfast Estate Limited, 111, 115-117
Belgium, 257

INDEX

Bellevue-Magalda Distillery, 108-110
Bentinck Estate Ltd., 172
Bequia, 171
Bermúdez Blanco, 243, 244
Bermúdez Distillery, 242-244, 246, 297
Bermúdez Dorado Rum, 243, 244
Bielle Distillery, 105-108
Bielle Hors-d'Age, 108
Bielle Rhum Blanc, 107, **C6**
Bielle Rhum Vieux, 107
Big B's, 212
Bitter End Yacht Club, 48
Black Label, 221
Blackbeard Five Star Dark Rum, 58
Blackbeard Five Star Gold Rum, 58
Blackbeard Five Star White Rum, 58
Blackbeard's, 57-59, 296
blending, 21-22
Bligh, Captain William, 297
Blue Curacao, 307, 309, 310
Blue Lagoon, 307
Blue Virgin, 309
Bocas, 216
Bois Bande, 58, 115, 170
Bolans Post Office, 71
Bolans Village, 71-72
Bolivar, 269
Bolivar, General Simon, 217
Bologne, 53, 61, 79-83
Bonaparte, Josephine, 152
Bonaparte, Napoleon, 152
Bordeaux, 160
Bossa Nova, 310
Boston, 4
Bouillante, 80
Bounty Crystal White Rum, 169, 307, 310
Bounty Rum, 169
Bowen, Gerald, 196
Brazil, 3, 6, 79, 93, 295
Breion, Giles, 53
Brewer's Bay, 43
Bridgetown, 198, 205, 206, 212
Briggs, Charles, 301
Brighton, 208
Britain, 4, 165, 267, 297, 298
British proof, 24
British Virgin Islands, 39-48
British West Indies, 218, 296
Brownies, 319, 320
Brugal, 242, 245-246
Brugal Añejo, 246
Brugal Gold Label, 246
Brugal White Label, 246
Buccaneer Rum, 169, **C11**
Bundaberg Black, 266
Bundaberg or "Bundy" Distilling Company, 265-266, 298
Bundy & Cola, 266
Burgess-Simpson, Hamish 73
Busco, 52
Busco Rhum Blanc Agricole de Plantation, 52, **C2**
Busco Rhum Vieux, 52

Bush, George, 143
Bushwhacker, 310
Bushy Barreto's Blends, 72
Bushy's Best Matured Rum, 71, 72, **C3**

C. J. Wray Dry Rum, 251, 253
C.O.D.E.R.U.M, 155
Caballero Rum, 67
Cacique, 269
Cadenhead, 267
Callwood Distillery, 40-42
Callwood, Michael, 40, 41
Callwood, Mikey 40
Callwood, Philicianno "Foxy," 46
Callwood, Styles, 42
Cambelton, 267
Campari, 305
Camuy, 239
Canada, 20, 116, 207, 224, 235, 239, 257
Canary Islands, 3, 270
Cane Garden Bay, 40, 42
cane juice, 17-18
Cane Spirit Rothschild (CSR), 63, 64
Canefield Airport, 115
Cannonball, 307
Capesterre, 90, 92, 108, 110
Captain Bligh, 173, 174, 297
Captain Morgan, 242
Carbet, 123, 124, 125, 127, 142
Carib beer, 191
Cariba Nativa Antigua Rum, 60
Cariba Nativa Barbados Rum, 60
Cariba Nativa Guadeloupe Rum, 60
Cariba Nativa Jamaica Rum, 60
Cariba Nativa Rums, 59-60
Cariba Nativa Trinidad Rum, 60
Cariba Nativa Virgin Islands Rum, 60
Caribbean, xv, 3, 4, 5, 6, 7, 8, 13, 32, 39, 42, 46, 54, 55, 57, 58, 61, 64, 67, 70, 83, 85, 112, 113, 119, 131, 139, 156, 165, 166, 180, 198, 218, 224, 225, 228, 229, 231, 234, 237, 241, 242, 247, 248, 249, 255, 259, 267, 269, 271, 275, 298, 299, 300, 310, 312, 313, 317
Caribbean Liquors, 56
Caribbean Sea, 216, 238
Caribbean Sky Cocktail, 310
Caribbean Week Rum Testing Competition, 174, 199, 213
Carlisle Bay, 198, 212, 296
Caroni (1975) Ltd., 47, 222-226
Caroni Puncheon Rum, 225
Caroni Special Old Cask Rum, 226, **C16**
Caroni Sugar Factory, 222
Carreau Blends, 52
Carreau, Christian, 52
Carrere Distillery, 93-96
Carriacou, 175-178, 180, 186, 189
Carriacou Regatta, 176
Carta Viejo, 247
Cassinelli, Avna Paiewonsky, 37
Cassinelli, Filippo, 37

329

INDEX

Cassinelli, Sebastiano, 37
Castaways Hotel, 113
Castries, 165, 168
Castro, Fidel, 264
Catalona, 237
Cataño, 229, 235
Cavalier Antigua Dark Rum, 69, 302
Cavalier Antigua Light Rum, 69, 311
Cavalier Five-Year-Old Rum, 69, 72, **C3**
Cavalier Muscovado Rum, 67
Cavalier Rums, 68-72
Centerline Road, 32
Central America, 33, 92, 299
Chaguaramas, 217, 220
Champagne, 52, 53
Charity Hospital of Monks, 118
Charles Simonnet Rhum Vieux, 89
Charlotte Amalie, 316, 319
Chateaubouef, 147
Chelsea Gin, 206
Chester, The, 118
Chez Paulette, 151
Chicago World Fair, 37
China, 3, 9
Christ Church, 210, 213, 215
Christiansted, 31
Civil War (English), 295
Clarke's Court, 189-193
Clarke's Court Dark Rum, 193
Clarke's Court Kalypso White Rum, 191, 192
Clarke's Court Old Grog, 193
Clarke's Court Pure White Rum, 190, 192, 194, 195, 196, **C13**
Clarke's Court Superior Light Rum, 193
classification of rum, 16-26
Claude Marsolle & Cie, 78
Clément, 56, 61, 141-144
Clément, Homère, 143
Clément Rhum Blanc, 144
Clément Rhum Vieux, 144, **C9**
Clewiston, 259
Cockspur Five Star Fine Rum, 209, 311
Cockspur Gold Cup, 210
Cockspur Old Gold Reserve, 209, **C15**
Cockspur Rums, 53, 206-209, 211
Cockspur Very Special Old Rum (V.S.O.R.), 209
Coconut Complex, 115
Coconut Water & Rum, 306
Coeur de Chauffe, 134, 136, **C8**
Coffey, Aeneas, 15
Coffey still, 15-16, 200, 222, 229, 297
Cole Bay, 315
Colombia, 56
Colón, Don Juan Serrallès, 237
Columbus, 3, 52, 61, 216, 228, 255, 295, 298
Conch Republic Rum Company, 260-263
Concours Général Agricole de Paris, 78, 86

Connoisseurs Shop, 56
Conquering Lion Overproof, 254
continuous distillation column, 13-14
Convention of Paris, 297
Cool Runnings, 306
Copenhagen, 37
Copper and Lumber Store Hotel, 72, 73
Coral Bay, xvi
Corn Alley, 69
Coruba, 251, 153
Courlander, 216
Court of Connecticut, 6, 295
Courville, 151
Creme de Banana, 306
Creme de Cacao, 310
Croatia, 54
Crosstown Traffic, 319
Cruzan 151 Gold, 35
Cruzan 151 White, 35
Cruzan Clipper Spiced Rum, 36
Cruzan Dark-Dry, 35, **C1**
Cruzan Light-Dry, 35
Cruzan Rum Distillery, 32-36, 38, 321
Crystal White Rum, 222
Cuba, 229, 264-265, 298
Culebra, xiii
Culture, 63-64
Cumucarapo, 216
Curacao, 309
Customs and Excise Division, 224

D Special Rum, 117
daiquiris, 303
Damiens, 256
Damoiseau Distillery, 96-99
Damoiseau, Evre, 97, 98
Damoiseau, Jean Luc, 97, 98
Damoiseau Rhum Blanc, 99
Damoiseau Rhum Paille, 97, 99
Damoiseau Rhum Vieux, 98, 99, **C5**
Damoiseau, Roger, 97
Danish West India Company, 31
Dark and Stormy, 266
de Bologne, Guillaume, 79
de Bologne, Joseph Samuel, 79
de Bologne, Louis, 79
de Bologne, Pierre, 79
de Grasse, Admiral, 119, 296
Deadman's Chest, 39
Demarra Rums, 269
Denmark, 296, 298
Dennery Factory Company, 166
Denros Strong Rum, 168
Denrose Overproof, 254
Department of Agriculture, 8
DePaz Distillery, 119-122
DePaz, Victor, 119
Deshaies, 81
Dillon, Colonel Arthur, 152
Dillon Distillery, 152-155
distillation, 9-11
Distillerie Bellevue, 96, 108
Distillerie Carbet Neisson, 125-128
Distillerie DePaz, 119-123
Distillerie Dillon, 152-155

330

INDEX

Distillerie du Galion, 145-147
Distillerie G. Hardy, 137-141
Distillerie J. M, 128-131
Distillerie La Favorite, 147-151
Distillerie La Mauny, 156-158
Distillerie Poisson, 101-104
Distillerie Simon, 124, 141, 142, 144
Distillerie St. James, 131-136
Distillerie Trois Rivières, 159-163
Doctor Frankie, 210
Domain de Séverin Distillery, 83-86
Dominica, ix, 108, 111-117, 241, 296, 298
Dominican Republic, 241-247, 297
Don Armando, 243
Don Q Gold, 239, 240
Don Q Rums, 237-240
Don Q White, 239, 240
Doorly's Fine Old Barbados, 214
Doorly's Five Year Old, 214
Doorly's Harbour Policeman, 212, 215
Doorly's Macaw, 214, **C15**
Doorly's Rums, 211, 214-215
Dr. Siegert's Aromatic Bitters, 217
Drake, Sir Francis, 39, 241
Drunken Fruit, 315, 317
Dubuc family, 145
Duncan, Gilbey and Matheson International Limited, 167
Dunfermline Estate, 183-186
Dunfermline Rum, 186
Duquesne, Ange, 161
Duquesne, Augustin-Marie, 161
Duquesne Très Vieux Rhum, 162, 163
Duquesne Trois Rivières, 160
Durdy White Rum, 261, 262
Dutch, 6, 31, 49, 79, 216

E. S. A. Field, 211
East Caribbean Distilleries Limited, 167
East Main Road, 218
Eastern Caribbean, 5, 19, 21, 33, 40, 41, 69, 78, 116, 118, 152, 177, 179, 219, 221, 229, 295
Ecuador, 243, 257
Edmundo B. Fernandez, Inc., 233-236
El Dorado, 237, 239
Elisabeth, 318
England, 31, 66, 68, 72, 111, 164, 169 , 172, 187, 198, 216, 241, 243, 248, 249, 259, 267-268, 295, 296, 300
English Army, 54
English Harbour, 71-75
English Harbour Antigua Rum, 70
Erstin Sanford and Friends, 211
Esperanza Estate, 222
Estate Diamond, 36
Etang Noir, 108
Europe, 3, 4, 9, 20, 24, 39, 53, 68, 77, 79, 91, 104, 116, 143, 155, 161, 167, 169, 213, 216, 217, 224, 228, 234, 249, 267, 268, 295

Eustache, Eugène, 145
Express Ribs, 315

Fajou Rhum Blanc Assemblage, 89
Falernum, 212, 309
Fat Rice Bar, 180
Felicite Gold, 225
Ferdi's, 222
fermentation, 9
Fernandes Distillers (1973) Ltd., 219-222
Fernández, Edmundo, 234, 235
Fernández, Manuel B., 235
Fernández, Pedro B., 233, 234, 235
Five Islands, 65, 66
Flamin' Fruit, 317
Flaming Shrimp, 316
Florida, 54, 68, 249, 259-263, 264
Florida Distillers Company, 259-263
Fonds-Preville, 129
Fontabelle, 206, 209
Food Center, 315
Food Fair, 196
Forres Park Puncheon Rum, 221
Fort de France 142, 147, 150, 152, 154, 161, 162
Fort Duquesne, 161
Fort Wine and Liquors, 48
Fort Wine Gourmet, 48
Fouquet, Nicholas, 159
Foxy's, 45-47
Foxy's Fire Water, 46, 47, **C2**
Foxy's Tamarind Bar, 46
France, 4, 5, 7, 20, 31, 49, 77, 79, 88, 89, 91, 92, 95, 98, 99, 103, 107, 111, 121, 130, 131, 132, 134, 138, 142, 145, 146, 147, 153, 154, 155, 157, 160, 161, 163, 164, 216, 233, 237, 241, 255, 259, 268, 271, 296
Frangelica, 310
Fredricksted, 31, 32
French Revolution, 79, 80, 297
French West Indies, 52, 77, 91, 98, 118, 130, 140, 155, 156, 167, 325
Front Street, 58, 59

G and P Dormoy, 167
G. Hardy Distillery, 137-141
Galion, 147
Galion Bay, 145
Galion Sugar Factory, 145
Gay, Ensign Abel, 199
Gay, Lt. William, 199
Geest Distillery, 166
George, Ken, 113, 114
Georges, John, 219
Georgetown, 171, 172, 174
Germany, 156, 207, 211, 257
Gilbert Overproof, 254
Gilbey and Matheson International Ltd., 167
Gilbey's Gin, 206
Ginger Syrup, 304
Girardin, 152
Golden Eagle Bar, 178
Gondleau, 147
Gourmet Chocolate Fudge, 59

INDEX

Gracias, 235
Grand Anse Beach, 191
Grand Arome Le Galion, 147, **C10**
Grand Bourg, 101, 104, 105, 108
Grand Rhums Charles Simonnet Distillery, 87-89
Grand-Terre, 96, 99
Grands Vin de France, 130
Grappe Blanche Saint James, 133, 135, **C9**
Great Bay, 47
Great Harbour, 45, 46
Grenada, 3, 175, 179-197, 217, 298
Grenada National Marketing Board, 195
Grenada Sugar Factory Ltd., 189, 192
Grenadian Shandy, 191
Grenadine, 302, 305, 306, 309, 312
Grenadines, 171-174, 298
Grenville, 180, 183, 184
Guadeloupe, ix, 3, 50, 52, 53, 59, 60, 62, 65, 67, 76-99, 100, 103, 105, 111
Guatemala, 271
Guavaberry Liqueurs, 59
Gustavia, 61
Guyana, 6, 45, 116, 172, 267, 269

H.M.S. Diamond Rock, 164
H.M.S. Libra, 216
Habitation Clément, 143-144
Hacienda Santa Ana, 233
Hacienda Teresa, 237
Haiti, 241, 255-258, 264, 297, 302
Haitian Planter's Punch, 302
Hammond, 63, 323
Hanschell Inniss Limited, 206-209
Hanschell, Valdemar, 206
Havana Club, 264-265
Hawaii, 271
heavy rum, 18-20
Hemingway, Ernest, 264
Heritiers, Rameau, 103
Highway 5, 235
Highway 64, 32
Hillsborough, 178
Hindustani, 300
Hispaniola, ix, 237, 241, 247, 255
History of the Island of Barbados, 12, 295
Holiday Eggnog, 312
Holland, 79
Honduras, 243
Hood, Admiral, 164
Hopefield, 211
Hopefield Sugar Plantation, 210
Hot Buttered Rum, 313
Hot Punch, 313
Hot Toddy, 312
Hurricane Hugo, 299
Hurricane Janet, 298
Hurricane Luis, 299
Hurricane Marilyn, 299

Imperial Blanc Saint James, 133, 135
India, 300, 317
Indians, 3, 11, 216

International Distillers and Vintners, 207
Islamorada Light Rum, 261, 262
Island Planter, 302
Italy, 243, 257

J Armando Bermúdez & Company, Inc., 242-244, 245, 246, 297
J. Bally Distillery, 53, 56, 61, 123-125, 142
J. Bally Rhum Blanc, 125, **C8**
J. Bally Rhum Paille, 125
J. Bally Rhum Vieux, 125
Jack Iron, 175-178, 186, 189, **C12**
Jack's Favorite Chocolate Malt, 319
Jamaica, ix, 23, 59, 60, 170, 171, 248-254, 296, 297
James, Andrea, 267
James, Mike, 267
Japan, 156, 207
Jeyes, Alan, 73
Jim Beam Brands, 45
John D. Taylor's Famous White Falernum, 212
John Dore and Company, 68, 172
John's Brownies, 319
Jolly Harbour Marina, 69, 71
Jones, John Paul, 39
Jost Van Dyke, 45-48

Kahlua, 310
Kentucky, 157, 206, 259, 268
Key West, 261
Kilo 1.6, 235
Kimbe Rand, 98
Kingston, 171, 253
Kingstown, 171
Knights of Malta, 31
Knockemdown Key Rum, 261, 263, **C16**
Krishna Stores, 53
Kweyol Spice Rum, 170

La Belle Creole, 167
La Cava, 239
La Favorite, 147-151
La Favorite Cuvée spéciale de la Flibuste, 151
La Favorite Rhum Blanc, 150, **C10**
La Favorite Rhum Vieux, 151
La Fortuneand, 161
La Loire, 118
La Mauny Distillery, 156-159
La Palapa, 56, 57
La Société des Grands Rhums Duquesnes (S.G.R.D.), 160
Labat, Père Jean-Baptiste, 118, 296
labels, 22-23
Lady Hamilton, 308
Lagoon, The, 56
Lake Alfred, 259, 260
Lamentin, 142
Le Dentu and Cie, 81
Le Dentu, M. Emile, 81
Le Francois, 141, 142, 143, 144
Le Galion, 145-147

INDEX

Le Marquis Rhum, 170
Le Moule, 98
Lebenho, 307
Leeward Islands, 72, 299
Lemon Hart, 267
Les Rhumeries Duquesne, 160
light rum, 18-20
Ligon, Richard, 12, 295
Limes, 117, 316
Limousin, 257
Little Jost, 45
Little Spain, 255
London, 304
Long Street, 69
Longueteau, Francois, 91, 92
Louis XIV, 159
Lucian Rum, 170

M. E. R. Bourne & Company, Limited, 215
Macouba, 129, 130, 151
Macoucherie, 112-115
Macoucherie Elixir of Bois Bandé, 115
Macoucherie Rum, 114, **C7**
Macronix, 247
Madagascar, 270
Madeira, 71, 255
Madras label, 88
Magalda, 108-110
Magalda Rhum Blanc, 110, **C6**
Magalda Rhum Vieux, 110
Magical Rum, 305
Mai-Tai, 309
Mailbox, 57
Mainstay label, 270
Malays, 6
Malibu Coconut Rum, 206
Malu, 316
Mango Chutney, 317
Mango Rum Punch, 301
Manoel Street, 165
Manuel Dias Liquor Store, 69
Margeta, 175
Marie Galante, 3, 53, 100-110
Marigot, 52, 166
Marina Royale, 49, 53
Market Street, 69
Marley, Bob, 248
Marraud-Desgrottes, 161
Marseilles, 134
Marsolle, Alain, 93
Marsolle family, 84, 93
Martin Doorly & Co., Ltd., 212
Martin, Jean-Marie, 129
Martin, Remy, 202
Martini and Rossi, 160
Martinique, ix, 50, 53, 56, 62, 79, 90, 107, 111, 118-164, 167, 296, 316
Martinique Parliament, 143
Maso, Facundo Bacardi, 229
Matecumbe Dark Rum, 261, 263
Mauritius, 271
Maynard, Lieutenant Robert, 57, 296
Médaille d'Or, 78, 86
Mediterranean, 70
Meeling, 319

Mercedita, 237, 239
Miami, 65, 260. 306, 319
Millaquin, 265
Miramar, 239
Mississippi Valley, 259
Missouri, 268
Mitterrand, Francois, 143
Modern Navy Grog, 309
molasses, 17-18
Molasses Act, 296
Mon Repos Distillery, 90-92
Mon Repos Rhum Blanc, 92, **C5**
Mon Repos Rhum Vieux, 92
Montebello Distillery, 78, 93-96
Montebello Rhum Blanc, 94, 96, **C5**
Montebello Rhum Vieux, 94, 96
Montpelier Estate, 67
Morne Rouge, 128
Morne Vert, 125
Mount Gay Barbados Sugar Cane Brandy, 202, 203
Mount Gay Distilleries Limited, 199-203, 205, 206, 211
Mount Gay Extra Old Barbados Rum, 202, 203
Mount Gay Premium White Rum, 22, 202, 203, **C14**
Mount Gay Refined Eclipse Barbados Rum, 22, 199, 202, 203
Mt. Pelee, 119, 122, 132, 143, 298
Mucarapo, 216
Myer's Rum, 254

Naked Lady, 312
Napoleonic Wars, 217
Narrows, The, 45
National Rums of Jamaica, 249, 254
National Sugar Company Ltd., 254
National Weather Service, 65
Navigation Act, 295
Negrita, 271
Neisson Rums, 125-128
Nelson, Horatio Viscount, 72, 308
Nelson's Blood, 308
Nelson's Dockyard, 72
Nelthropp family, 32, 33
Nero, 113
Neuf Chateau, 90
Nevis, 299, 322, 323
New England, 4, 5, 6, 31, 70, 259
New Orleans Exposition, 37
New World, 143, 216, 241
North America, 4, 131, 259
North Carolina, 57, 296

Ogoun Feray Grog, 305
Old Brigand Black, 214
Old Brigand Black Superior, 214
Old Brigand Rums, 211, 212, 214-215
Old Brigand White, 214, **C15**
Old Florida Rum Company, 260-263
Old Fort Reserve Rum, 170, 310
Old Oak Gold and White, 220
Old San Juan, 229
Old St. Croix, 36
Old St. Pierre, 122

333

INDEX

Old Years Night, 46
Orgeat syrup, 308, 309
Orinoco River, 217

Pacific, 156, 271
Paiewonsky, Charlotte, 37
Paiewonsky, Isaac, 37
Paiewonsky, Isidor, 37
Paiewonsky, Ralph, 37
Paladin, 73
Palo Viejo, 239
Pampero, 269
Panama, 257
Papayas & Bananas, 317
Papuea New Guinea, 3
Paris, 8, 80, 143
Party Punch, 301
Père Labat, 53, 54, 101-104
Peru, 243
Petit Bourg, 93, 96
Philippines, 271
Philipsburg, 54-56, 58, 59
Pineapple Delight, 311
Pitons, ix, 170
Pitt, Fitz-Stephen, 173
Pittsburgh, 161
Pizza Panoramique, 159
Point-à-Pitre 78, 87, 88
Ponce, 228, 237, 238, 240
Poncho de Crema 318
Port of Spain, 16
Port Royal, 249, 296
Port-au-Prince, 256, 258
Port-au-Prince Cocktail, 305
Portsmouth, 112, 115, 116
Portugal, 3, 67, 79, 270, 295
pot still, 11
Potts distillery, 49
Poulsen, Olaf, 37
Prince Rupert Bay, 115
Prince William Henry, 198
Pringle, Rachel, 198
Pris d'Eau, 87, 89
Prohibition, 238, 298
Puerto Plata, 242, 245
Puerto Rico, ix, 31, 228-240, 260, 264, 295, 298
Puerto Rico Distillers, 239
Puncheon, 217, 221
punches, 300-302
Pusser's, 43-45, 47
Pusser's Blue Label, 45, 73, **C1**
Pusser's Co. Store, 44
Pusser's Navy Rum, 44, 298, 307, 308, 309
Pusser's Painkiller, 47
Pusser's Red Label, 45
Pusser's Reef Juice, 309
Pusser's Traditional Rum Punch, 301

Que Rico, 235
Queen Anne's Revenge, 57
Queensland, 265, 266, 297
Quin Farara's Liquor Stores, 69

R. L. Seale & Company Limited, 210-215
Rat Island, 67

Red Cap, 117, **C7**
Red Heart label, 270
Remonique, M., 87
Renault, M. E., 103
Resort blends, 48
Reunion, 271
Revolutionary War, 32
Rhum Ambre Saint James, 134, 135
Rhum Barbancourt, 256-258
Rhum Blanc DePaz, 122, **C7**
Rhum Blanc Dillon, 154
Rhum Blanc Duquesne, 163
Rhum Blanc G. Hardy, 139, **C9**
Rhum Blanc J. M, 131, **C7**
Rhum Blanc La Mauny, 158, **C11**
Rhum Blanc Neisson, 128
Rhum Blanc Trois Rivières, 163, **C11**
Rhum Bologne, 83, **C4**
Rhum Charles Simonnet, 89, **C4**
Rhum du Père Labat, 104
Rhum Longueteau, 91
Rhum Marsolle, 78, **C3**
Rhum Paille DePaz, 122
Rhum Paille Dillon, 154
Rhum Paille du Père Labat, 104
Rhum Paille G. Hardy, 139
Rhum Paille J. M, 131
Rhum Paille Saint James, 133, 135
Rhum Runner, 194-195
Rhum Runner Rhum Punch, 194-195, **C14**
Rhum Saint James Hors D'Age, 134, 136
Rhum Traditionnel Le Galion, 147
Rhum Très Vieux Duquesne, 162, 163
Rhum Vieux Agricole Hors d'Age, 159
Rhum Vieux DePaz, 122, 123
Rhum Vieux DePaz Reserve, 123
Rhum Vieux Dillon, 155
Rhum Vieux du Père Labat, 104, **C6**
Rhum Vieux G. Hardy, 140
Rhum Vieux J. M, 131
Rhum Vieux La Mauny, 158
Rhum Vieux Neisson, 128
Rhum Vieux Plantation Millésimé DePaz, 123
Rhum Vieux Saint James, 53, 133, 136
Rhum Vieux Trois Rivières, 162, 163
Rhumerie J. M, 128-131
Riise, Albert Heinrich, 37
Riise, Valdemar, 37
Rita's Rum Cake, 319
River Antoine Estate, 180-183
Rivers, 183, 186
Rivière du Carbet, 126
Rivière Goyaves, 84
Rivière Pilote, 156, 158
Riviere-Salee, 161
Road Town, 40, 48
Rodney, Admiral George, 111, 296
Roland, 185
Ron Barceló Añejo, 247